THE CULTURE OF CRAFT

MANCHESTER
UNIVERSITY PRESS

STUDIES IN
DESIGN

general editor
CHRISTOPHER BREWARD
founding editor
PAUL GREENHALGH

THE✦CULTURE ✦OF✦CRAFT

Status and future

EDITED BY PETER DORMER

Manchester University Press

Manchester and New York

distributed exclusively in the USA by Palgrave

Published by Manchester University Press
Oxford Road, Manchester M13 9NR, UK
and Room 400, 175 Fifth Avenue, New York, NY 10010, USA
www.manchesteruniversitypress.co.uk

Distributed exclusively in the USA
by Palgrave, 175 Fifth Avenue, New York, 10010, USA

Distributed exclusively in Canada
by UBC Press, University of British Columbia, 2029 West Mall,
Vancouver, BC, Canada V6T 1Z2

British Library Cataloguing-in-Publication Data
A catalogue record is available from the British Library

Library of Congress Cataloging-in-Publication Data
The culture of craft : status and future / edited by Peter Dormer.
        p.   cm. — (Studies in design and material culture)
      ISBN 0-7190-4617-3 (hardback). — ISBN 0-7190-4618-1 (pbk.)
        1. Handicraft. I. Dormer, Peter. II. Series.
    TT145.C84   1997   96-31364
    745.5'01—dc20

ISBN 0 7190 4617 3 *hardback*

ISBN 0 7190 4618 1 *paperback*

First published in 1997

06   05   04   03   10   9   8   7   6   5   4

Designed by Max Nettleton FCSD
in ITC Giovanni

Typeset by Koinonia Ltd, Manchester

Printed in Great Britain
by Bell & Bain Limited, Glasgow

CONTENTS

Contents

NOTES ON CONTRIBUTORS

PETER DORMER was a journalist and author specialising in contemporary applied art, design and architecture.

NEAL FRENCH trained as a sculptor at the Royal College of Art, worked at Royal Worcester from 1958 to 1972, and was subsequently Head of Ceramics at Hornsey College of Art until his retirement in 1991. He has contributed articles to *Ceramic Review*, and his *Industrial Ceramics/Tableware* was published by Oxford University Press in 1971. He was joint author of *Worcester Blue and White Porcelain* (1981) and his *Ceramic Painting* is to be published by Batsford in 1997.

PAUL GREENHALGH is Head of Research at the Victoria and Albert Museum. He was formerly Head of Art and Design History at Camberwell College of Arts, a curator of ceramics at the V&A, and a Tutor at the Royal College of Art. He has published many articles and three books, *Ephemeral Vistas* (1988), *Modernism in Design* (ed.) (1990) and *Quotations and Sources on Design and the Decorative Arts* (1993).

T. A. HESLOP is currently Dean of the Schools of World Art Studies and Music at the University of East Anglia, where he teaches and researches the history of medieval art and architecture. Recent publications include *Norwich Castle Keep: Romanesque Architecture and Social Context* (1994) and *The Eadwine Psalter: Text, Image and Monastic Culture in Twelfth-Century Canterbury* (1992).

GLORIA HICKEY is a freelance curator and writer living in St John's, Newfoundland, Canada. She has published more than two hundred articles on art and craft for magazines in Canada and the USA, and has edited the book *Making and Metaphor: A Discussion of Meaning in Contemporary Craft* (1994).

ROSEMARY HILL is contributing editor of *Crafts* magazine. She writes about applied art for *The Times Literary Supplement*, *The London Review of Books* and

Perspectives on Architecture. At present she is writing a biography of A. W. N. Pugin for which she received V. S. Naipaul's award for work in progress on the history of art and ideas.

BRUCE METCALF is a jeweller and writer living in Philadelphia, Pennsylvania, USA. His jewellery has been exhibited widely in Europe and the United States, and his writing has appeared in *American Craft, Metalsmith, Studio Potter* and other publications. He has received two National Endowment for Arts Fellowships and a Fulbright Teaching and Research Scholarship.

JONATHAN MEULI is an artist and art historian. He is interested in how and why made objects are viewed at different times by different peoples. His most recent work has been on Native American art. He received his doctorate from the University of East Anglia.

JEREMY MYERSON is a design writer, editor and researcher. He studied at the Royal College of Art and was Founder-Editor of *DesignWeek*. He is affiliated to De Montfort University, Leicester, where he is Professor of Contemporary Design.

HELEN REES is a doctoral student at the University of Manchester and a free-lance writer, lecturer and exhibitions organiser. She is a former Director of the Design Museum, London.

GENERAL EDITOR'S FOREWORD

The essays gathered here are dedicated to the exploration of the philosophy of craft. Despite its undoubted importance as an area within the visual arts, 'craft' has floundered recently between many partially-formed definitions. It has displayed what one could describe, if one were being generous, as a plurality of meanings; less charitably, the word has been the epitome of confusion.

Consequently, the crafts have been, to a considerable extent, pushed to the margins of intellectual life in Europe and North America. They have suffered imposed definitions that have served to reinforce this marginalisation. This is not a problem merely for aesthetes and historians. The commercial, institutional and creative survival of craft practices are threatened by the lack of confidence and clarity buried within the term itself.

This volume deals with a number of issues, including the position and meaning of craft within culture and society, the nature of its previous history, the economy of hand-making, the role of technology and the function of critical writing. The volume is markedly interdisciplinary in its approach to the subject, with strategies from anthropology, economics, literary studies, design history, sociology and philosophy all in evidence. Many of the authors are internationally recognised authorities and all have clear and sometimes controversial views on their subjects.

The persistence of hand-making as a method of manufacture is one of the most interesting aspects of visual culture in the twentieth century. It is the function of volumes such as this one to make this truth abundantly clear.

The editor of the texts, Peter Dormer, has long been considered one of the most important thinkers on contemporary craft in the world. Over the last twenty years he published a number of seminal books and articles, curated several vitally important exhibitions and taught thousands of students. There could not have been a more appropriate editor for this project.

Peter Dormer died on Christmas Eve 1996, as this volume entered its final proofing stage. He leaves behind him many friends and countless admirers of his many contributions to the history and theory of the visual arts. We will all miss him.

PAUL GREENHALGH

ACKNOWLEDGEMENTS

The editor would like to thank the Eastern Arts Board for its generous assistance, the Crafts Council and the University of East Anglia. He would also like to express his gratitude to all those who have contributed to the volume and to Ed Barber for the photographs.

Richard La Trobe-Bateman is a designer and maker of wooden structures: furniture, bridges and fencing. His business embraces hand- as well as batch- and mass-production work; he demonstrates that 'craft' is a fluid, technological activity that cannot easily be categorised into one set of attitudes or life-styles. In one sense the existence of a *salon de refuse* suits La Trobe-Bateman: it provides him with a home.

INTRODUCTION

1 ✧ *The* salon de refuse?

PETER DORMER

After the Bauhaus

Many of us have come across works of art that thrill us. Such objects may include, although not necessarily, those 'masterpieces' or monuments promoted by museums or national tourist boards. Whatever they are, they will have for us the status of being *defining objects*, objects which we think reach (and exemplify) the highest standard. For example, the ceramic and metal functional wares produced by students and teachers in the workshops of the Bauhaus possess this exemplary status in twentieth-century craftsmanship; they are objects that demonstrate so many of the qualities that are desirable in everyday design.

The Bauhaus Archive in Berlin is an intriguing place to visit for anyone who had the fortune or misfortune to undergo the Foundation Year in a British art school after the Second World War. The Bauhaus invented the foundation course, in which every student would go back to first principles in understanding form, texture, line and colour. It produced much work that was modern, innovative and experimental. Moreover, what the Bauhaus foundation or basic course demonstrated was an absolute commitment to craftsmanship. The quality of the experimental drawings, paintings, textiles, sculptures, ceramics and metalware is underpinned by craft knowledge. Here were students and teachers who knew how to draw or paint or make things of a high quality. They needed this knowledge and the clarity of expression it brought in order to give conviction to their ideas.

Years later British foundation courses were a poor version of the

Bauhaus: it was enough to encourage work that had the appearance of innovation or the look of the experimental. The general idea of the foundation or basic course was accepted but the teachers who led these courses were either not versed in craft or they had taken an ideological position against it. By the end of the 1960s craftsmanship was barely taught at all, nor was it valued.

Arguably there has been an immense amount of talented scholarship and polemic published about the Bauhaus and the role of craftsmanship. But while generally craftsmanship at the Bauhaus is acknowledged, it is also downplayed as though it were an intellectually inconvenient fact of design history.

Why is craft intellectually incovenient in modern and contemporary art? Why did it go out of fashion as an interesting concept and activity to argue about and to practise? Certainly the highly intelligent but at times Swiftian scepticism that has constantly probed and taunted the question of what art is has had its effect on crafts over the last seventy years. The questions tempt and beguile us with their implicit answers: why should art be this? Why does art need craft? Why make something when you find a ready-made and present it as art? It is your ability to choose and select, not your ability to make, that marks you as an artist, as a connoisseur. Why have the object at all? And in the face of these questions craft in art collapsed. Craft just seemed so *tedious* because it was almost inelegant in its demands.

There has also been an assumption that ever-improving technology replaces craft. In some areas technology has indeed replaced craft in efficiency and aesthetics: ask almost any devotee of the top ranges of BMW motor cars. Or indeed ask the owner of a pair of Nike shoes. What they drive and what they wear is art.

Yet technology's achievements are not godlike, they are variable and flawed. When I visited the Bauhaus Archive I was struck by the contrast that exists between the quality of the exhibits and the quality of the building housing them. The building, created in 1989, is of a conventional, pre-cast slab concrete construction. Its quality and its design are neither above nor below the average that we encounter throughout Europe at the end of the twentieth century: it is a building of expediency created from a kit of parts, with no finesse and no detailing.

Inside, however, and in contrast, the exhibits, especially the textiles, furniture, metal and ceramic ware, are a treasury of information on the nuances of line, texture and surface finishes which offer a surprising combination of shapes and forms. The contradiction between the aesthetic ideals exhibited in the Archive and what we tolerate in building or manufacturing sixty years later is striking.

The Bauhaus was not the only institution in the 1920s which was exploring new design through craftsmanship; there were other art schools, especially in Switzerland, such as the Kunstgewerbeschule, Zurich, and the Ecole des Beaux Arts in Geneva, taking similar approaches. But what followed from all this workmanship was something of an anti-climax: we had the post-Second-World-War phenomenon of the studio crafts. The serious endeavours of technology and design went their own ways and craft became 'the Crafts': people who enjoyed making things found themselves left, not with the yeast of culture, but the crumbs. They had to make do with the unsatisfactory world of studio craft and art craft. It is unsatisfactory because, to borrow a phrase from one of my co-authors, it has become a *salon de refuse* of low status.

However, as the art historian T. A. Heslop, an expert on medieval art, demonstrates in chapter 3, the collapse in status of one kind of art in favour of another is not new; nor is it easily explainable. For the collapse in status is less like a simple change in fashion (fashions tend to get rediscovered) but amounts to a real shift in aesthetic appreciation. Whole generations are no longer moved by that which enthralled earlier generations.

Heslop's chapter draws attention to a substantial shift in the perceptions of artists and (his term) craftists around the twelfth century. In this time there was a relative decline in the status of those arts associated with the forge and the furnace, goldsmithing and enamelling, for example, and the relative rise of arts which were concerned with figuration, such as painting and sculpture. He takes as his particular example stained glass.

Heslop is too experienced a scholar to create direct comparisons between what happened in the twelfth century and what is happening in the twentieth century. On the other hand, he is bold enough to want us to draw conclusions from history to see how they fit and whether they inform us today. Indeed, his belief in history's ability to shed light on our contemporary world is stated in his first paragraph:

Perspective can also, usually, provide a contributory explanation for some quite recent 'event' from deep in historical time; in my own view a good case can be made for regarding the Treaty of Verdun in 843 as a major cause of the First World War.

Heslop discusses where stained glass got its prestige from and draws attention to its captivating display and the craft virtuosity upon which it rests. He then moves on to a consideration of the way in which taste changed away from the pleasures of 'dazzling the senses' to the mimetic games of painting. He describes this, interestingly, as a shift from the sensual to the intellectual – as a shift which, of course, artists and art critics today insist distinguishes the move of art away from craft. Heslop also says that stained glass 'attempted increasingly to play the games of painting'. Observers of the contemporary relationship between the studio crafts and 'fine' art can only mutter 'plus ça change'.

Definitions and their implications

Craft

General definitions of 'craft', 'technology' or 'design' tend to be pretty hopeless, in the same way that definitions of art tend to be. To be of any real use definitions should not proceed through generalities, but, like the legal system, evolve through case law by taking account of previous examples and the judgements of connoisseurs. Paul Greenhalgh uses the case-law approach when he tackles the slippery history of what the term 'craft' means in chapter 2. He begins by noting that there are many partially-formed definitions of craft creating a confusion whose ambiguity, he notes wryly, is often to the advantage of makers and writers: they (we) make the word mean whatever is convenient for the moment.

Greenhalgh demonstrates how, in the last three centuries, the word 'craft' has changed its meaning; in the eighteenth century the word was used to describe political acumen and shrewdness, it was not related to a particular way of making things but rather a way of doing things, especially in politics. In some applications, as with the Freemasons, Greenhalgh points out that the phrase 'the craft' had (and still retains) the meaning of power and secret knowledge.

The more contemporary sense of 'craft', 'craftsman' and 'craftswoman' does not appear as common currency until the last quarter of the nineteenth century and the beginnings of the Arts and Crafts movements. By that time, Greenhalgh notes, one of the categories of art – 'the decorative arts' – is in the process of being disenfranchised from fine art. With the disenfranchisement of the decorative arts comes that most familiar question: is art a quality that can be applied to any object regardless of genre, or not?

As Greenhalgh traces his history through to the twentieth century he describes how craft becomes divorced from design in the 1920s. Thus 'craft' becomes intellectually isolated from both the pursuit of beauty (art) and purpose (design).

For so many contemporary craftspeople the most important question related to their status is that question – 'is art a concept that can be applied to any manufactured object?' The practical importance of this question comes into focus once one recognises its sociological aspects.

For instance, some people want to claim that their motor car or their motor cycle is 'a work of art'; others would be content if they could get their pots accepted as art. Conversely, I would like to have entire movements of painting and sculpture discussed in terms of craft. None of these objectives is attainable because the institutions of contemporary art set the definitions of what fine art is and what it is not.

For European and North American makers of pots and other craft objects the 'is it art?' question is a practical one of status that has to do with money: anything with the status of art is potentially more valuable than a thing without that status. Moreover, people want the status of being an artist as a value in its own right. The status of being an artist is almost a tradable 'invisible' commodity within the art, craft and design world. Its value is kept high by protectionism. Being an 'artist' may not make you wealthy but it enables you to be considered for the more important exhibitions and public collections, as well as mainstream news media coverage and consideration by the critics.

Whether or not 'being an artist' any longer has high status with the general public is a different issue, but that hardly matters; the tradable value of 'being an artist' is with the art-going public and, above all, the institutions of art.

No amount of talking or writing up by designers of motor bikes or makers of pots (or by design or craft writers) has the slightest effect on the status quo. This is because at the heart of the argument lie questions, not of connoisseurship, but of cultural politics, and behind them is an art world economy. Bruce Metcalf in chapter 4 raises this issue when he talks about the 'institutional theory of art', a theory which he attributes to the American philosopher and art critic Arthur Danto. More controversially, Metcalf, himself a craftsman, sees contemporary craft and contemporary art as radically different from each other and states: 'I propose that contemporary art and craft are rooted, at least in part, in different biological and social contexts.'

With regard to the definition of craft used by most of us in this book there are two dominant definitions, both of them unavoidably sloppy. Either craft means 'studio crafts' covering everyone working with a craft medium. This includes producers of functional ware as well as abstractionist sculptors working in textiles, clay or glass. Or craft means a process over which a person has detailed control, control that is the consequence of craft knowledge. I shall discuss this more fully in chapter 8.

Technology

Technology is as slippery to define as craft. Most craft activities involve 'a technology' – using a brush, a palette and a set of colours is a technology. Our contemporary use of the term, however, refers to means of making or doing things which have a certain order of magnitude. Technology is the integration of machines and information to create processes of manufacture or the distribution of knowledge in ways that are increasingly independent of the vagaries, whims or decisions of individual employees or, indeed, employers.

There is a debate, among sociologists for example, regarding how far technology shapes us and how much we shape technology. On the one hand, there is an understandable reluctance to accept the deterministic view that technology drives us in one direction regardless of our individual desires and political or moral values. On the other hand, it does appear that technology has its own impetus and logic and that various new ways of manufacturing or organising our institutions or our lives are imposed upon us in ways that we did not choose. This 'us' upon which technology is imposed also includes the managers, directors and owners of technology. For instance, the board of a newspaper publishing company has no choice but to adopt computerised technology if the

7

company is to stay competitive. The alternative would be if all publishers agreed as a cartel not to adopt new technology, but such agreements would not be credible; someone would break the agreement and steal an advantage in the market.

In principle human beings can organise themselves to change the course of a technology but in practice it is difficult. Consider how embedded the 'car culture' has become; any attempt to limit the effects of this one technology becomes a cultural revolution.

Yet just because a technology exists does not mean that a society is fated to adopt it. Take the technology of firearms and handguns. One of the marked differences between north-west European societies and that of the USA is that the USA has a gun culture and the Europeans do not. There are complex historical and constitutional reasons why this is so, but the point remains that choices about technology *can* be made. However, once a technology is entrenched in a society it seems that nothing will dislodge it except another technology.

Technology may advance as a series of inventions, but it also proceeds organically with a mass of tiny alterations and improvements taken by thousands of individuals. The interesting thing about working in any kind of technology, including craft, is the way in which an improvement will 'suggest' itself to someone. Therein lies technology's power: one set of ideas leads 'naturally' to another set and this natural growth happens not in one place at one time but is going on all the time and everywhere that the technology is used. It takes a very determined political initiative to interrupt such growth. Additionally, the notion that any one person has power to determine the direction of technology, given the diffused nature of its development, becomes less credible.

Not all studio crafts are ill at ease with contemporary technology, and far from all (or even many) craftspeople are in opposition to the machine (whether mechanical or electronic). In chapter 10 I discuss the ease with which craft weaving fits in with factory processes and how there is a conceptual core to the structure of weaving that gives it a central position in computerised design and manufacture. Additionally, Paul Greenhalgh in chapter 6 corrects the historical misconception that categorises crafts-people as Luddites. He also clarifies what the term 'Luddite' should properly mean.

Some people have become pessimistic about the effects of technology on certain arts. Regarding architecture, for example, it is arguable that both craft and art have been driven out from the design of most buildings by technology.

Take the argument and example set by the Dutch architect Rem Koolhaas. He has raised the issue of the deterministic effects of technology upon architecture in his book titled *S, M, L, XL* (Rotterdam, 010 Publishers, 1995). The title stands for small, medium, large, and extra large. *S, M, L, XL* makes one recognise how architecture has been changed by the single issue of size and how size is the product of a developing building industry interested in being efficient and in offering as much quantity per dollar or Deutschmark as possible.

Consider his own experience in Lille in northern France. Lille fell upon hard times in the 1980s, but the Mayor, recognising that his city sat between Brussels, London and Paris and knowing that the Channel Tunnel was to be built, lobbied France's central government to allow Lille to become France's most important railway junction. Turning Lille into a transport artery puts Lille at the centre of a potential audience or consumer market of 100 million Europeans. International companies are encouraged to settle in Lille, and Lille is being marketed as the natural meeting-place for international conferences.

Koolhaas became the city planner in 1989. He says the key to Lille's success is size. There had to be big conference and trade venues, big offices, and big shopping centres. Current technology means that extra large can be very economical. He says: 'Cheapness is ideological in this situation because the virtual community of 100 million can work only if Lille remains cheaper than the surrounding cities' (p. 1198). He also had the insight to realise that the new Lille had to have a big-bang beginning: it could not afford to evolve; it had to achieve a critical mass as quickly as possible. Quantity – getting the maximum from every franc – was a necessity.

Koolhaas believes that the 'art' of architecture is useless in bigness. It is not just that art is squeezed out from the building through the need to get as much building as possible per franc but because the technology of bigness has no place for art. Big buildings have their own systems-led, pre-formed, component-orientated logic. It barely needs an architect to direct it.

Thus Koolhaas writes,

9

Without a theory of Bigness, architects are in the position of Frankenstein's creators: instigators of a partly successful experiment whose results are running amok and are therefore discredited. Because there is no theory of Bigness, we don't know what to do with it, we don't know where to put it, we don't know when to use it, we don't know how to plan it, Big mistakes are the only connection to Bigness. (p. 509)

Technology has given us the economics and scale, but in achieving this it has necessarily adopted the strategy of simplification and removal of the possibility for human error. This is discussed in chapter 8. Where there is art in architecture, it remains in the craftsmanship or workmanship of high-status, one-off, hand-crafted buildings.

Bigness, however, is not all that technology is good at. Chapter 8 also discusses the fact that, on a smaller scale, technology is beginning to challenge craftsmanship by its ability to mimic the 'look' of handworkmanship, especially in areas such as textiles. At the moment this ability to mimic craft has its aesthetic limitations.

In chapter 9, Neal French offers an example of an aesthetic limitation which may seem predictable coming from a man who was a noted designer of tableware and whose experience was based on the more traditional relationship of a designer working with a modeller (rather than a computer operator). The old way of doing things involved freehand drawing and carved and turned plaster models. There were weeks available for thinking and the readjustment of nuances. Neal French believes it created a livelier, more aesthetic product because it allowed the possibility of art to enter the design. The old way meant that a design for a set of tableware took two years to bring on to the market; using CADCAM it takes twelve weeks.

French's experience receives endorsement in Professor Jeremy Myerson's chapter 11, which discusses whether or not using computers is a craft. Myerson reveals that a number of people using elaborate computer software to model designs believe that in order to get the best out of the software – to get some 'art' out of it – one needs to know how to make things oneself. One needs a separate experience of making in order to use the computer software knowingly.

One of the reasons why people purchase CADCAM is that it has two virtues: it can be very fast and, more important, it produces consistent results. In the ceramics industry this consistency has encouraged manufacturers to produce work that is indistinguishable in quality from its competitors. This is deliberate because market researchers employed by the tableware and giftware manufacturers have confirmed that the public wants consistency and desires a dependable, almost hygienic neatness in the quality of tableware.

This news, if correct, bodes ill for studio crafts since it limits their appeal both as consumer objects and as gifts: how can you give an 'untidy' pot to an aunt who prefers something neat and smooth? Anthropologists sometimes refer to gifts as 'exchange commodities', which would imply an even bleaker outlook for the sales of craft. For if most consumers are wary of buying handmade untidiness for themselves then they may be even more wary about offering it as gift to someone else: they'd never know what they would receive in return. This is one of the questions that Gloria Hickey, a Canadian writer, has researched in chapter 5. It appears that the studio crafts have no market at all other than the rather small constituency of studio craft collectors. If craftspeople who cannot sell to collectors want to earn a living then they have to make giftware. They need to discover the difference between giftware and art–craft. They should read Hickey's chapter. On the other hand, making giftware will do nothing for an artist's status.

Interestingly, Tony Ford, Director of the British Crafts Council, regards such research as Hickey's and speculation such as my own as unduly pessimistic. Research undertaken on behalf of the Crafts Council apparently shows that one in four adults in Britain has an interest in the crafts. Some of this interest includes buying work that other people have made. This divergence of opinion is probably resolvable by defining our terminology more closely, i.e. craft that is made as giftware is not the same as studio craft, which is made as art. Hickey's research encourages this distinction.

Design

Design is the most difficult term of all to define. In one sense I was quite jolted by Paul Greenhalgh's observation that craft had become divorced from design. Surely design enters *everything* one makes? He is, however, historically right that the new profession of design divorced itself from craft. Helen Rees, in chapter 7, describes how, from the 1920s onwards, we see the aggressive growth of a new business called 'Design' in which creative people with an eye to making money created the lucrative idea of consultancy. It was like slicing a salami sausage: one takes the business of manufacturing and one sees how many separate businesses can be created from it – the design profession was one of them, public relations was another.

Nevertheless, in a practical sense you cannot divorce craft from design. The craftsman or craftswoman is as much a designer as any product designer: to make something requires choices regarding the structure and appearance of the object as well as a strategy for making it.

Even so, from the designer's point of view, the craftsperson has become expendable: computer-guided machines increasingly inhabit factories (unless labour costs are so low that the machines are uneconomic). Moreover, even model-making and prototyping are under threat because of advances in automated rapid prototyping techniques. However, as Neal French points out, there is still a role for model-making and prototyping but for how long and in what form it will last is impossible to predict.

Designers do not think that they are expendable. Here they may be making a mistake. In a world in which quality that is 'good enough' generally passes muster, there is no reason why the majority of designers should not be replaced by computer operators guided by salesmen and saleswomen. Software menus of shape, form, line and colour, together with databases on materials, costs and manufacturing methods, are ideal for the computer.

Designers do not agree. They claim they are in the business of satisfying human desires and, indeed, creating new ones. Computers cannot compete. As Helen Rees describes matters, design is more socially orientated than the studio crafts because designers are constantly thinking about consumers. The studio crafts are characterised by inwardlookingness because so many practitioners claim they are making (and designing) for themselves. A designer who does not seriously consider whether other people will respond as he or she does to a given design is probably gambling with unemployability. Meanwhile, being unemployable is one of the characteristics of the majority of those practising studio crafts, which is why there are so few links between them and industry (or architecture).

Yet Helen Rees also argues that the division between the studio crafts and design is no longer as sharp as a divorce. There is some interesting evidence for this in that for the last thirty years a succession of high-status designers such as Ettore Sottsass, Andrea Branzi and Daniel Weil have merged studio crafts with design in their pursuit of more 'humane' design.

Ettore Sottsass is one of Italy's most famous 'industrial' or product designers; yet he has produced 'art' ceramics for forty years, beginning in 1956 when an American businessman asked him to design some modern, upbeat pots for young, upwardly mobile Americans. Since then Sottsass's pots have certainly looked like studio ceramics; they are not primarily functional, some have thick, custard-like glazes, and others are highly textured or incised with deep cuts that only just catch the glaze – and they are handmade, but not by him. He draws; artisans produce the work.

Sottsass has always had a problem with design. He wants to address

> the problem of making things that wouldn't yield too quickly to the pleasure people get from filling their homes with a thousand small trophies of personal status, objects that would not in any way sacrifice themselves to currency values; that would not yield too quickly to the rhythm of consumerism. (Ettore Sottsass, *Ceramics*, London, Thames & Hudson, 1995, p. 8)

That is why he took to handcrafted ceramics. Sottsass's instincts were right. As Gloria Hickey discovered, very few shoppers (at least in Canada where she did her research) accept studio ceramics as being within the giftware or the consumer market. They don't know what they are – maybe art, maybe not – but they're not seen as things you can show off as trophies or treat as an investment. And, certainly, Sottsass's ceramics fit no clear category of consumables.

Andrea Branzi, another Italian designer, has through his exhibitions and books explored the idea of adding meaning and symbolism to objects in the home. His pursuit has led him to create a series of studio-craft designs for furniture and other objects which he has called 'domestic animals'. Domestic animals, or pets, are lovable and have personality. This is what Branzi has sought in his designs. However, it has to be said that his designs are impractical, probably unmarketable, and exist as rhetorical objects; they are part of an argument among philosophers of design, nor a service for the public.

But it is Daniel Weil, who worked for a while with Sottsass's studio, and who in the early 1990s was Professor of Design at the Royal College of Art, London, who has given the clearest demonstration of how design and the studio crafts can dissolve into one another.

All Weil's postgraduate students, many of them from Holland,

13

Germany and Scandinavia, were encouraged to explore metaphor in design and to think of their work as small expressions of art, desire, wit or sensuality. The result was that the aspirant designers took their visual language from the studio crafts and also from classical English workmanship. There is still in England a strong artisanal culture in high-quality shoemaking, hatmaking, and gifts for the rich such as small leather boxes for cufflinks and finely crafted combs and brushes for a 'gentleman's toilette'. All these things were seized upon by the students as sources of tactile and even symbolic information which they could incorporate in their own designs for clocks, watches, computers, mobile telephones, furniture and domestic accessories.

Whether or not Sottsass, Branzi or Weil (or their followers) have made or will make a big impact upon design for manufacturing is hard to gauge, probably not. What is interesting (and heartening from the viewpoint of the studio crafts) is that when designers want to make a rhetorical cultural comment about the shortcomings of design and technology they have borrowed an argument from the crafts. In so doing they also showed how fluid is the definition of design.

Another department at the Royal College of Art has demonstrated that the *rapprochement* between design and craft is not one-sided. Professor David Watkins, head of the jewellery and metalsmithing department, has for ten years been building a course for postgraduates in which they consider all the aspects of making a design in metal for batch or mass production. What has emerged is that, in metalsmithing at least, practitioners of a craft can invent new ranges of highly desirable consumer objects (or gifts) that neither compromise on quality of manufacture nor ignore the logic of economics. Watkins has enabled his students successfully to break out of the *salon de refuse* of studio crafts.

Rhetoric and writing

The studio crafts may be of marginal importance in a Western or Westernised national economy but, as Helen Rees points out, they constitute a cultural phenomenon which pursues a set of values. These values ought to be of some interest philosophically and socially: they include the freedom that comes through the possession of skill and the freedom that is attainable when one is in a position to direct the content, pace and quality of the way one earns one's living. Practitioners 'state' or rather demonstrate their arguments and values through what they do and how they live. I discuss one of the several ways in which this happens in chapter 14. However, objects and ways of life, whilst they provide a demonstration of values, do not really argue for them in the sense in which now most people commonly understand advocacy. Showing is different from speaking or writing.

Writing has assumed considerable importance in the battle of the status of the crafts because the written text has itself a high cultural status. From the craftsperson's point of view no writing is more important than the catalogue essay. As is the case in contemporary fine art, the catalogue essay exists as a form of propaganda. It is the vehicle through which the artist or craftsperson can see his or her own glowingly positive obituary. For the catalogue essay is an attempt both at convincing the doubters of the present and providing the future with a particular view of the maker's status.

Yet the question remains: whom does it convince? Is anyone, other than the craftsperson's friends and relatives, inclined to believe the often over-elaborate philosophical and art-historical claims made on behalf of the work? Surely not. Additionally, there is the broader question of whether any writing that seeks to draw attention to the nature of craft, its virtues, values and continuing relevance, actually does any good in terms of raising craft's status in the eyes of those who are not interested in the subject or who have dismissed it as second-rate. If the craftspeople are in a *salon de refuse*, then are not those who write on the subject in there with them? Almost certainly.

No amount of writing can reverse a cultural trend. When T. A. Heslop outlines the change from higher to lower status of 'crafts' such as stained glass, metalware and embroidery, one cannot imagine that a small band of writers, still less theorists, would have been able to argue the trend into reverse.

The simple truth, and it seems to hold for all *salons de refuse*, is that the work and rhetoric is of interest and significance mainly to the members of the *salon*. If others from time to time peep in and discover an idea or two that takes their imagination (like Messrs Sottsass, Branzi and Weil), then that is a bonus. And if, like David Watkins's students, craft practitioners can broaden the scope and interest in their own works,

15

then that too is very welcome. For the rest of the time we must pursue our own interest talking among ourselves.

In stating this I am not ignoring Tony Ford's opinion (see above) that the constituency for 'craft' is quite large – one in four of British adults. Yet my intuition is that only a small number of this constituency are interested in the debate about what craft is and why tacit knowledge matters. Perhaps such debates are regarded as too recondite or simply too silly to attend to. What does concern and surprise me is the rigidity of middlebrow art criticism with regard to craft. For instance, as I write, the British art critic Andrew Graham-Dixon is presenting a six-part television series on the history of British art since the sixteenth century. Graham-Dixon's arguments are revisionist and provocative. They provoke me in so far as he ignores 'the crafts'. It is apparently all right to admire a painting of Elizabeth I in which her lavish dress, jewellery and headwear are so well-executed in paint. It is not, however, thought relevant to show the jewellery or clothing of the period and discuss the art of these crafts in their own right.

Consequently I regard all the chapters in this book as a contribution to a family argument provided either by members or friends of the family. This does not, however, remove the necessity or the desire for good-quality writing and argument. For if we value the subject, and all of us, for reasons as diverse as the subject itself, do so value it, then we must see to it that we give ourselves as good a diet of writing as we can, and I believe the chapters contributed by Rosemary Hill and Jonathan Meuli in Part III of this book are good examples of this desired quality.

Alan Peters is an internationally famous designer-maker in wood, whose education and aesthetic are rooted in the English nineteenth/early-twentieth-century craft revival. To understand what his work – and that of other makers like him – represents, one must explore, as this section does, the shifts of meaning in the history of craft.

THE STATUS OF CRAFT

The separation of craft from art and design is one of the phenomena of late-twentieth-century Western culture. The consequences of this split have been quite startling. It has led to the separation of 'having ideas' from 'making objects'. It has also led to the idea that there exists some sort of mental attribute known as 'creativity' that precedes or can be divorced from a knowledge of how to make things. This has led to art without craft.

The fact that the practitioners of essay-writing, dance, theatre and music, for example, have not accepted that creativity can be defined as 'art without craft' has been ignored in the visual arts. In the visual arts 'I don't want the craft to get in the way of my creativity' is a perfectly meaningful statement.

At the same time there has been the evolution of 'the crafts' as a separate art form. Enough people have wanted to go on making things. Enough people believe that they can expand their ideas and knowledge about the world through learning and practising a craft. Some people believe that if you want to truly understand a thing you have to make a version of that thing – a model, representation or piece of mimetic art. This belief accounts for why the crafts of the figurative arts persist (although not to the same standards of the past).

Many of the practitioners of 'the crafts' have found themselves caught in a contradiction. For one thing, although the makers of pots, textiles and furniture have many understanding admirers, they have not found themselves admired as much as other 'artists'. Potters do not earn the same regard as sculptors, for example; and jewellery, for all its virtuosity, invention and ideas, remains a minor art. This is hurtful to the practitioners concerned but it is not a sudden development, it has been growing since the late nineteenth century.

But as if this were not bad enough, they have also found that the 'ordinary consumer' does not admire them so much either, or rather, the ordinary consumer is puzzled by what the value of 'the crafts' is supposed to be (or, put yet another way, why are 'the crafts' so expensive!). The contradiction is that it appears to many intelligent craftspeople that they have actually to renege on craftsmanship to pursue their craft. The admirers of 'high art' are not interested in craft and the consumers of decorative objects and other trophies for the home do not see that high craft is really worth paying for. So what is a maker to do if he or she is to gain status or earn a living?

To summarise then, there are three aspects which contribute to the ambiguity of the status of 'the crafts':

 (i) the separation of making from meaning;
 (ii) the separation of the arts into categories of 'higher' and 'lower' (pottery is low art, sculpture isn't);
(iii) puzzled 'ordinary' consumers.

These three aspects are among the those discussed by Paul Greenhalgh, T. A. Heslop and Gloria Hickey in their respective chapters.

For craftsmen and -women who are worried about the status of craft, and yet remain hopeful that categories such as the prevailing distinction between 'art' and 'the crafts' are really quite arbitrary and can be made to disappear one into the other – as water in water as it were – there is interesting news. Bruce Metcalf's chapter, which is also concerned with status, argues that 'craft' and 'art' are fundamentally different activities and that their difference is rooted in the biology of the brain.

2 ✧ The history of craft

PAUL GREENHALGH

> All art has been rigidly divided into classes, like the society it reflects .... We have the arts all ticketed and pigeon-holed on the shelves behind us. (Walter Crane, 1892)[1]

> When we establish a considered classification, when we say that a cat and a dog resemble each other less than two greyhounds do ... what is the ground on which we are able to establish the validity of this classification with complete certainty? On what 'table', according to what grid of identities, similitudes, analogies, have we become accustomed to sort out so many different and similar things? (Michel Foucault, 1974)[2]

For several decades now the major debate within the craft world has been to do with the status of the word itself.[3] Some makers and thinkers have revealed themselves unhappy with the nomenclature 'craftsperson'. Others have worn it with undisguised pride. Whether for or against it, however, most have professed an unsureness as to what exactly it means. Despite its undoubted importance as a descriptor in the visual arts, it seems to bounce between many partially-formed meanings, exuding a plurality which is more to do with confusion than complexity. This can have its advantages to makers and thinkers alike. One can take possession of the word, latch on to any number of previous and partial definitions and develop an individualised philosophy, aesthetics, technology, ethnology or economy of craft. We can all hunt for clothing in this wardrobe of meanings and emerge dressed as the craftsperson of our choice. But there are grave disadvantages also in a signifier that has no stable significance. The fractionalised confusion of craft prevents those practices placed within its boundaries from forming a cohesive lobby. The commercial, institutional and creative survival of the practices held within its empire are threatened by the lack of clarity and confidence buried within the term itself.

This is the first and most important point to hold in mind. Craft is an empire. It is a constituency within the late-modern system of the arts, a naming-word and a major class in a professional world that is underpinned by a rigorous classificatory structure. For some time it has stood alongside two other classes, of design and fine art.

The crafts have not been well served by historians for much of the twentieth century. The lack of detailed historical analysis has been a contributory factor to what is undoubtedly a contemporary crisis of confidence. I will attempt to do two things in this chapter to help remedy this situation. I will take the word 'craft' and briefly chart its history from the Enlightenment onwards. Then I will look at craft as a class and examine the historical formation of its theoretical elements.

My main argument will be that the fundamental problem with the word is that it is being used to collectively describe genres and ideas that formerly were not grouped together and that grew from quite separate circumstances. I will also suggest that 'craft' as a naming-word is an unstable compound at this time because there is a disjuncture between its etymology and the constituency it is expected to represent. These problems are best addressed by history, prior to any recourse to theory.

The etymology of three craftsmen

Caleb D'Anvers could no longer keep quiet. In 1729 he published a news-sheet, which he himself had almost entirely written. He called his publication *The Country Journal or the Craftsman*, shortening this after several months to *The Craftsman*.[4] It was the first publication ever to bear that name. *The Craftsman* averaged some four pages per week of topical discussion, unequivocally promoting the principle of free speech and using most of its column-space to wrestle with the great problems of the time. Anglo-Spanish relations were a main subject of the first issue, for example. The flavour of the whole was acrimonious, a bastion of xenophobic aggression. Caleb's writers hated most races of which they were aware: 'Irishmen [are] ridiculous and offensive ... Scotch impudence is of a different species.'[5] Several of them also had an endearing if pompous disrespect for political power, constantly castigating an aristocracy they suspected of decadence and cosmopolitanism: 'the little regard you pay to the laws and religion of your country ... has produced such a deluge of vice and profanity, as may soon overwhelm the whole nation'.[6] The entire intellectual structure of the news-sheet was formed through Whiggishly aggressive replies to, or attacks upon, other publications. A piece of verse in an early issue captured the spirit of the whole:

> Once upon a time in sunshine weather,
> Falshood and truth walk'd together,
> The neighbouring Woods and Lawns to view,
> As opposites sometimes do.[7]

The abrasive style made *The Craftsman* popular. It survived Caleb and rolled on for almost six decades, finally petering out in the 1780s.

Caleb's title is particularly interesting in the present context, because it carried no references at all to making processes of any kind. Its connection to modern usage of the word is in the general sense of 'crafty', or 'shrewd', although the strongest implication of craft in the journal is of a sort of political acumen. Other mid-century texts used the word in this sense, often with an added sense of criminality: 'The unequal distribution of property must have been as ancient as craft, fraud and violence.'[8]

Samuel Johnson's *Dictionary of the English Language* (1773) shows that these earlier references had not wholly characterised the meaning of the word, and that it could include the concepts of making and skill. One of his four definitions of craft is 'manual art or trade'.[9] A craftsman could be 'an artificer, manufacturer, a mechanick'.[10] Craft did not imply specific methods, trades or object types, however. It had no constituency, it could be applied to any form of practice within the culture. It was not a thing *in itself*. Ben Jonson was cited to explain the word, for example, showing that it could be applied to poetry, the most cerebral of the arts: 'A poem is the work of a poet, poetry is his skill or craft of making.'[11] In Johnson's volume, the word was still clearly centred on the meanings that are apparent in Caleb's journal, these dominating the entry as a whole. Craft was 'fraud, cunning, artifice, full of artifices, fraudulent, sly', the verb derived from it meant 'to play tricks, to practice artifice'.

Taken collectively, the sources I cite here generate the flavour, if not the specificity, of a further sense of the word. Its use by Freemasons, preserved probably from the language of the guilds, combined trade with politics to imply power. Control of skill and labour, after all, had far less to do with aesthetics or technics, and far more to do with politics and economy. Craft as ungovernable power is also the implication of witchcraft.[12]

The reuse of *The Craftsman* as a title after the decline of the original is most revealing. During the nineteenth century there was no recorded publication of that name at all.[13] The words 'craft' and 'craftsman' are not widely used in any context until the last quarter of the century, when both became powerful signifiers in advanced debates in the visual arts and relatively common in institutional circles. 'Handicraft' was used as frequently as craft. One writer noted of museum facilities, for example, that 'the handicraftsman pursuing his industry in one or other such divisions, could come to South Kensington and consult the works which belonged to his craft'.[14]

As a name to publish under, Caleb's word, therefore, had a conspicuous absence through much of the nineteenth century; it was destined to be omnipresent in the twentieth. In 1901 Gustave Stickley founded *The Craftsman* in New York.[15] Picking up on contemporary developments in Britain, his publication became a principal means through which American producers and consumers of goods became completely familiar with developments in the visual arts, and especially the Arts and Crafts movement. Published by the United Crafts, an Arts and Crafts group based in Eastwood, the journal unashamedly supported the economic and political positions associated with that movement. The first two issues were dedicated to William Morris and John Ruskin respectively and carried lengthy discussions of their lives and work.[16] Once it settled into a pattern, Stickley's journal simultaneously maintained a powerful polemic and styled itself as a broad-based visual arts magazine. The October 1906 issue carried articles on books, cabinet-making, city planning, etching, opera, painting, poetry, vernacular industries and religion.

At least six journals or series after Stickley's carried the name up to 1981, when Paul and Angie Boyer launched their *Craftsman*. Their version was far less catholic than Stickley's. Servicing what has proven to be a substantial and persistent readership, it appears every two months and concentrates its attention on the processes and products of hand-making. In some senses it is a trade magazine, offering support to those who manufacture goods by hand using what are thought to be traditional methods. Issue 65 of 1995, for example, featured batik, knitting, pottery, spinning and stick-making. The magazine also has an ethical agenda, to protect a constituency it perceives to be under threat:

> our traditional crafts are being forgotten in favour of something requiring less skill and creativity. There is, certainly, room for everything in the marketplace, but surely that is what traditional crafts should not be seen as – a marketplace.[17]

Having said this, there can be little doubt that the main function of the magazine is to sell and promote this manufacturing sector. The bulk of the pages are devoted to craft fairs and retail outlets, and articles such as 'I want to sell more, what do I do?'[18] and 'Why and how to make changes in your business'[19] offer advice.

Taken collectively, the most striking feature about all three of these publications is the shift in meaning of the word itself. The 'craftsman' implied by Caleb's title, in so far as he can be characterised, was a confident, arrogant, self-reliant, free-living Englishman. A century after his belligerence, Gustave Stickley's craftsman was an ethical aesthete. He clearly understood craft to principally relate to processes of making, but there were no limitations on what techniques or genres the word applied to. Craft for him was a broad, generic signifier that might be applied to any area of the arts or humanities; it could be used in the context of theology, opera or easel painting. Paul and Angie Boyer do not share this vision. For them, craft implies a particular type of person, environment, genre, technique and market. Pottery, weaving, basket-making, metalsmithing, stick-making; their craftsman makes things by hand using pre-industrial technologies and sells them to make a living. He is an eco-friendly small businessman.

The three examples could be added to. I have cited them as archetypes simply to make the point that whilst craft has represented specific ideas at any one time over the past three centuries, it has continually developed and changed. Time-laden and traditional as it might seem, the years have not bestowed the word with a solitary or even consistent meaning. It has acquired fresh ones on several occasions and has inherited constituencies that did not formerly belong to it. It has moved from being an adjective to being a noun; from being a description of things to being a thing in itself. Yet it has managed, as it has rolled on, to hold on to shades of meaning from its earlier lives. Once it acquired a meaning, craft never wholly lost it. As Paul and Angie Boyer edit their copy in the late 1990s, the brutish nonconformism of Caleb D'Anvers belies their vision of tradition, and the high cultural aspirations of Gustave Stickley oppose the modesty of their aesthetic aims. In like manner, those who have inherited the mantle of Stickley feel uncomfortable in the shadow of the canvas awnings of country fairs.

The elements of craft

If it can be said that the word itself has been forming for over two and a half centuries, the constituency it is now used to represent is far younger. When the total range of genres presently described as crafts are put together and scrutinised, it becomes clear that there is a certain arbitrariness in the gathering. They arrived in that category from different beginnings, gathered by forces that emanated from without.

More important than this, the ideological and intellectual underpinning of the craft constituency is not a consistent whole, but has several distinct threads to it, which have only become intertwined relatively recently. It is these threads, or elements, that I will deal with here. There are three. I will describe them as *decorative art*, the *vernacular* and the *politics of work*. The first of these categories is a feature of all civilisations. Its importance in the present context is that it took on a particular set of meanings in Europe in the later eighteenth century. The other elements were formed, or perhaps transformed, during the nineteenth century. In the last years of that century the three elements were brought together by thinkers connected with the Arts and Crafts movement in order to form the concept of craft as it has existed throughout the twentieth century. I will analyse the three before describing what I believe to be the implications of their union.

There has always been decoration. There always will be. Decoration is a wide, amorphous practice engaged in by all cultures. It would be a mistake therefore to see the *decorative arts* as a natural grouping with an internal

25

logic. Their collectivisation in the present context is to do with negative circumstances, with the consolidation of a hierarchical classification system within the European visual arts. There came to be, to use Walter Crane's phrase, 'the fine arts, and the arts not fine'.[20] The decorative arts were, and are, disenfranchised art: *the arts not fine*. They bring two things simultaneously to craft: art, and the crisis of being denied the status of art.

There has been disagreement amongst scholars as to the historical point at which fine art as a fully-formed grouping could be said to be in general usage. There is wide acknowledgement, however, that distinctions did not exist before the sixteenth century. Rudolf Wittkower summarises the consensus:

> In Classical Antiquity and the Middle Ages the visual arts were regarded as purely imitative occupations in contrast to the speculative and intellectual occupations of the Liberal Arts [sciences], for which reason a separation of the arts and crafts was unknown and, in a scale of absolute values the visual arts ranked below the liberal arts.[21]

Erwin Panofsky believed the formulation of fine art had effectively occurred by the sixteenth century, during the Renaissance:

> the arts of painting (plus the 'graphic arts') sculpture and architecture, still commonly understood as the 'Fine Arts' in the narrower sense … were firmly established as a unit by the middle of the sixteenth century. Vasari, the first to define them as the three 'arti del disegno' because of the fact that 'design is their common foundation', consistently treats them *pari passu* both from a biographical and from a systematic point of view.[22]

This would seem now to be an over-simplification. Others have demonstrated that fine art as such continued well after the sixteenth century to routinely include other disciplines such as poetry, music, rhetoric and eloquence, and that the Renaissance groupings were not in any way systematic.[23] Paul Oscar Kristellar asserted firmly that 'the Renaissance did not formulate a system of the fine arts or a comprehensive theory of aesthetics'.[24] He identified the eighteenth century to be when a system emerged:

> The fundamental importance of the eighteenth century in the history of aesthetics is generally recognised … all the changes and controversies of the more recent past presuppose certain fundamental notions which go back to that classical century of modern aesthetics. It is known that the

very term 'aesthetics' was coined at that time ... it is generally agreed that such dominating concepts of modern aesthetics as taste and sentiment, genius, originality and creative imagination did not assume their definitive modern meaning before the eighteenth century ... scholars have noticed that the term 'Art' with a capital 'A' and in its modern sense, the related term 'Fine Arts' (Beaux Arts) originated in all probability in the eighteenth century.[25]

Much evidence would support the idea that it was during the Enlightenment that the status and divinity of the arts was first assessed in absolutist terms. It was then that the Academies were created. Under their auspice the system of the five fine arts, of painting, sculpture, architecture, music and poetry, was formulated and brought to maturity. In the manner of Diderot's *Encyclopédie*, what was irrational was made rational and what had little order was ordered.

It would be a mistake however to assume that even then this structure was universally understood or adhered to. In his *Present State of the Arts in England* (1756), for example, M. Rouquet privileges some types of painting, which he divides into ten distinct types, but he reveals no understanding of a hierarchical system or even a sense of what the borders of 'art' might be. He discusses sixteen genres apart from painting, including the more predictable luxury trades of silk manufacture, engraving on stone, porcelain, chinaware, architecture, jewellery and the 'decoration of shops', but also the less familiar arts of 'declaiming', 'preparation of aliments', 'physic' and 'surgery'.[26] Contrary to Panofsky's view, the compilers of *The Builder's Magazine* (1774) insisted on lamenting the fact that architecture was generally not considered a fine art. In a combative editorial the editors complained bitterly about the lack of support and recognition afforded to the profession in relation to the more prestigious arts, and especially poetry:

> It appears a matter of astonishment that, while the Professors of Literature have monthly increased their intellectual treasures, the Architects, Surveyors, Carpenters, and Masons, have been unnoticed, and passed by as unworthy of the instruction or assistance of those who are eminent in their respective professions.[27]

Nevertheless, by the opening of the nineteenth century, a hierarchy was broadly in place. The developing infrastructure of European professional culture facilitated the further rise of academies, professional thinkers and connoisseurs, who further clarified a system from the amorphous, rolling actuality of object manufacture. The decorative arts steadily congealed into a *salon de refuse* of genres that cohered only by virtue of their exclusion. Outside the fine arts, there was no fixed nomenclature or hierarchy. Variously – and interchangeably – known as the decorative, useful, industrial, applied or ornamental arts, they struggled to maintain a place in intellectual life at exactly the time when intellectual life was being classified and consolidated in museums, academies and universities.[28]

Supporters did not accept this fate quietly. The issue of status was widely and loudly debated, so much so that it was deemed important enough to be raised and recorded at governmental level. The following exchange between C. R. Cockerell and Richard Redgrave in a committee of 1846 exposed key aspects of the debate:

Cockerell There has been a great deal said about the principles of art. It is very difficult to know what these principles are; but you have no doubt considered what the differences are between poetical and prose art?

Redgrave Decidedly.

Cockerell Would you not say that the painter's art with the knowledge of anatomy, the power of exact imitation, the knowledge of position, color [*sic*], perspective, foreshortening, illusion, movement and action, all these may be called a poetical art?

Redgrave Yes.

Cockerell Whereas the architect's art, or the art of the designer for manufactures, is truly a prosaic art?

Redgrave I should be sorry to take such a low ground. I conceive that the architect's art is as much addressed to the object of making poetical impressions upon the mind as that of the painter.

Cockerell Would you say the same of design as applied to manufactures, to chinzes [*sic*], to jewellery, to vases, to calico printing and china painting?

Redgrave Even there I conceive that the power of making an impression upon the mind may be exerted as well as in the painter's art. If the poetry of invention does not enter into these designs, we shall never have proper designers.[29]

Cockerell's division of the arts into poetry and prose revealed the continuing sense that poetry was one of the fine arts. It also identified high art with non-functional objects. For Cockerell, in order to be a truly disinterested vehicle of artistic ideas, a genre had to be severed from perceivable use-value. For this reason, he positions architecture alongside the decorative arts.

For Redgrave, utility was irrelevant. The intention behind the creation of the object was the key to its status as art. Using a position usually associated with John Ruskin, he was arguing that *art* was a quality that could be applied to any object and was not genre-specific.[30] Poetry could manifest itself anywhere if the conceptual will was there. For the rest of the century, discussion on the status of the decorative arts revolved around this point. Either art was specific to the genres allocated the status of fine art, following the logic that 'Designing, decorating, and the like, have each their important functions ... but no sane man ever claimed for them a very high place in art',[31] or it was a quality capable of emerging in any form of practice, a universally applicable quality that could make 'poetical impressions upon the mind'.

The pejorative connotation of function led to a lack of stability at the edges of fine art. Much in the way that Cockerell questioned the status of architecture on these grounds, some forms of sculpture tended to be excluded. In a similar spirit the reverse could happen, and non-functional decorative arts, such as gem-carving, tapestry and porcelain manufacture, could, on occasion, gain admission. Oil-painting was the only absolute constant. It held sway over all other genres in that it was always unequivocally a high art. Some felt it was the *only* high art, but this was rare. Usually, other genres were sited alongside it to complete the class.

The privilege was not always an exclusive one. The Fine Art sections of the South Kensington International Exhibition of 1871, for example, included the following:

> Paintings of all kinds including oil, water-colour, distemper, wax, enamel, on glass and porcelain; sculpture including modelling, carving, chasing in marble, stone, wood, terracotta, metal, ivory, glass, precious stones; mosaic; engraving, lithography, photography, architectural designs and drawings, photographs of recently completed buildings, restorations and models; tapestries, carpets, embroideries, shawls, lace; designs of all kinds for decorative manufactures; reproductions, i.e. exact, full life-size copies

29

of ancient and medieval pictures painted before 1556, reproductions of mosaics and enamels, copies in plaster and fictile ivory, electrotypes of ancient works of art.[32]

This gathering showed alternative yardsticks in operation for the measuring of fine art: the cost of production, the value of materials and the status of the patron. In the exhibition of 1871, porcelain, an expensive material selling into high markets, was a fine art, earthenware was not.

It also revealed the relative strength of the decorative arts in the nineteenth century. Compared with, say, the second half of the twentieth century, they enjoyed a healthy patronage and a substantial critical literature. A generation of designer-writers continually made the case, with considerable success. Richard Redgrave, Christopher Dresser, John Ruskin, William Morris, Walter Crane and many others wrote and spoke eloquently in their defence as arts worthy of consideration alongside all others. The decorative arts enjoyed prestige and patronage. Ruskin, always the maverick, was confident enough to place them above all other arts: 'There is no existing highest-order art but that it is decorative .... Get rid, then, at once of any idea of decorative art being a degraded or a separate kind of art.'[33] With or without their place in the canon, the decorative arts were certainly not a beleaguered force. Indeed, the radical and progressive makers at work in Britain, Europe and North America in the twenty-five-year period which ended with the First World War were, in retrospect, participating in a golden age of ornamentation.

The suffering of the decorative arts within the cultural hegemony thus had nothing to do with quality or confidence, but the abundant presence of both could not reverse the ideological tide. A space had opened up between the actuality of practice and the discourse of classification. By 1890 the category of fine art occupied a clear space on its own, and for many commentators it had narrowed its range to exclude poetry and architecture. Whilst acknowledging that there was no historical precedent for it, one writer confirmed that 'unless the context shows that it must have a wider meaning, [fine art] is taken to mean the arts of painting and sculpture alone'.[34]

The decorative arts were disenfranchised art. The high end of the furniture, ceramics, glass, metalwork, tapestry and jewellery worlds had the same pretensions and served the same patrons as, for example, sculpture or portrait-painting. This was hardly the case with the genres represented by the second element I have identified within the craft constituency, the *vernacular*.

The vernacular refers to the cultural produce of a community, the things collectively made, spoken and performed. It is as close to nature as a culture can get; the unselfconscious and collective products of a social group, unpolluted by outside influence. It carries the mystique of being the authentic voice of society. There has been a tendency to associate this authenticity with pre-industrial, rural communities:

> the work of country craftsmen was believed to have evolved 'naturally' as the direct and honest expression of simple functional requirements and solid virtues. This vernacular tradition was construed as something static and timeless, in contrast to the dynamic and progressive modern world.[35]

The vernacular was noticed only when other forms of living began to destroy it. The beginnings of vernacularism as a cultural phenomenon can be clearly identified in the writings of the Gothic revivalists in the early nineteenth century, as urbanism and industry took their inexorable toll on older forms of life. Its real significance in the present context dates from the last quarter of the century. It was of great symbolic importance to William Morris and the founders of the Arts and Crafts movement. The rural and handmade aspects of craft production arose at least partly as a result of the desire to return to the vernacular world.

There is a powerful irony, therefore, in the fact that it was the modernisation of European culture which gave the vernacular a presence on the cultural scene. Its status as being 'authentic' culture has made it attractive to a surprisingly wide range of opinion over a long period of time, the Romantic vision of pure simplicity affecting the cultural sphere up to the present day. Victor Papanek observed of the persistence of vernacular models in architecture, for example, that 'Rousseau's "Noble Savage" has spilled over into the concept of the "Noble Savage's House"'.[36]

It supplied modernists as varied as Wassily Kandinsky and Bernard Leach with forms whilst simultaneously providing a model for anti-modernist lobby groups committed to the preservation of tradition. Socialists admired it as being an appropriate way of developing and maintaining a community; fascists admired its blood-ties and its racial purity. It has furnished the Utopias of the left and the right in Europe and

North America since the onset of mass industrialisation. Its attractiveness to all lay in the fact that it stood outside such notions as professionalism, specialisation, authorship or academicism. It could make legitimate claims to universal honesty, that most desirable of normative values.

Real people through the millennia have unconsciously generated styles and techniques based on local values and economic necessity. People make things and entertain themselves in ethnic groupings well capable of cultural creativity in the absence of universities and museums. On one level, then, the vernacular is no more than the popular culture of an ethnic grouping. In the hands of some, however, it has been taken well beyond this simple reality, into the realm of myth. For over a century now it has become subject to nostalgic invention, it has been made into a beautiful, rustic land in which one can hide from an ever more alien world. As often as forms could claim to be the authentic expression of an unaffected culture, they could also be shown to be completely invented or the result of outside influence. Vernacular costumes, songs, histories, artefacts, architecture and foodstuffs, when they became tools of socialist or nationalist propaganda, could be distorted or fabricated.[37] G. K. Chesterton's xenophobia was typical:

> The ordinary Englishman [was] duped out of his old possessions, such as they were, and always in the name of progress …. They took away his maypole, and his original rural life, and promised him instead the Golden Age of peace and commerce.[38]

Walter Crane's internationalist socialism had a more generous though no less fictitious spirit to it:

> we want a vernacular in art, a consentaneousness of thought and feeling throughout society. As it was … in the days of Homer, of Phideas, or even of Dante. No mere verbal or formal agreement, or dead level of uniformity, but that comprehensive and harmonising unity with individual variety, which can only be developed among a people politically and socially free.[39]

Many political groups in Europe and North America have found, in the vernacular, a template for existence. In the closing decades of the nineteenth century, it was especially attractive to the third element I have identified as being part of the constituency of craft: the *politics of work*.

Work was a key area of politico-economic debate during the nineteenth century. For some, work actually defined the human condition. Thomas Carlyle believed that it not only underpinned the structure of society, but also lent psychological stability to the individual. Samuel Smiles saw in it national progress. For Karl Marx, they who controlled work – the means of production – controlled the world. It was logical, if not inevitable, therefore, that work would become an issue in that most prestigious area of commodity production, the visual arts.

Marx's theory of alienation established a causal relationship between work conditions and the degradation of the human personality:

> What constitutes the alienation of labour? First, that the work is external to the worker, that it is not part of his nature; and that consequently, he does not fulfil himself in his work but denies himself, has a feeling of misery rather than well-being, does not develop freely his physical and mental energies but is physically exhausted and mentally debased ....
>
> We arrive at the result that the man (the worker) feels himself to be freely active only in his animal functions – eating, drinking, procreating, or at most also in his dwelling and in his personal adornment – whilst in his human functions he is reduced to an animal. The animal becomes human and the human becomes animal.[40]

More influential in the British and the Arts and Crafts context, John Ruskin's 'The Nature of the Gothic', published in 1851, was strikingly close in its reasoning:

> You must make a tool of the creature or a man of him. You cannot make both. Men were not intended to work with the accuracy of tools, to be precise and perfect in all their actions. If you will have that precision out of them, and make their fingers measure degrees like cog-wheels and their arms strike curves like compasses, you must unhumanise them.[41]

In effect, the way that people work, the conditions they work under and the way they make things, is fundamental to the well-being of society. It is not possible to have a proper society if its inhabitants are not humanely and creatively employed. William Morris was centrally responsible for generating out of this position what I will term a *politics of craft*. His socialism was deceptively simple. He channelled the whole of his vision of a better society through the need to engage in creative

33

work. Creative work would improve the environment, lead to an equitable system of the distribution of wealth and generate psychologically fulfilled peoples. In this sense, craft – creative work – was about the empowering of individual workers, about the political control of the work situation. The objects produced were a by-product of this larger ideal:

> It was essential to the [capitalist] system that the free-labourer should no longer be free in his work; he must be furnished with a master having complete control of that work, as a consequence of his owning the raw material and tools of labour; and with a universal market for the sale of the wares with which he had nothing to do directly, and the very existence of which he was unconscious of. He thus gradually ceased to be a craftsman, a man who in order to accomplish his work must necessarily take an interest in it …. Instead of a craftsman he must now become a hand, responsible for nothing but carrying out the orders of his foreman.[42]

Morris, Ruskin and indeed Marx were tapping a rich vein within British social life. Rebellion against the constraints of machinery and the division of labour were far from new in the mid nineteenth century. The heritage of Luddism – resistance to mechanical and political control of the workplace – went back to the origins of the Industrial Revolution itself.[43] It embraced the most basic of all political ideals: the right to be human. This vision of craft, as unalienated labour, provided the intellectual and emotional underpinning to left-wing thought in British society throughout the entire period. The Trade Union movement and the Independent Labour Party, for example, were more squarely based on the politics of work than on any wider ideological struggle. The metaphysics of work provided craft with its moral core.

These three elements, *decorative art*, the *vernacular* and the *politics of work*, were brought together in the last two decades of the nineteenth century by makers and thinkers associated with the Arts and Crafts movement. Gillian Naylor has summed up the movement as being 'inspired by a crisis of conscience. Its motivations were social and moral, and its aesthetic values derived from the conviction that society produces the art and architecture it deserves.'[44] The core ideal was that art should become life through the process of work. Walter Crane defined it along these lines:

> this revival of handicraft, this claim of the workman to have some share

of the joy of the artist in his work ... this claim is ... a protest against the domination of our modern commercial and industrial system of production for profit.[45]

As I have described them, these elements were pulled together for specific reasons in a particular ideological climate. They had little common ground in any previous existence. The high *decorative arts* were not intrinsically political and they hardly contained many of the qualities of the *vernacular*. For many centuries they had been produced and traded in a highly sophisticated international environment. The *politics of work* had evolved through a century of political and philosophical discourse, its natural milieu being the corridors of radical education establishments and working-men's meeting-halls.

But the historical moment was right, the combination in this context dynamic and compelling. The nineteenth century had seen widespread and protracted debate on the relationship of morality to culture. The Arts and Crafts movement, in retrospect, can be seen to be the most successful construction of a theory and practice of ethical art. The crafts were to be a politicised form of work which produced art objects to decorate society. The *vernacular* was the model, unalienated *work* was the means and *art* was the goal. The larger ideal pulled the three elements into proximity. It was a brilliant formulation: humankind would be liberated through communal creativity. Ultimately, for craft pioneers, the movement was centred on physical and mental freedom. By uniting the work process directly to the demand for a higher quality of life, they had regenerated the idea that craft was synonymous with power. A. H. MacMurdo eloquently outlined the agenda in a lecture of 1891:

> If the tongue does not give itself to song, the mind to imaginative interest, we are at best sound animals, healthily stabled ... we give the people only that which we provide for the lunatic in the asylum. Unless then, we also increase our opportunities and possibilities for the higher life of the imaginative interest, and make life no less beautiful than healthy, we are not alive to this great tendency about us making for the *completeness* of existence.[46]

The Arts and Crafts movement enjoyed its best moments at the opening of the twentieth century, by which time it had become a fully international movement. Europe, North America and many nations within the then British Empire had powerful craft movements of their own, motivated along similar lines to those formulated by the pioneers.

It would not be an exaggeration to say that craft was invented at this time, in the sense that there came into being a generally recognised sense of craft as a thing *in itself*. It was now a noun as well as an adjective. The word had travelled from Caleb D'Anvers's sense of guile and political intrigue, to Gustave Stickley's vision of art and life.

After the First World War, when the original Arts and Crafts movement had dwindled into confusion and decline, it made its next, and possibly final move, by entering into common usage.

The formation of a new system of the arts

In the twentieth century, all definitions and movements within the craft world were derivations from and combinations of the three elements I have described. When craft was an issue in any sphere, the underlying motive forces would be one or a combination of these. The wardrobe of meanings I referred to in my introduction comes from the three, the confusion and complexity being a result of endless selections from these three broad churches.

A few managed to hold the three together very much in the Arts and Crafts spirit. Amongst these were the great studio-craftspeople such as Michael Cardew, Eric Gill, Bernard Leach and Ethel Mairet. Most inheritors of the mantle, however, quite deliberately decided to settle for a partial rather than a pure model. After 1918, therefore, craft began simultaneously to expand, fragment and factionalise. This degenerative process is the key to the condition of craft as we have it at the end of the twentieth century. Three very variant examples will show that all combinations and outcomes were possible.

First, the Bauhaus. The founders of the Bauhaus professed a debt to William Morris and the Arts and Crafts movement and passionately declared that:

> Architects, sculptors, painters, we must all turn to the crafts .... There is no essential difference between the artist and the craftsman .... Let us create a new guild of craftsmen, without the class distinctions which raise an arrogant barrier between craftsman and artist.[47]

This vision of craft laid emphasis on the political and ideological aspects of the word. It recognised and attacked the class of fine art, and sought to reanimate the disenfranchised art forms. It also wished to use the practice of art as a weapon in the struggle towards human equality. As the school settled down, however, hand-making and the vernacular were aspects of the canon that went into steep decline. As far as the Bauhaus theorists were concerned, the politics of craft remained central; the sources and methods of craft were, however, far more open to doubt. Emphasis on hand-making appeared to be anti-progress and the vernacular politically reactionary.

If the Bauhaus combined the elements of decorative art and the politics of work, my second example, the Woodcraft Folk movement, developed a craft ethic that had little use for art. Ernest Thompson Seton, an American naturalist and folklorist, promoted the idea of a 'Woodcraft' life-style from the first years of the century. His *Book of Woodcraft* (1912) became rapidly known all over the world and a primary influence on a generation of parents who wished to educate their children following ecologically sound, humanist principles. In 1925, the Woodcraft Folk was founded in Britain as a deliberate alternative to Baden-Powell's imperially inspired Boy Scouts. Thompson Seton and William Morris were cited as the inspiration behind the British movement, which was sponsored by the Co-operative Society and supported by the Labour Party. Combining socialism with a love of nature and the vernacular, the Woodcraft Folk were, in effect, simply making use of the idea of craft as it had been formed thirty years earlier, without recourse to the element of decorative art. They wished to find Morris's Nowhere. By 1940, the Woodcraft movement was a huge international presence amongst children's organisations. It still is.[48]

My third example, the Women's Institutes, passionately promoted the crafts on an amateur and semi-professional level. Craft here was a skilled pastime, or something which was in effect a rarefied form of household husbandry. This remains the single most common usage of the term. It is a vision of craft void of the original political commitment, a vernacular ruralism with pretensions to decorative art. The Women's Institutes are to do with making things in order to enhance the quality of life. They promoted and preserved the world of rural and domestic crafts. The Countess of Albemarle, a patron of the WI, recognised in 1950 that:

We owe to William Morris and other pioneers of the Arts and Crafts Movement in the last century the spread of this doctrine that we cannot afford to let craftsmanship perish .... Handicrafts, primarily in the form of home crafts (those that can be practised without a special workshop), have been amongst the activities of the Women's Institutes from the early days of the movement. Thousands of countrywomen have ... learnt a technique of a craft and find joy in practising it.[49]

The Bauhaus (craft without the vernacular), the Woodcraft Folk (craft without art) and the Women's Institutes (craft without its politics) are all examples from the inter-war period of selective visions from within the meaning of craft as it had been earlier formulated. The signs of strain between the three elements had surfaced; the confused plurality of what it was to be a craftsperson began to grow.

Craft expanded on the institutional front dramatically after the First World War. The *Arts and Crafts Yearbooks* through the 1920s cited thirteen national organisations considering themselves to be centrally involved in the crafts. Some of them, such as the Rural Industries Bureau (founded 1921), the Home Arts and Industries Association (founded 1884) and the Church Crafts League were well funded and powerful.[50] There can be no doubt that they helped form a particular vision of life in Britain. The Art Schools became more overtly concerned with craft as a constituency and museums generally awoke to the issue of craft.[51]

Thus the transmutation of craft into a major class within a new system of the arts was a staged process. It began with the rise and triumph of the Arts and Crafts movement. In the Edwardian period, the movement began to lose its revolutionary edge to become embroiled in the fabrics of the various national cultures.[52] In the inter-war years, the pioneer generation of thinkers and makers gradually died off and the conceptual unity of craft was undermined by factionalism and partial readings. The process of its stabilisation and institutionalisation gathered pace then, as did the idea that craft was a distinct class based upon processes and genres rather than ideas. After the Second World War, and particularly after 1960, institutional recognition of the class was complete.

A class within any hierarchy, however, does not simply arrive through its vulgar omnipresence. It is formed in relation to other classes and groupings. The new system was a tripartite affair – *art – craft – design* – and was largely a result of the perceived need to clarify problems of status, meaning and control of the decorative arts. As I have demonstrated, the decorative arts were an amorphous collection of practices fashioned from the disenfranchised when the original concept of fine art was formed in the eighteenth century. Towards the end of the nineteenth century a further rift began to open up within the decorative arts, between those practices connected closely with the craft ethic and those seen to be centrally part of the world of large-scale manufacturing. The latter would ultimately become collectivised as *design*.

The space between design and craft – a space which we now use to organise our education systems, media networks, industries and cultural organisations – was opened up for ideological and political reasons by Arts and Crafts thinkers. It is not at all clear that, for example, the real methods and conditions used, say, in the furniture industry in the later nineteenth century, were fundamentally different from those used by Arts and Crafts studios. The difference was in the attitude to work, labour, politics and art. The decorative arts, therefore, were gradually pulled in two by the ideological wars waged in the intellectually aware workshops of Britain, mainland Europe and North America.

The evolution of design as a phenomenon is outside the scope of the present chapter, but suffice it to say here that, as with craft, it began its steady rise as a distinct area of activity from the later nineteenth century. It had been formerly used as a general term which implied a drawing, a plan or a preparatory study. As with craft, it had older roots in mental activity. To have a design on something, or someone, suggested an insatiable desire.

Deriving from the Italian (Latin) word for drawing, *disegno*, it was used to mean drawing or preparatory study throughout the European tradition. It is especially common in this regard throughout the nineteenth century. Thus the Schools of Design established in Britain from 1836 onwards, and the endless books written on design, broadly and loosely referred to the idea of preparing a study or design for a finished piece of work. Painters or sculptors might talk about a design for a painting, as much as an engineer or a potter would refer to designs for steam engines or pots.

Steadily through the closing decades of the century its meaning began to embrace the idea of the preparation of templates for longer runs of objects: to make a design *for* something. It also came to imply a problem-solving activity lodged between art and science, a phenomenon akin to the Renaissance notion of the liberal arts.[53] The term *industrial design* was occasionally used to suggest a pattern applicable to objects manufactured in long runs, such as textiles. Again, as with craft, it would be wrong to argue that design was a distinct area of activity or a constituency within the visual arts in this period. It was not. Indeed, many writers between 1880 and 1914 used the word 'design' far more often than 'craft', and used the former virtually interchangeably with art.

It was in the twentieth century that the idea fully evolved of a designer as a professional who saw an entire process of manufacture through from drawing-board to finished artefact. It was only then that 'design' became exclusively tied to the idea of industry and designers clearly distinguished from artists and craftspeople. They are now irrevocably associated with mass production, or at least highly-mechanised production.

As the fine arts had split from the decorative, so the decorative, under the aegis of craft, split from design. By the end of the 1920s, supporters of the various classes could bullishly support their causes with a growing sense of clarity. One could assert with authority that 'craft promises to be more important than fine art',[54] or that 'the design of machine-made goods naturally belongs, of course, to an order entirely distinct from that of hand-made objects'.[55]

Due to the unstructured nature of the decorative arts, however, the constituencies of craft and design could never be separated out with clarity. Most written histories of design place the decorative arts within its empire, yet clearly these are at the heart of the history of craft also. Only at the extremities are the divisions clear. Design exclusively includes package, automotive and corporate design, as well as large-scale engineering and most forms of architecture.[56]

The genius and the mechanick

At the turn of the century, it could easily be argued that the crafts boasted the most advanced and vociferous theoretical, critical and historical writing. Indeed, Roger Fry, as he brought to maturity his own brand of formalism in the last years before the First World War, felt he had to specifically address and attack this intellectual powerhouse, as he perceived its influence to be the decisive one in visual culture.[57] It all declined with alarming suddenness after the First World War.

By contrast, writing on the fine arts blossomed dramatically, and can now be seen as one of the most potent areas of discourse in twentieth century European and North American literary culture. So it tended to be that when the crafts received analysis of any kind after 1918, it was usually filtrated through ideas associated with the latter. There was a powerfully pejorative aspect to this discussion, in that it was invariably premised on the notion that it was important to distinguish the creativity of art from the worthiness of craft.

By the outbreak of the Second World War, the internal hegemony of the new classification system was justified using intellectual means. The classes were given an intelligence test, as it were, the questions being written by forces usually associated with fine art. When this was not the case, the parameters were set by the Modern movement in design. Predictably, and ironically, the intellectual rigour which had underpinned the idea of craft in the *fin-de-siècle* period was now identified as being non-intellectual. The borders of craft were going to be policed by discourses dedicated to its containment. Like sheepdogs circling a fold, these were going to check the odd gathering of jostling and uncomfortable genres and hold them in proximity.

The philosophy of craft developed by the Arts and Crafts pioneers had a core of immutable ideas. Perhaps the most important of these posited that creative practice – art – was inseparably part of the physical process of making. In short, craft was premised on the understanding that *cognitive* and *manual* activity were effectively the same. Indeed, the politics of craft were premised on their congruence. However, after 1918, aestheticians and practitioners associated with the fine arts steadily legitimised the idea that the two were two wholly separate realms. This had a drastic effect on the standing of craft. Two main types of discussion have dominated. The first relates to the process of making art and the role in that of the artist. The second is to do with where exactly the phenomenon 'art' resides in relation to 'art objects'.

The first of these has, perhaps, been the key site of any rift between fine art and craft. Dominated by the seemingly everlasting heritage of Romanticism, the majority of recent thinkers have considered art to be a state of mind, an outlook, a way of seeing things rather than a way of doing things. Art is centred in the artist, the absolute individual, rather than in the object or in society. This vision of the artist has been the key to much avant-garde activity. Dada, Surrealism, Art Brut, NeoDada and Arte Povera, for example, all pushed Romantic anarchism and individualism to an extreme and inevitable conclusion. For them, art resided in the mind, it emanated out of life-style, welling up out of the intensity of *being*: 'The mere word freedom is the only one that still excites me …. To reduce the imagination to a state of slavery … is to betray all sense of absolute justice within oneself.'[58] This intensity of being could be manifested in an expressionistic way or as an ironic critique of the world and of previous developments in art.

The celebration of unfettered creative thought led inevitably to the development of artistic processes that eliminated the manual vehicle of artistic expression: skill. Whilst usually declining to define it, the Romanticist avant-garde wrested skill from the artistic process, made it into a relative value and then dispensed with any sense that there could be a useful heritage behind it. Skill was presented as a regimented pheno-menon because it is mediated externally and is therefore potentially detrimental to subjective consciousness and innovation.[59] Within the visual arts, skill has been characterised as the antithesis of the self. Jean Dubuffet, for example, talking of Art Brut, asserted that:

> We mean by this the works executed by people untouched by artistic culture … so that their makers derive everything (subjects, choice of materials used, means of transposition, rhythms, ways of patterning, etc.) from their own resources and not from the conventions of classic art or the art that happens to be fashionable. Here we find art at its purest and crudest; we see it being wholly reinvented at every stage of the operation by its maker, acting entirely on his own.[60]

Any technique that achieved the sought-after end was legitimate. Art as a profession was dispensed with in an effort to capture its essence, which was believed to be a property buried within all of us.

A parallel and equally significant development occurred when Marcel Duchamp arrived at his concept of the 'ready-made' between 1912 and 1916. The ready-made – an object chosen by the artist, signed and put on display – was art because the artist declared it to be so. Thus, technical skill, indeed, physical process of any kind, was replaced by intellect. Duchamp altered the context of an otherwise banal object, claimed it as a manifestation of his intellect by applying his signature to it. By successfully adding this process to the canon of twentieth-century art, he made irony a central vehicle for modern visual culture. His non-physical intervention was also intended to be a biting critique of the artist as a maker of things.

But as I have already demonstrated, as created by the Arts and Crafts movement, craft stood exactly *for* the making of things. Artistic expression *through* the making process was at the heart of craft aesthetics and politics. For them, skill – regardless of how one characterised it – was part of the infrastructure of making which empowered communities and allowed for the creation of a free, creative society. Skill as an actual phenomenon was far less important than what it represented on the ideological plane. For the craftsperson it was to do with empowerment, for the avant-garde fine artist it was to do with constraint. Indeed, for followers of Duchamp and Dubuffet, the idea of the 'artist-craftsman' is a contradiction in terms.

Much avant-garde practice has been dedicated to the subversion and transformation of normative values in art and life. One of the central features of the avant-garde has been its opposition. Renato Poggioli referred to a 'spirit of hostility and opposition' that was a 'permanent tendency … of the avant garde movement'.[61] The philosophical positivism of craft as defined by the pioneers of the Arts and Crafts movement resulted in objects without irony or critique. Rather, they made exemplars of an appropriate way of living. Their politics, which were as radical as any within the fine-art world, emerged in the processes they made and lived by. It was this positivism that fed one of the other great threads of modernist practice, the Modern movement in design. The Utopianism of the various schools within the Modern movement stood alongside – and distinct from – the Romantic individualism of Surrealism. The tendency amongst historians of architecture and design has been to depict craft as the forebear that lost its way by the time of the First World War.

The second issue, of where exactly the phenomenon 'art' resides in relation to 'art objects', has had the effect of reinforcing the space between the physical and cognitive realms even further. It has been a concern of philosophers of all persuasions since the middle of the century. Jean-Paul Sartre, for example, confidently asserted that: 'We can at once formulate the law that the work of art is an unreality …. What is "beautiful" is something which cannot be experienced as a perception and which, by its very nature, is out of the world.'[62] By 1968, the space between aesthetic experience and the art object had become such a truism that Richard Wollheim could uncontroversially ask of works of art 'Are they mental? or physical? Are they constructs of the mind?'[63]

In the present context, by far the most important discourse along these lines was provided by R. G. Collingwood. In his *Principles of Art* Collingwood set himself the task of clearly defining the nature of art. To this end he dedicated a considerable portion of his book to the philosophical separation of art from craft.

He was committed to the idea that art is not a physical but a cerebral quality:

> We must disabuse ourselves of the notion that the business of an artist consists in producing a special kind of artifact, so-called 'works of art' or *objets d'art*, which are bodily and perceptible things (painted canvases, carved stones and so forth). We shall have, later on, to consider in some detail what it is that the artist, as such and essentially, produces. We shall find that it is two things. Primarily, it is an internal or mental thing, something (as we commonly say) 'existing in his head' and there only: something of the kind we would commonly call an experience. Secondarily, it is a bodily or perceptible thing (a picture, a statue etc.) whose exact relation to this 'mental' thing will need very careful definition.[64]

The 'mental thing' was in his view by far the most significant. He goes on to call it 'the work of art proper'. The object gets far shorter shrift:

> The making of it is therefore not the activity in virtue of which a man is an artist, but only a subsidiary activity, incidental to that …. There is no such thing as an *objet d'art* in itself; if we call any bodily and perceptible thing by that name or an equivalent we do so only because of the relation in which it stands to the aesthetic experience which is the work of art proper.[65]

'The work of art proper' denied any inherent link between mind and body and divided the physical realm, processes and objects, off from art.

For Collingwood, art and craft were fundamentally different activities. Craft was 'the power to produce a preconceived result by means of consciously controlled and directed action'. Moreover, they could not be left in proximity: 'in order to take the first step towards a sound aesthetic, it is necessary to disentangle the notion of craft from that of art proper.'[66]

In effect, Collingwood believed craft to be the technical (physical) means through which art (the cerebral) could be manifested. The two were linked only by the journey from conception to realisation. 'Art proper' could be made physical through the 'subsidiary activity' of craft, but craft was not intrinsic to the achievement of art. Of course, those held within the perimeters of craft have not been the only ones to suffer from this. Much contemporary painting and sculpture was also intellectually undermined.

Collingwood – indeed, most defenders of this type of discourse – was dependent on a Cartesian duality that had been under attack since the turn of the century. But despite the eventual discrediting of what Gilbert Ryle was to call 'the dogma of the Ghost in the Machine',[67] the rift between the cerebral and the physical, the manual and the mental, has persisted in the visual arts.

Collingwood did not separate out the genres themselves into 'arts' and 'crafts' and he did not like the term 'fine art'. He was opposed to a class system of arts based upon traditions and practices. It has been common practice throughout the century, however, to use his Cartesian-ism to reinforce the space between fine art and craft as classes. By taking his definition of craft as 'subsidiary activity', as non-intellectual manual skill, and simply applying it to craft as a class, one could define all of those genres contained therein as non-intellectual practices. In a similar way, ready-mades, *objets trouvés*, installations and happenings, acquire cognitive status by virtue of being in the fine-art class. They have been collectivised as intellectual, in contradistinction to the crafts, the *mechanical* practices. Individual objects are thus not judged by their inherent ingenuity, but rather by a generalised claim to cognitive status. In the same way as social class, gender and race, the genres are judged in advance and positioned within the hierarchy. In the absence of serious critical response from the craft world this situation has consolidated into a truism.

The image of being *merely* a maker of things has been reinforced by the issue of function. Much in the way that C. R. Cockerell, cited earlier, separated out the 'poetical' from the 'prosaic' principally according to whether they were 'useful' or 'non-useful' arts, so the crafts in the twentieth century have had the continual demand laid upon them to be functional. Cockerell's idea of 'useful' was catholic and non-ideological; the modern notion of 'functional' is neither. The pressure to eliminate

45

what critic Peter Fuller called 'singularly useless' idioms has further reduced the range and role of one of the three elements of craft, the decorative arts.[68] Ornamentation has always had a role; it has rarely had a material function. The demand for function has severed the tie back to the actuality of the decorative heritage and intensified the sense that craft is a purely technical activity.

Postscript: the order of things

The interesting thing about craft over the last century is that the further it consolidated into a classification – the more it became a naturalised and institutionalised signifier of a certain range of practices and attitudes – the less of a serious player it became. We have endured fifty years of embarrassed, apologetic explication on the meaning of craft. In the *fin-de-siècle* period, no apologies were necessary; craft was a set of principles and practices, it was a potent force on the international scene. Since then, as a way of classifying the arts and humanities, it has largely been a negative force. It was invented for good reasons; it has been held together for bad ones.

Nomenclature is vital in all this. How we name things determines what they are perceived to be, how they are used and thought about. How you are called is what you are. Nomenclature is the key product of the process of classification through which we order our lives. This process results in a hierarchy that is used to rank cultural produce so that value – ethical, aesthetic and economic – can be attached to classes and to individual objects within classes. *Craft* is a very important name.

The name of any class, of course, might eventually come to have little relationship to the things within it, and the objects within it may relate to one another only *because* they are in the same class. Situations might arise in which the cat and dog Foucault refers to on the opening page of this chapter are believed to sit logically together. If the pressure of class were strong enough, the two would undoubtedly start to look alike even to the least jaded of veterinarians. Indeed, it has to be said that a cat is more like a dog than a Meissen figurine is like a Welsh coracle, or a Tiffany vase is like a granite headstone. But these are all clearly discernible as craft, and are more firmly held together than a *designed* table and a *crafted* one.

We create orders according to the way we understand things. In due course we come to understand things by their position in the order. A pot, a chair, a picture, a shoe, a motor car, a window, a brooch, whilst they have an infinite variety of relational meanings within culture, acquire an absolute status within the scheme of things.

I have attempted to demonstrate that the actual forces which gave craft cultural meaning in the nineteenth century were split in the twentieth century and exploited in isolation. The original combination of *decorative arts*, the *vernacular* and the *politics of work* had a dynamism which proved important on a global basis. They had an ideological power that was generated from within. In our own times, that power has been lost and replaced by one from without.

The fractionalisation of craft has caused it to become an unstable compound but I do not think that we should contemplate abandoning it as a term just yet. Indeed, it is a class system and therefore by definition its disbandment would prove extremely difficult. Thinkers have struggled for a generation to determine whether in fact we *need* to classify things before we can understand and use them. If this is the case, then we should hang on to craft for dear life. Rather, the time has come to analyse the three elements in order to determine their usefulness in our present context. Craft needs to be *de-* and then *re-*classified. It needs to become internally dynamic once more, rather than allowing itself to be externally constrained.

Questions need to be asked. Are these elements the ones craft needs at this point in time? How do they relate to wider socio-cultural issues? Do they work with or against each other? What exactly constitutes the vernacular in the present international framework? What is the real difference between the decorative art that is held within the empires of fine art, design and craft? What forms of work are the most appropriate to our times? Is morality intrinsic to the artistic process – as the pioneers believed – and, if it is, how is it made manifest through the artistic process? What concept of craft can be developed to allow it to generate a philosophy and aesthetics for the next century?

I believe that we are about to decide that the constituency and intellectual make-up of craft needs to change. Perhaps we will conclude, like our illustrious forebears of 1890, that this is part of the process of change within civilisation. Whatever form the change takes, we should constantly remind ourselves that, as it was handed to us at the base of the

47

century, craft was first and foremost the most articulate material outcome of a generation of brilliant positivist activity. Its elements had an ethical and aesthetic logic beyond the circumscribed world of art practice.

The art historian has an ethical role in this process of change, to attempt to expose the actuality of history. The crafts have been misunderstood too long by those who have been exposed only to halcyon myths and wishful thinking.

Notes

1 *The Claims of Decorative Art* (London, Lawrence & Bullen, 1892), p. 109.

2 *The Order of Things* (London, Tavistock/Routledge, 1974), p. xx.

3 See, for example, Elinor Richardson, Thomas Scott and John A. Walker, *Women and Craft* (London, Virago, 1987); C. Frayling and H. Snowdon, 'Perspectives on Craft' (1982), in John Huston (ed.), *Craft Classics Since the 1940's* (London, Crafts Council, 1988); Norris Ioannou (ed.), *Craft in Society: An Anthology of Perspectives* (Western Australia, FACP, 1992); G. A. Hickey (ed.), *Making and Metaphor: A Discussion of Meaning in Contemporary Craft* (Quebec, CMC, 1994).

4 The journal occasionally changed its subheading through its long run. These were: *The Gray's Inn Journal; Say's Weekly Journal; Being a Critique of the Times; Weekly Journalist; The London Intelligencer.* See also Paul Langford, *A Polite and Commercial People: England 1727–1783* (Oxford, Clarendon, 1989), pp. 24–6. Langford dates the first issue as being in 1726. I have remained with 1729, as the run held at the British Library does indicate this later start date.

5 Saturday 7 March 1729.

6 Saturday 7 March 1729.

7 Anon., *Truth and Falshood: A Fable* (18 January 1729).

8 M. Rouquet, *The Present State of the Arts in England* (London, 1756).

9 Samuel Johnson, *A Dictionary of the English Language*, 4th edition (London, 1773).

10 *Ibid.*

11 *Ibid.*

12 I am grateful to Michael Archer, Malcolm Baker, Linda Parry and Clive Wainwright, colleagues in the Research Department of the V&A, for the points made in this paragraph.

13 There is nothing listed in the British or National Art Libraries.

14 Anon., 'The Educational and Technical Value of Public Collections', *The*

Builder, 5 November 1881, Abrams, New York, pp. 564–5, quoted from Antony Burton, *The V&A: Politics and People* (forthcoming), p. 23.

15 It ran from 1901 to 1906 through nine volumes.

16 'William Morris: Some Thoughts upon his Life, Work and Influence' (October 1901), 'John Ruskin: A Word regarding his Life and Public Service' (November 1901).

17 *Ibid.*, p. 5.

18 Issue 65, August/September 1995, p. 24.

19 *Ibid.*, p. 51.

20 Crane, *The Claims of Decorative Art*, p. 109.

21 Rudolf Wittkower, *The Artist and the Liberal Arts* (London, UCL, 1950), p. 12. See also Indra Kagis McEwen, *Socrates Ancestor: An Essay On Architectural Beginnings* (Chicago, MIT, 1993).

22 Erwin Panofsky, *Galileo as a Critic of the Arts* (The Hague, Martinus Nijhoff, 1954), pp. 2–3.

23 H. Parker, *The Nature of the Fine Arts* (London, Macmillan, 1885), p. 1.

24 P. O. Kristellar, 'The Modern System of the Arts', *Journal of the History of Ideas* 1951, p. 510.

25 *Ibid.*, p. 496.

26 M. Rouquet, *The Present State of the Arts in England* (London, 1756, reprinted 1970 by Cornmarket Press).

27 *The Builder's Magazine or Monthly Companion* (London, 1774), Preface.

28 The history of these various other terms is outside the scope of the present chapter. I use 'decorative arts' mainly for convenience, but also because it has been the longest-standing, the most widely understood and the least ambiguous of the available terms.

29 Report of a *Special Committee of the Council of the Government School of Design*, appointed November 1846 (London, Clowes & Sons, 1847), p. 41.

30 Though he accepted further into this interview with Cockerell that painting was special and exceptional, demanding a higher intellectual calibre and artistic quality in greater degree: p. 42.

31 James Stanley Little, *What is Art?* (London, Swan & Sonnenschein, 1883), p. 26.

32 The international exhibitions often revealed a broad plurality. See Paul Greenhalgh, *Ephemeral Vistas: Expositions Universelles, Great Exhibitions and World's Fairs 1851–1939* (Manchester, Manchester University Press, 1988), Chapter 8.

33 John Ruskin, 'Modern Manufacture and Design', from *Sesame and Lilies, The*

Two Paths and The King of the Golden River (London, Everyman, 1859), quoted from Paul Greenhalgh (ed.), *Quotations and Sources from Design and the Decorative Arts 1800–1990* (Manchester, Manchester University Press, 1993).

34 Parker, *Nature of the Fine Arts*, p. 1.

35 Darron Dean, 'A Slipware Dish by Samuel Malkin: An Analysis of Vernacular Design', *Journal of Design History*, 7:3, 1994, p. 153.

36 Victor Papanek, *The Green Imperative* (London, Thames & Hudson, 1995), p. 114.

37 See Wendy Kaplan (ed.), *The Arts of Reform and Persuasion* (London, Thames & Hudson, 1995).

38 G. K. Chesterton, *A Short History of England* (London, Chatto, 1917), p. 131, quoted from Alun Hoskins, 'The Discovery of Rural England', in Colls and Dodd (eds), *Englishness: Politics and Culture 1880–1920* (London, Croom Helm, 1986), p. 69.

39 Crane, *The Claims of Decorative Art*, p. 15.

40 Karl Marx, *Extracts from the Economic and Philosophical Manuscripts*, quoted from Paul Greenhalgh, *Quotations and Sources from Design and the Decorative Arts 1800–1939* (Manchester, Manchester University Press, 1993), p. 35.

41 John Ruskin, *The Stones of Venice* (London, 1851), quoted from Alasdair Clayre (ed.), *Nature and Industrialization* (Milton Keynes, Open University Press, 1977), p. 255.

42 William Morris, *Art and its Producers*, The National Association for the Advancement of Art and its Application to Industry, Liverpool Conference Papers 1888 (London, 1889), p. 231.

43 See Charles Poulsen, *The English Rebels* (London, Journeyman, 1984).

44 Gillian Naylor, *The Arts and Crafts Movement: A Study of its Sources, Ideals and Influence of Design Theory* (London, Studio Vista, 1970), p. 7; for other histories of the movement see I. Anscombe and C. Gere, *The Arts and Crafts in Britain and America* (London, Academy, 1978), Alan Crawford (ed.), *By Hammer and by Hand: The Arts and Crafts Movement in Birmingham* (Birmingham, Museum and Art Gallery, 1984), W. Kaplan and E. Cummings, *The Arts and Crafts Movement* (London, Thames & Hudson, 1991).

45 Crane, *The Claims of Decorative Art*, p. 64.

46 A. H. MacMurdo, Presidential Address to the Birmingham Conference of the National Association for the Advancement of Art and its Application to Industry (London, 1891), p. 165.

47 'The First Proclamation of the Bauhaus, 1919', quoted from Herbert Bayer, Walter Gropius and Ise Gropius (eds), *The Bauhaus 1919–1928*, exhibition catalogue, MOMA, New York (New York, 1938), p. 16.

48 See *We are of One Blood* (London, CRS, 1985).

49 From Mavis Fitzrandolph (ed.), *30 Crafts* (London, The National Federation of Women's Institutes, 1950), p. 9.

50 See Holly Tebbutt, 'The Rural Industries Bureau' (MA thesis, Royal College of Art, 1990).

51 See David Jeremiah, 'The Culture and Style of British Art School Buildings', *Point*, 1, winter 1995, pp. 34–47.

52 See, for example, Paul Greenhalgh, 'The English Compromise: Modern Design and National Consciousness', in Wendy Kaplan (ed.), *Experiencing Modernity: The Arts of Reform and Persuasion* (London, Thames & Hudson, 1995).

53 Wittkower, note 21.

54 *Arts and Crafts Yearbook* (London, 1929), p. 21.

55 W. B. Honey in W. J. Turner (ed.), *British Craftsmanship* (London, Collins, 1948), p. 6.

56 I should make it clear here that my history of craft is only true of those nations which adopted the central principles of the Arts and Crafts movement, and then went on to allow a space to open up between industrial and craft production. The French, Italian and Scandinavian stories, for example, are quite different. My narrative rings true of America, Australia, Canada and Germany, however. The wider picture should be the subject of another study.

57 See Stella Tillyard, *The Impact of Modernism: The Visual Arts in Edwardian England* (London, Routledge, 1988).

58 André Breton, 'First Manifesto of Surrealism', in *Manifestoes of Surrealism* (Michigan, Ann Arbor, 1972 edn), pp. 4–5.

59 Some of these issues are taken up in Peter Dormer, *The Art of the Maker* (London, Thames & Hudson, 1994); Peter Fuller, 'The Proper Work of the Potter', in *Images of God* (London, Chatto & Windus, 1986).

60 Jean Dubuffet, 'L'Art Brut Préféré aux Arts Culturels', in *L'Homme du Commun à l'Ouvrage* (Paris, Gallimard, 1972).

61 Renato Poggioli, *The Theory of the Avant Garde* (New York, Belknap, 1968), p. 26.

62 Jean-Paul Sartre, *The Psychology of the Imagination* (1948), originally published as *L'Imaginaire* (Paris, Gallimard, 1940). Quoted from Methuen edn, 1972, p. 219.

63 Richard Wollheim, *Art and its Objects* (1968), this edn London, Penguin, 1970, p. 50.

64 R. G. Collingwood, *The Principles of Art* (Oxford, OUP, 1938), pp. 36–7.

65 *Ibid.*, p. 37.

66 *Ibid.*, p. 15.

67 Gilbert Ryle, *The Concept of Mind* (London, Hutchinson, 1949), quoted from Penguin edn, 1973, p. 17.

68 Fuller, 'The Proper Work of the Potter', p. 240.

3 ✧ How strange the change from major to minor: hierarchies and medieval art

T. A. HESLOP

Historical perspective is a terrifying thing. One reason is that it can place hard-won political or religious beliefs in a context which makes them seem like a normal or recurrent phenomenon. An example relating to the visual arts would be iconoclasm, which has cropped up in similar forms in widely different cultures. Perspective can also, usually, provide a contributory explanation for some quite recent 'event' from deep in historical time; in my own view a good case can be made for regarding the Treaty of Verdun in 843 as a major cause of the First World War. Patterns of human behaviour and of history *longue durée* can thus, in theory at least, aid our understanding of any number of social, political or cultural developments. The fluctuating perceptions of the status of the visual arts and crafts (if one chooses to distinguish between the two) and their practitioners are arguably no exception, and it is the aim of this chapter to try to place the issue in a context of European cultural behaviour from Antiquity onwards. This will not be potted history nor even, really, broad-brush history. Indeed, perhaps it is too polemical to be history at all, but I hope that its inclusion in a book on the status of the crafts will help to open up a debate about the anomalies and curiosities evident in hierarchies of artistic endeavour.

From the standpoint of the late twentieth century, the visual arts of medieval Europe can be regarded as remote indeed. The distance is not just one of time, but also more crucially of changes in perception of what the arts are for in a contemporary context and indeed significant shifts in our views of what art was for in the Middle Ages. To give an example of the latter, I believe it is very difficult for us to perceive Gothic art and architecture without the various glosses put upon it in the nineteenth century by 'ecclesiologists' on the one hand and Utopian socialists on the other. The combined image, if I may caricature it, of happy and fulfilled artisans labouring for the love of God, dies hard. But if we see the Middle Ages through that gloss, we hardly discern it in its own terms.

It would clearly be pointless, however, to pass judgement on historical shifts over which we can have no control. Indeed, it might be doubly pointless to bemoan the distorting effect of time on our understanding of a state of affairs more than half a millennium ago, since the fact that we bother to think anything much at all about the art of the Middle Ages can be attributed to precisely those more recent attempts to understand it which now seem to stand in our way. Fortunately, in the context of this chapter, these circumstances are no more of a hindrance than they are a help. While they may serve to depress the seeker after absolute historical understanding, they help to overcome the prejudices of those who regard as irrelevant things that happened long ago and far away.

It could be argued in the context of understanding the status of the crafts that the Middle Ages has a particular importance, for a number of reasons. The most immediately obvious is the extent to which the 'revival' of the crafts over the last century and a half took inspiration of various kinds from perceptions of medieval craft production, whether as regards training, design ideas or even, as it were, a supposed philosophy of life. Less apparent and thus less discussed is the importance of the medieval legacy for categorising the visual arts in ways which still influence us today. I want in particular to draw attention to a substantial shift in the perceptions of artists/craftists around the twelfth century. Put simply, this period saw the beginning of a relative decline in the importance of the arts associated with the forge and the furnace (goldsmithing, enamelling, etc.) and the relative rise of those which seemed to privilege figuration (painting and sculpture).

Outlining the circumstances which influenced these, largely tacit, shifts in perception will be one purpose of what follows. But I also want to put some flesh on these bones, as it were, by looking at the vicissitudes of an art form that arguably would have sat as uncomfortably within the medieval view of art, between the furnace and the figure, as it has ever since, the art of the stained-glass window. I have divided these two sections, the general context and the exemplary art, for reasons of clarity but both contribute essentially to my overall conclusions.

The tendencies to categorise and prioritise are fundamental to cognition. The ways in which humans understand their own place in the scheme of creation, in the social (and spiritual) order of culture, in the pattern of events, is based on sets of well-developed but quite artificial hierarchies and taxonomies. Many of these are so deeply structured in our thinking that we rarely question them. In many cases this is very convenient. We need to agree, for example, that there are sixty seconds in a minute, sixty minutes in an hour, and so on, but there was a time when this was not so. Such agreement has become particularly important to support the scientific predisposition of modern Western thought, but even when there was less unanimity (as, for example, in the Middle Ages) there was still a predisposition to categorise.

It is perhaps inevitably those things which defy measurement or logical classification which are seen as most threatening to a sense of order on microcosmic or macrocosmic scales. The tidy-mindedness of modern bureaucracy is constantly jeopardised by the uncomfortable realities of those cases which refuse to fit into the spaces provided on the form or which technically defy the intention of legislation. And in the theocentric past as much as the scientific present, the desire to find immutable physical laws which reveal the workings of universal systems was often thwarted by exceptional data which demonstrated the fallibility of the model. We may laugh, now, at those schemes which attempted to classify the ages of man, and correlate them with the ages of the world, or which conceived of learning on the basis of the seven liberal arts, or of society in terms of three groupings of those that worked, those that fought and those that prayed. But we still largely accept other constructs such as the notion of four seasons, even in those places where the transition from winter to summer lasts but a few days!

The borderline between rational and arbitrary classification is ill-defined. This is particularly the case as one moves from natural to social systems. We can generally agree about which heavenly bodies are suns, planets or moons, for example. We agree less about which states are democracies or dictatorships, or what constitutes public ownership. Even leaving precise definition aside, if one part of the problem is a matter of perspective (one person's terrorist is another's freedom-fighter) another is that such things are very susceptible to changing perception brought about by shifts in the historical context, be they political, economic or cultural.

Fluctuating fortunes have certainly affected perceptions of art and craft. As generally understood within Western culture over the last two centuries or so, art has tended to mean painting on certain kinds of support (not glass, not ceramic) and sculpture in certain media (not precious metal; that would be jewellery). The categories of applied art and craft are more fluid and vary rather more from country to country for micro-cultural and economic reasons; however, they can be regarded as those elements of traditional material culture which are not art. Defining something in terms of what it is not is a far from satisfactory state of affairs, especially when the thing that it is not is itself such an irrational category. It seems to me that the only method available to us to explain this bizarre situation is historical analysis, but for a number of reasons that is not straightforward. The complexity of the problem is well exemplified by an examination of medieval European attitudes which, quite apart from their innate interest, are relevant as an influential antecedent to more recent thinking.

Latin Christendom was heir to two distinct literary traditions concerning the visual arts: the Classical (essentially Greek) and the Judaeo-Christian. The former was particularly concerned with mimesis, that is to say the similarity between the representation and what was represented. This concern was expressed philosophically, for example by Plato, in the context of imitations of reality, anecdotally through stories of people (or animals) being deceived by painted or sculpted images which were mistaken for the thing they depicted (birds pecking at a painted bunch of grapes), and through the tradition of ekphrasis, a literary convention which used an object or a visual narrative as the point of entrance to a historical or mythological subject (the shield of Achilles). By contrast, the Judaic tradition concentrated on the relationship of the visual arts and divine authority. Prohibitions, such as the second commandment's, on the making of graven images were overcome only by the specific intervention of the godhead either in the form of a set of instructions to patrons,

Moses or David for example, to make things in a certain way, or through the 'inspiration' of the artist:

> And the Lord spake unto Moses, saying, 'See, I have called by name Bezaleel the son of Uri … and have filled him with the spirit of God in wisdom, and in understanding and in knowledge, and in all manner of workmanship, to devise cunning works, to work in gold and in silver and in brass, and in cutting of stones, to set them, and in carving of timber, to work in all manner of workmanship. (Exodus 31:1–5).

The list of artefacts which Bezaleel and his assistant produced for the tabernacle, essentially ornaments, furniture and vestments, thus had divine complicity. Crucially too, for the Christian Middle Ages, they were works normally associated with the arts of precious metalworking, gem-setting and the loom. Much of the reputation of goldsmiths' work, tapestry and embroidery in the medieval West derived from biblical support of this kind.

Also pointing in the same direction were the very positive comments about the materials themselves. The implications of Genesis (2:11–12) are that gold and gems come from those countries watered by the rivers that flow out of the Garden of Eden, and that these precious materials are thus the accessible deposits of earthly paradise. There were certainly those in the Middle Ages that drew this conclusion. The names of these lands, imbued with almost magical associations, were Havilah, Ophir and Tarshish, the latter being a source of ivory as well as gold and silver (I Kings 10:22). Given such authority, it is little wonder that the crafts which relied on these materials had a status which outstripped the painter's. As a consequence we know the names of significantly more goldsmiths, for example, from the central Middle Ages than we do of painters. Indeed, up until the eleventh century, the working of metal was of sufficient status for the skill to be attributed to senior churchmen and even saints. The patron saint of goldsmiths throughout most of continental Europe was St Eligius or Eloy (a seventh-century bishop of Noyon) and in England it was St Dunstan (a tenth-century archbishop of Canterbury), both of whom practised the craft.

This situation really only changed in the late eleventh and twelfth centuries with the proliferation of luxury production of all sorts, including the visual arts. The expansion was almost entirely secular and urban. That is to say the providers of fine metalwork, painting, embroidery, and so on were increasingly a part of a growth in numbers of the artisan classes concentrated within the greater cities and new towns that were a fundamental part of the twelfth-century renaissance. True, to begin with the principal patrons remained the great churches and their wealthy prelates, but gradually this too was supplemented and then supplanted by the larger civic parish churches and their parishioners and eventually, too, by the rural churches and their congregations and the lords of the manors who often had responsibility for them. And the growth in the decoration of secular places (a merchant's house with patterned floor tiles) and persons (heraldic embroidery for dress or enamels for the horse harness) increasingly evidenced the separation of patronage from the realm of the great who were godlike.

It is necessary to sketch out these general developments if one is to begin to understand the changing status of the manufacturers of the different visual arts during the later Middle Ages. The change from a command to a consumer economy meant that artists were no longer necessarily associated with the prestige of major patrons. The concomitant controls of training, through legal apprenticeship systems, and of quality of materials and manufacture, succeeded in lowering the cachet of the work-force, now subject to regulation little different from those of, for example, bakers. As the makers were rarely churchmen (certainly never major churchmen) and the patrons might be quite lowly too, and as there was a prescribed and rather menial pattern to the development of a career, the idea that the spirit of God filled the artist with understanding became less and less plausible, indeed it could be a potential embarrassment. Consequently the magic for so long associated with those who worked at, for example, the furnace or the forge was gradually eroded, although the smiths who worked in precious metals and gemstones continued to bask in some of the reflected glory of their raw materials. And while the ladies of a noble household continued to ply their needles for domestic consumption, the production of elaborate ecclesiastical embroidery, such as *Opus Anglicanum*, was increasingly concentrated in the medieval equivalent of the sweatshop.

The reverse of this coin may be considered to be the rise of the artist as a maker of the human image, pre-eminently the painter and the sculptor whose products simulated the likeness of mankind. There is some empirical evidence to support such a view. It was in the twelfth century, when the status of the metalworker as artist began its relative decline, that texts lauding the figurative arts started to become more common – revelling in that deception of the senses which had previously been regarded as so problematic. Many classical ekphrastic topoi were revived. Pictures and sculptures were supposed sufficiently lifelike to affect the spectator by causing him or her to suspend their disbelief and imagine they were witnessing the event itself. Even fantastic invention had its supporters. As Alan ab Insulis wrote in his *Anticlaudianus* in the early 1180s:

> Oh painting with your new wonders; what can have no existence comes into being, and painting, aping reality and diverting itself with a strange skill, turns the shadows of things into things and changes every lie to a truth.

The same period saw the rise of figure sculpture on an unprecedented scale, *pace* classical Antiquity, and furthermore much of that sculpture was painted in quasi-naturalistic colours. Whereas earlier cult images had been clothed in gold foil and gems, from the twelfth century onwards they increasingly stunned the emotions through empathy, not by splendour.

One may argue, then, that social and economic changes in the century either side of AD 1100, saw a gradual reversal of major and minor in the visual arts. Before that date the art of the goldsmith, in particular, had been in the ascendant to such a degree that painting had frequently imitated the interlacing and *cloisonné* stone-setting and enamelling of the goldsmith, whereas after that date the position was gradually reversed, and forms of what we would call naturalism, most readily associated with painting and sculpture, came to dominate to such an extent that goldsmiths had to cultivate the arts of drawing and modelling as never before.

However neat such a formulation may appear, it is only right to sound a few cautionary notes. One is that the rate of change was slow enough to be practically imperceptible and another that it was very low-key. Although the twelfth century saw the first major explanatory and justificatory treatise on the visual arts, the *De diversis artibus* written around 1125 by a north German ecclesiastic who called himself Theophilus, they found no place in the schema of the mechanical arts devised at the same period by Hugh of St Victor. Although three of Hugh's seven categories, working with fibres, defensive and offensive arms, and the theatrical arts of entertainment, might all, as he perceived them, have impinged upon the margins of the visual arts as we might now regard them, he himself did not make the connection except in the case of architecture. A final point to make here is also that there was, of course, no absolute need for painting and sculpture to gain at the expense of smithing or embroidery: they could all have risen, or fallen, together. It is, however, my view that there was such a reversal and, for all that I have given some explanations of its context, it remains a very odd phenomenon. It is not, after all, as though gold, jewels or silk embroidery suddenly became cheap. They remained relatively sumptuous and exclusive. Furthermore, at the highest level, some at least of the practitioners must have retained the potential levels of technical skill which had always been essential.

One art form, the stained-glass window, is in my view potentially particularly informative since it sits uncomfortably between the priorities of image and technique. It can succeed as a conveyer of imagery in that it has the capacity to represent on a public scale the natural world in a way that is quasi-illusionistic. Its illusion is hampered, though, by the windows' being semi-transparent (there is always interference from beyond) and by the black lines (that is the lead cames which hold the pieces of glass) surrounding or crossing almost every coloured element. Technically it can be a vehicle for demonstrations of great skill, virtuosity and knowledge, whether in the colouring, cutting or assembling of the glass, but in practice the demonstration of such ability invariably works against mimetic illusionism since it tends to fragment the image and interfere with an understanding of the subject-matter. Thus, if I am right in seeing a shift in status from dazzling display to figuration, stained glass is probably best-placed to reveal how a major art might become a minor one while remaining essentially the same thing it always was.

The stained-glass window, as we have come to know it in subsequent centuries, was a medieval invention. It is hard to say quite where, when and how the idea came about of combining areas of coloured glass with selective painting and using lead cames to help delineate the design and hold the pieces together within a window surround. Theophilus (mentioned above), writing in around 1125, regarded the technique as French and expected his local German audience to know little or nothing of it. As a consequence he devoted an entire 'book' to it in his treatise, and was painstaking in his descriptions of the technology and engrossing on certain aesthetic aspects of the medium (of 'white' figures on a coloured ground, or coloured ones on a 'white' ground, and of a subtractive technique for creating scrollwork and flowers by removing soft paint from lightly painted areas of coloured glass). The impression he gives is that the idea is a novelty, or at least a relative rarity until recent times. His contemporary, the English monk William of Malmesbury, commented on the effects of the new windows in the splendidly enlarged eastern arm of Canterbury Cathedral, then nearing completion. 'It was not possible to see anything in England comparable', he said, 'to the light of the glass windows.' Another contemporary, Abbot Suger of St-Denis, near Paris, went out of his way to have constructed a new east end to his abbey in which the windows were placed so close together that the effect was of *lux continua*, uninterrupted light. Fortunately enough of Suger's glass survives for us to be able to gauge the effect which he felt it worthwhile recording – an effect which we might regard as coloured glass suffused with light, rather than a translucence which illuminates the interior of the building.

These comments, and several more which could be cited, amount to a remarkable quantity of writing on any art form, given the general paucity of such information from this period. Interestingly, all three authors suggest elements, at least, of innovation in what they are describing. And if one reads Theophilus, even in quite a cursory way, one cannot help but be struck by the sheer experimental technology of it all. There is no direct suggestion that this art was ancient, or that it had biblical authority.

The question thus arises: where did its prestige come from? The answer, I would suggest, lies in a complex amalgam of factors. Although not an ancient art as such, it was an art of the furnace like those practised by Bezaleel. Furthermore it reused some ancient materials, such as glass from ancient mosaic tesserae. The materials themselves were regarded as precious not just because of their rarity and expense, but apparently because of their similarity to gemstones, like those fragments of the earthly paradise found in the lands of Havilah and so on. Abbot Suger even calls his blue glass *opus sapphirorum*, and the phrase 'sapphire glass'

61

appears elsewhere in the Middle Ages. This association in turn brought to mind the walls of the New Jerusalem, described at the end of the Bible, in Revelation 21, 'And the foundations of the wall of the city were garnished with all manner of precious stones. The first foundation was jasper: the second sapphire'. Stained glass allowed its twelfth-century admirers to realise the effect of walls made of jewels like the heavenly city.

But to these factors should be added the formidable aesthetic qualities of the medium – the ravishing effects of the flashing colour, and the astonishing skill of the designers and makers. Several examples could be cited, but perhaps the most impressive is the surviving glass from the rebuilding of the choir of Canterbury Cathedral after a disastrous fire in 1174. The range and purity of the colour and the minuteness of the execution, most apparent in some of the foliate borders and backgrounds, are remarkable. Although we do not have a contemporary appreciation of these qualities in glass, descriptions of an ancient illuminated gospel book (by Gerald of Wales) and of an equally venerable silk textile (by Reginald of Durham) indicate that intricate virtuosity was noticed, even though often attributed to the products of a former age. The view that such things seemed 'more like the work of angels than of men' suggests the supernatural qualities that were associated with virtuoso performance in the visual arts.

Just how difficult it was to accomplish some of these designs can perhaps be appreciated if one examines a single element of foliate scroll-work and analyses the number of individual cut shapes of glass that constitute it. The stems themselves are frequently only about a centimetre across and scroll in volutes or 'S' curves that would be difficult enough to cut from a sheet of glass with a modern diamond glass-cutter. But, as Theophilus makes clear, the medieval glazier was dependent on 'cutting' his glass with a hot iron, a bit like a poker. The resulting scroll had then to be leaded up with the other colours constituting the small, flowering tips and, of course, with the intervening background colour which had to follow the same serpentine contours. When one realises that the design might be repeated dozens of times, even a hundred times, in a single window, and that each element was intended to be and indeed appears to be identical, one can gauge not only the sheer skill involved but also that this 'degree of difficulty' was actually being designed into most of the hundred or so windows from the outset. This is what, in this context, I take virtuosity to be – it is the conception of the execution as a performance both when it was designed (i.e. before it was made) and in the reception of the finished product. The audiences for such work, whether churchmen or laity, whether artisans or clerks, would have needed little imagination to understand and probably none at all to sense that the consistent repetition of designedly complicated technical feats was awesome.

As a commission and as accomplished it was a prodigious scheme – but one which was rivalled at other great and wealthy churches in the late twelfth and early thirteenth centuries, such as Chartres Cathedral. The commitment of time and resources, of skill and expensive raw materials, is breathtaking (a square foot of coloured glass might cost the equivalent of a week's wages for one of the artists), far more so than for any collection of wall paintings of the period. The vast mural spaces of southern European churches in the Gothic period could be painted at a fraction of the cost, using a smaller work-force and cheaper materials. I would argue that the technical virtuosity evident even in the most accomplished of fresco cycles is hardly a patch on early Gothic glass. And yet it is self-evident from consulting almost any book on medieval art that it is painting in manuscripts, on walls and panels that is preferred for illustration and discussion.

There are a number of reasons for this. We are ignorant of the names of early glass painters – so 'personalities' seem to be ellusive (why do we persist in thinking people need to be named before their character is apparent?). To our eyes, glass painting lacks that illusionism which we have been taught to value in the other figurative arts. And then of course there is the status of the art or craft itself. What is it?

It is tempting to suppose that it is in some sense our fault that we are so puzzled by the medium, how to categorise and assess its place within some artistic hierarchy. But on what grounds could we do this? The Middle Ages had no hierarchy which we can adopt to help us, and our own scales for assessing such things are virtually nonexistent – we have no experience of perhaps fifty or sixty artistically trained technicians working simultaneously on a commission to produce more than 5,000 square feet of intricately patterned glass.

The indications are, though, that the kind of ambition that led to the glazing of a Canterbury or a Chartres were themselves quite short-lived. By the early fourteenth century the design of the borders and backgrounds had been noticeably simplified – the tight, thin curls of separately leaded scrollwork a thing of the distant past. The figure panels, too, were far less complex in design, and the colours by the fifteenth century were paler. Money was apparently being saved on the quantity of expensive metal compounds used to tint the glass, and the amount of plain white glass in use had increased to the point where it might occupy over half the area of even a quite prestigious window. Perhaps even more interestingly (since economy is not of itself very interesting in an aesthetic context), the designing of the windows approximated more and more closely to painting in general, whether on panels, wall or in books. That is to say, the representation of the human figure rose in importance as the other attractions of the medium declined. Stained glass no longer had the minuteness of fine goldsmiths' work, no longer matched the richness of translucent gold *cloisonné* enamelling and filigree scrolls. It is as though it had been sucked out of the realm of Bezaleel, the arts of the furnace, and was now placed uncomfortably on the margins of the kingdom of Apelles – where mimesis, not splendour, attempts to influence the emotions of the onlooker.

It does, then, seem that glass (and one could indeed make many of the same points about, for example, embroidery) demonstrates a general shift, visible in many of the other visual arts. It attempted increasingly to play the games of painting, and in the process lost that power to amaze the senses by a dazzling display of colour and virtuosity. It opted, or more likely its patron did, for another role – one that was didactic, that appealed to sentiment through narrative, that was primarily intellectual rather than primarily aesthetic. As one looks at the glass in the aisles of the eastern arm of Canterbury Cathedral one is captivated by the array of colours, the variety, the intricacy. It is very difficult to read the subject-matter, especially of the scenes placed nearest the tops of the windows. So perhaps that really was not quite the point. The narratives were there to justify the expense and to edify the resolute interpreter, but for the vast majority they must simply have been a marvel.

The change in aesthetic, for want of a better word, away from this predilection for dazzling the senses, was for glass or for goldsmiths' work the beginning of a gradual change in status. If we call it a change from major to minor we are, of course, using our own evaluative system. But then we have little option. As a medievalist, and one who particularly thrills to the art of the twelfth century, placed as it is so interestingly on the cusp between privileging the sensual rather than the intellectual, it seems to me unfortunate that the shift which occurred then has continued to have a deleterious effect on the status of those visual arts which are best able to astonish us. Why should it be that we think a designer or maker who is clever enough to overpower our responses by displays of light, colour and craftsmanship is in any way inferior to one who leaves us sufficiently unaffected that we can react with the measure of our minds?

It is a moot point how far the status of the crafts in the modern world has been affected by the changes in aesthetic which I have been discussing. So much else has changed too. Those who wish to have their senses dazzled can witness displays of pyrotechnics not available five centuries ago, perhaps even co-ordinated with the performance of a symphony orchestra. And those who wish to see complexity of design and precision in its technical realisation have thousands of examples of often very beautiful machines or engineering projects to look at. What would previously have seemed tremendous is now quite commonplace, and with that familiarity has come if not contempt for then at least a marginalisation of the knowledge, skill and virtuosity associated with craft and design in earlier centuries.

But in the process so much has been lost, particularly the audience's capacity to look with an informed imagination or even to sense the qualities of things and their makers from the forms of the things themselves. In part this is inexperience – we lack the background to understand how difficult it would be to make something like that; and in a world where so much else is so much more obviously tremendous, why should we give it a second thought? But even if we overcome this and look at a great cathedral and its windows and marvel at the accomplishment ('incredible given the resources at their disposal', 'we have probably lost the ability to do that kind of thing now'), we find it almost impossible to transcend the perceived notions of 'art' as they have hardened over the centuries and see what a comprehensively aesthetic experience hovers before our eyes. It is symptomatic of the stranglehold of the cognitive process and its need for categories that so many steps forward come with steps backward attached. The crafts, as narrowly defined, are a victim of this process. There are, however, a number of strategies for overcoming the disadvantage. One is to contribute to redefinitions, as such things as CADCAM will undoubtedly do, or as the chapters in this book might conceivably do; another is to exercise imagination, to try for an 'out of contemporary mindset experience', and to see ourselves as others might have seen us.

4 ✧ Craft and art, culture and biology

BRUCE METCALF

Defining and evaluating contemporary craft is a vexing business, especially if one also claims that craft is a type of art. Of course, craft practitioners have been making exactly that claim ever since Ruskin penned 'The Nature of Gothic' (1853). To assert that craft is art assumes that the two are comparable, and implies that the conceptual tools and vocabulary of the fine arts can be applied directly to any craft object, and vice versa. But is that so? Are art and craft similar enough, philosophically, to validate such comparisons? The stock answer would hold that both craft and art are visual, and thus subject to the same formalist visual analysis. However, an examination limited to the formal aspects of craft overlooks the way craft objects are made and used, resulting in a highly distorted view.[1]

In this chapter, I propose that contemporary art and craft are rooted, at least in part, in different biological and social contexts. I will investigate recent theories about human nature and culture, and connect them to one of the foundations of craft practice – the choice and mastery of a single medium. In the end, the very human basis for craft practice remains unrecognised by the narratives that explain and empower art, and the resulting cultural clash restricts any comparison between the two.

Western art in the twentieth century has undergone a series of mutations, to the point where there are few characteristics that are shared by all of the different types of art now being produced. However, philosopher-critic Arthur Danto offers an all-encompassing theory, in which he defines art as embodied meaning.[2] Danto was trying to come to grips with examples of art as diverse as Andy Warhol's imitation Brillo boxes, Arakawa's enigmatic text-paintings, or the persistent survival of monochrome painting. The only shared element among these different varieties of art was the way in which all of them were meaningful objects or acts, even if they were highly coded. To Danto, the artness of art is located in its essential transaction with meaning. (He now implies that art has effectively become a branch of philosophy.) Any other characteristics – for instance, the elements of line, space, colour and composition that anchor formalist theories of art – are secondary at best. From Danto's point of view, art can be anything at all. Of course, much of what passes for avant-garde art these days confirms Danto's perception, with artworks taking forms as diverse as self-mutilation, petty theft, extended lectures, and steam. Danto thus offers a cogent explanation for the dematerialistion of art. The art product can mutate into any imaginable form because art consists primarily of meaning. Objecthood is no longer a necessary criterion for art status.

Danto adds one proviso: art can indeed be anything, but only if a loosely organised community of artists, art professionals and interested bystanders, which he called the artworld, recognise it as such. The average citizen cannot go to a plumbing supplies shop, point to a porcelain urinal, and believably proclaim that this object is art: he or she simply doesn't have the requisite stature in the artworld. In order for Marcel Duchamp to transform his urinal into a work of art, a community of authoritative figures had to agree. As Danto puts it: 'To see something as art requires something the eye cannot descry – an atmosphere of artistic theory, a knowledge of the history of art: an artworld.'[3] When Duchamp first exhibited his *Fountain*, he had already established his credentials as an artist. Having achieved a modest reputation as an avant-garde painter, he earned enough credibility to speak directly to the larger social context in which a simple plumbing fixture could be understood as art: the various artists, critics, historians and museum professionals who believed him. Duchamp proposed, the artworld disposed. 'The eye cannot descry' this community, but it is essential to the way we conceive of art. (Danto would deny that the artworld simply decides what is and what is not art, but thousands of craftsmen would disagree.) The philosopher George Dickie and others[4] have further explored the idea of an art culture that must reach some measure of consensus, and it has become known as the institutional theory of art.

Danto is describing a culture, with its own value system(s), language and behaviours. It is a very bookish culture. Danto alone has written five books of art theory and criticism, along with four monographs. He adds to the body of literature about art that stretches back to Alberti's *De Pictura*; a body that can now fill whole buildings. Things have reached the point where a recent 1,189-page anthology of twentieth-century art theory doesn't contain a single image of an artwork. The artworld atmosphere of theory and history assumes a typically Western emphasis on literacy and logical analysis, which will render the philosophical aspects of any artwork far more interesting than an apparently irrational aspect. I will return to this point later.

At the same time, one could also postulate a craftworld, which is subject to a different set of conditions than the artworld. As the artworld concerns art, the craftworld concerns itself with craft. Perhaps I should clarify something here: apart from its connotation of cunning and guile, the word 'craft' has two distinct senses. First, it suggests skilful labour, the work of fabrication, but also any skill at all. In this sense, we speak of an entity having been made: crafted. So, there is a craft of pottery, but there is also a craft of welding nuclear containment vessels, a craft of cooking or a craft of writing. Each of these disciplines implies learning and expertise applied to work. This essay might be superbly crafted, or it might not. But the word 'craft' also denotes a class of objects. This sense of the word is used for institutional names like the British Crafts Council and the American Craft Museum, pointing towards 'studio' craft or 'art' craft. It is this second sense of the word that is the subject of this article: craft which includes ceramics, weaving, silversmithing, and so on. I wish to distinguish between craft-as-skilful-labour, which suggests a great many activities, from craft-as-a-class-of-objects, which is a restricted category with permeable boundaries.

I think of craft-as-a-class-of-objects as being defined by a matter of degree. A menu of characteristics can be described: the more an object exemplifies these characteristics, the more craftlike it is.

Most significantly, craft-as-a-class-of-object must be an object. On the surface, this is a circular definition. But craft is not infinitely mutable; it cannot take the form of the spoken word alone, text alone, performance alone, or many varieties of diffuse materialisation like fireworks, smoke and light. While art has dissolved most of its identities, craft *must* retain several limitations. Craft cannot be dematerialised: it must first and foremost remain a physical object. I can think of any number of performances, installations and ephemera that strike me as not being craft in any meaningful way. There is a famous picture in recent ceramic history, of four men sitting in a row, their heads coated with damp slip: an early-1970s attempt to demonstrate that ceramics was a legitimate art form (*Changes*, 22 August 1972, at the Amsterdam studio of Hetty Huisman). While this performance aped some aspects of the high art of the moment – drippiness on a grand scale, like an Yves Klein body-painting; process raised to subject-matter; emphemerality as noble gesture against the commodification of art – I fail to see how dumping a bucket of slip over somebody is craft. To do so is to shade into intellectual glibness wherein everything is everything, and words have no specific meaning. I may be unsuitably pre-postmodern for saying so, but I assert that words have meanings. And craft (as a class of objects) is not pouring slip over people. Nor is it dragging plaited structures on to a beach (Neda Al-Hilali, *Tongues*, 1975 – although the structures themselves probably were craft objects), arranging firebricks on a gallery floor (John Mason, *Irvine* and other works, 1973), or ladling molten glass on to railroad sleepers and watching them burn (Gene Koss, 1976). Such phenomena can profitably be thought of as performances and sculptures, but they strike me as being quite marginal to the centre of craft.

At any rate, craft-as-a-class-of-object is further identified by a menu of characteristics, as I mentioned above. I would submit, for instance, that a craft object must be made substantially by hand, utilising the hand itself, handtools, and to some degree, power tools. Objects made on an industrial assembly-line, partially or entirely with automated machinery, are not usually regarded as craft. Coca-Cola cans and most motor cars are not craft because they are not crafted: they are not fabricated with a significant amount of handwork. While a certain amount of machine work is now accepted – most woodworkers have long consented to the use of stationary and portable power tools in the fabrication of 'handmade' furniture – the involvement of handwork remains both a definition and a limitation of craft.

Furthermore, to some degree craft can be identified by the use of traditional craft materials, use of traditional craft techniques, and addressing a traditional craft context. By 'traditional', I mean the materials, techniques and formats that survive from pre-industrial production. For instance: clay as material, throwing on the potter's wheel, and vessels constitute a traditional locus of the craft of ceramics – because this triad has been employed by many of the ceramic-using cultures worldwide, long before the Industrial Revolution. Other traditions operate in the craft of ceramics as well: hand-building, pit-firing, glaze decoration and figurative sculpture, to name a few. But the triad of traditional material, technique and context continues to provide a centre and reference for contemporary ceramics-as-craft. In contrast, research into machinable ceramics for automotive engines does not.

These three identifying criteria are quite elastic: a craft object can retain only one out of three of these characteristics and still be recognised as craft. A woven nylon hanging, in which a non-traditional material is manipulated with a conventional craft technique to make a non-traditional form, remains a craft object. So does a spun titanium vessel, in which a machine acts on a very modern material to make an object that conforms to a traditional craft format. However, substantially handmade objects that fail to address at least one of these three characteristics are rarely regarded as craft. Paintings, racing cars and steel-forming dies may still be crafted – skilfully fabricated – but I do not regard them as craft objects. Again, I find it more useful to think of them in other contexts: art, specialised machinery and industrial toolmaking, respectively.

If craft (as-a-class-of-object) is necessarily tied to this menu of limitations, craft cannot fully partake of the infinite mutability that Danto identifies as a corollary of art-as-embodied-meaning. While an artist might freely choose any form for his or her artwork, the craftsman must make an object, must make it substantially by hand, and must utilise to some extent the traditional materials and usages of craft. In the craftworld, objecthood and material come prior to any other consideration; otherwise, the enterprise ceases to be craft. In the artworld value-system that prizes the open-ended manipulation of meaning above all else, such restrictions appear arbitrary and backward. If the first priority of art is to address ideas, and if form and material should be secondary to the idea in question, how can an artist justify working in only one medium? Why should the project of embodying meaning necessitate hand labour, or even making an object?

Thus far, the crafts community has advanced no satisfactory answer to these questions. The problem is further exacerbated by some craft practitioners who loudly claim to be making art, but who fail to account for the logical inconsistency of trying to embody meaning with such limited means. While craft certainly can embody meaning, and occasionally is recognised by the artworld for doing so, craft cannot be anything at all. Craft is limited. I believe that the artworld recognises this distinction intuitively, and the rejection that craft practitioners often suffer at the hands of art-gallery owners, art-museum curators, and art critics turns on this perception. The free field of art is compared to the restricted field of craft, and craft suffers in the comparison.

But then, is it reasonable to compare craft and art in these terms? If, as Danto implies, the essence of contemporary art is based on a culture of writing and reasoning, where are the roots of craft? I submit that craft grows directly from the human cognitive potential for fine motor control, and that this potential is actualised as a cultural response to late industrial conditions. While the artworld places its highest values on verbal and logical cognitive abilities, the craftworld places its value elsewhere. The logical inconsistency of craft makes sense only if measured by the artworld's values. These values, however, are far from universal, and may not apply to modern craft.

In the past fifteen years, cultural anthropologists, neurobiologists and psychologists have amassed a substantial amount of evidence indicating that a universal human nature actually exists, and the field of evolutionary biology has provided a persuasive theory to explain the evidence.[5] One body of data strongly suggests that the human mind has undergone an evolution formed by environmental conditions, just as the human body has, and human nature can be defined as the inherent cognitive capacities of the human brain. Some of the most persuasive research documents how brain lesions cause very specific losses of language, motor and even musical abilities; other research corroborates Noam Chomsky's theories about a deep structure to all human languages. Another line of research examines the anthropological record, and sorts out a number of behaviours that appear to occur in every known society. Unfortunately, the literature is much too complex to summarise here, and of course, this conclusion is hotly contested. But taken together, the case for a pancultural human nature is quite persuasive.[6] If we as a species are endowed with a biological mind and share common behaviours, then we all share a common human nature. The implications are profound.

The renewed confirmation of a universal human nature directly challenges the most extreme of postmodern positions. Language and culture, being influenced by a biological human nature, can no longer be seen as arbitrary constructions. Theories that assert the arbitrariness of language and culture are (again) too complex to adequately describe here, but they form the basis for much of the 'politically correct' thinking so fashionable in American academic circles. In brief, these positions are based on the declaration that science (with its inevitable cultural bias) is incapable of determining the difference between learned behaviour and behaviour emanating from a pan-cultural human nature. Some recent thinking rejects the possibility of a human nature altogether: 'nature' is eliminated completely in favour of 'nurture'. In doing so, the postmodern position typically declares the primacy of culture, and particularly the primacy of language.

These theories have the virtue of questioning all previous claims to discern a human universal, demanding a more rigorous proof than simply declaring that one can intuitively ascertain it. (Universality, of course, is one of the cornerstones of formalist aesthetics: Kant invented a universal 'common sense' [*sensus communis*] as the basis for his aesthetic theory in *Critique of Judgement*.) But since postmodern thought sees culture and language as essentially arbitrary cultural constructions, these theories also suffer the liability of being uncompromisingly relativist: if our culture is ultimately an arbitrary construction, we have no right to draw any conclusions about any other (arbitrarily constructed) culture. In an extreme relativist position, we would not even be allowed to condemn murder, because the cultural 'other' acts according to a set of rules every bit as valid as our own. Luckily, most people reject this kind of moral imbecility, and seek out a middle ground. We can redraw the circumstances upon which cultures can and cannot be compared, but must do so on the basis of sound evidence about human nature. If behaviours have a close and demonstrable basis in human nature, we can compare similar behaviours across cultural boundaries. If, however, behaviours are learned, or if behaviours are rooted in demonstrably different aspects of human nature, then comparisons are restricted.

Not surprisingly, as science carefully reconstructs our sense of a biological human nature, universalising aesthetic theories are starting to reappear. The implications of an innate human basis for art have been explored by two writers: Peter Fuller in England and Ellen Dissanayake in the USA. Fuller proposed an analysis of art based on the study of animal behaviour and human neonatal development,[7] and rejected the totalising relativism of some of his colleagues.[8] More recently, Dissanayake draws on a significant body of anthropological research, and concludes that art is a manifestation of a universal tendency rooted in human nature. She maintains that art springs from a desire to 'make special':

> [Art as a behavior] can result in artifacts and activities in people without expressed 'aesthetic' motivations as well as the most highly self-conscious creations of contemporary art. I call this tendency *making special* and claim that it is as distinguishing and universal in humankind as speech or the skillful manufacture and use of tools.[9]

Dissanayake claims that 'making special' was an evolutionary adaptation to the circumstances of early human culture. 'Making special' involves the separation of certain acts and objects from the ordinary, as dance is separated from mere walking and song is separated from mere conversation. The idea of 'making special' links art with ritual, and proposes that art is typically the vehicle of many important social meanings. Dissanayake also condemns contemporary art for having departed from its biological origins, becoming little more than an intellectual game for a privileged class of professionals and aficionados: that is, the artworld.

However, the concept of 'making special' explains little of the way in which art (or craft) is manifested within the confines of any given culture: the historical record shows such tremendous variation that few other constants are discernible. To say that art stands apart from day-to-day concerns doesn't tell us much about the way art is used and evaluated in present-day Europe or America. It's obvious that art is 'special': even a black-velvet Elvis Presley painting stands apart from refrigerators and doorknobs. Nor does the idea of 'making special' clarify the issue of comparing art and craft raised at the beginning of this chapter.

Recent theories about divisions of functions in the human brain offer a more useful reference. Howard Gardner, a professor at Harvard University, has advanced a theory of multiple intelligences,[10] which revises the standard hierarchy of mind over body and thought over physical labour.

Studying the loss of mental capacity caused by localised brain damage, neurobiologists have demonstrated that the human brain is divided into several regions in which specific cognitive functions take place. In most individuals, for instance, damage to the part of the left frontal lobe called Broca's area will cause difficulty in speaking grammatically, while verbal comprehension remains untouched. Damage to the part of the left temporal lobe called Wernicke's area will cause loss of language comprehension, while preserving fluent speech. These two types of aphasia show how capacity for speech and comprehension are located in specific parts of the brain. Similarly, brain damage in other locations causes other equally specific losses of cognitive ability. The biological evidence shows that human intelligence is divided into relatively discrete capacities, as if the brain consisted of several different computers, each assigned to a specific task.

Gardner proposes six distinct types of intelligence. While the categories themselves are fictions, they denote real properties of the brain. Linguistic intelligence and logical/mathematical intelligence are the capacities measured by IQ tests and the like, and almost exclusively form the Western conception of mental power. But Gardner also proposes musical intelligence, spatial intelligence, personal intelligence (which governs social and introspective skills), and bodily-kinaesthetic intelligence.

Because craft is so intimately tied to labour and the physical handling of material, bodily-kinaesthetic intelligence is particularly important to any consideration of craft. Motor activity is typically (in right-handed individuals) concentrated in the left hemisphere of the brain. Gardner remarks:

> Characteristic of [bodily] intelligence is the ability to use one's body in highly differentiated and skilled ways, for expressive as well as goal-directed purposes .... Characteristic as well is the capacity to work skillfully with objects, both those that involve the fine motor movements of one's fingers and hands and those that exploit gross motor movements of the body.[11]

To support his distinction of bodily intelligence from other types of cognition, Gardner cites various motor-control disorders caused by selective left-hemisphere injuries. Brain-damaged individuals have shown impairment of the ability to dress, to carry out verbal commands, or to sequentially execute certain directions, in spite of their being in good physical condition and in spite of their having understood the directions. Gardner also cites examples of severely autistic children who show extra-ordinary motor control or a gifted understanding of mechanical principles.[12] Interestingly, bodily intelligence appears to be linked to language. Gardner goes on to speculate about the evolutionary sources of bodily-kinesthetic intelligence, which he locates in the increasing sophis-tication of early hominid tool use.

Bodily intelligence is manifested in the skill of the athlete, the dancer, the mime – and the craftsman. All crafts demand exceptional motor control, from the precision demanded by jewellery-making to the subtle co-ordination required in throwing a pot. Bodily intelligence can thus be seen as a biological and cognitive foundation to all craft practice, and it becomes an important factor in the way individuals choose a single medium, and later develop a powerful loyalty to their craft.

It is important to realise that crafts are not taken up in the same manner as in pre-industrial times, when sons followed their father's trade and daughters learned household skills out of necessity. Few in the modern Western world are compelled by social pressure to learn a craft. People now make their commitment to craft voluntarily, with very different motivations than 150 years ago. Furthermore, the opportunities to learn a craft have moved out of the family and the neighbourhood, and into educational institutions. The choice to take up a craft is now a personal decision, in which consideration of one's internal state is paramount. Free of external compulsion, people can be motivated by intuitive recognition of their own innate abilities.

In the USA, one typically encounters crafts for the first time while attending a college or university. Students usually try out different craft courses casually and indiscriminately: each class is merely an alternative to be taken up and abandoned, unless a compelling reason emerges to continue. A predictable pattern occurs: most students never take a second course in any given medium; but of those who take the second class, the majority will major in that subject. The motivation of those who continue is based on a powerful intuitive response to the labour of manipulating a specific craft material. These students cannot offer logical reasons for their choice, but they are often powerfully moved.

Over a period of time, teachers discover that students' responses are highly particular. One student may react strongly to ceramics – usually the plasticity and earthiness of raw clay – but will find metalsmithing completely unattractive. Another student will respond in the opposite way. (In fact, I once witnessed identical twins enact precisely this scenario: one majored in ceramics, the other in jewellery.) Because most students have no prior experience with craft mediums, the responses cannot have been greatly formed by language or culture. Instead, the response must reflect some pre-existing interior condition of the individual. Psychology does not presently provide an adequate term for this condition, so I refer to it as sensibility. I do not use the word in the nineteenth-century meaning, where sensibility was related to artistic genius, a special gift with which few were endowed. In that language, the great artist had a unique sensibility, responsive to impressions and sensations to which ordinary mortals were deaf and blind. In my terms, sensibility refers to the set of capacities and sensitivities that each individual has, but which differ from one individual to another. One could conclude that an individual's sensibility reflects their particular disposition of the six intelligences Gardner defines.

My personal experience, and my work as a teacher for more than a decade, leads me to believe that the potent response exhibited by a young craft student is an intuitive recognition that the bodily-kinaesthetic intelligence has finally found an outlet. It's the mind speaking through the body. The student discovers a special gift of bodily intelligence, comparable to that of the athlete or the dancer, and it suddenly dawns on him or her that the exercise of their newly discovered sensibility is both pleasurable and powerful. To act in concert with one's own ability and sensibility brings a meaningfulness to life previously experienced by few of these students. Those who listen to their inner voice often discover an inexhaustible motivation to pursue craft as a life's work – as I found for myself in a jewellery class some twenty-five years ago.

The verbal and rational intelligences are not the primary faculty in action here. The motivation is felt: self-perceived as an emotion. Just as it would be when the musical, spatial or personal intelligences come into play, one cannot be strictly rational in dissecting the experience. Logic and language remain in the background, although the individual knows clearly that *something* is going on. Usually, a young student simply feels motivated to work. Theories of motivation are not presently well resolved: debate persists about subjects as simple as hunger and thirst. But two general observations can be made about the craft experience: that the motivation is largely intrinsic, that is, based on desire to do something for its own sake regardless of external reward; and that the motivation to learn and practise a craft is probably related to individualised needs of self-esteem and self-actualisation.[13]

In craft, a powerful motivation is essential. To gain control over a chosen medium, a student must persist in the face of many doubts and failures. A potter must become proficient in throwing and handbuilding, as well as learn about different clay bodies, glazes, firing practices and kiln-building. Much of this learning comes with frequent frustrations – every potter has stories of kiln-loads lost and glazes gone bad. And so it is with jewellery-making, weaving, glassblowing, and all the rest of the craft disciplines: one must serve a long apprenticeship to the material and its processes. It takes four to six years before a craft practitioner has enough experience to function as a professional or a teacher, and even then the learning never stops. The first intuitive glimmer of recognition matures into an investment in one's own life, but gaining this maturity demands an unwavering motivation. It should come as no surprise, then, that many craftsmen develop an unshakeable loyalty to their medium.

Most Western crafts practitioners follow the same trajectory. They first felt their bodily intelligence awaken upon contact with the clay, wood, fabric, glass or metal; they were moved to endure the long training; they developed an abiding love for their work. Such shared experiences lead directly to a shared value-system in which handwork, technical mastery, and passion in one's labour are all unstated but deeply meaningful. These three values have helped shape a new culture of craft.

I am not personally familiar with the craft associations in the UK and Europe, but in the USA the crafts are highly organised. Most of the American craft societies are based on medium or technique: jewellers, glassblowers, ceramists, each seek out their own kind. Most of these organisations have their own magazines and annual conventions. Some are internally divided between one group devoted to business and another group devoted to art, or, in a related schism, between functional and non-functional craftsmen. But beyond all the petty bickering, the societies represent individuals banded together with a specific, shared and often unstated value system.

This craft culture is not a pre-industrial throwback, but a distinctly twentieth-century phenomenon. It is rooted, initially, in the biology of the brain. People use craft to exercise a gifted bodily intelligence, partly because Western society provides few other vehicles for self-determined and dignified handwork. Having made a choice about their life's work, people then seek out others who share the same experiences, ultimately inventing an adaptive culture based on the value of handwork.

Here, I think, is the rub. Most Western thought, which distrusts the body and its underlying cognition as a source of valid meaning, fails to find any significance in hand labour. Western civilisation has privileged the linguistic and mathematical intelligences, probably because those two skills are most useful in business, war-making, politics and academic careerism. Wherever verbal and mathematical intelligence alone are claimed to predict failure and success (as in IQ tests and classroom grades), spatial and motor skills will be relegated to the lowest levels of a hierarchy.

However, Gardner's theory suggests that there is no biological basis for placing the various human intelligences in a hierarchy. Each type of cognition arose in response to specific environmental conditions, and is value-neutral. Thus, it becomes much more difficult to assign an absolute priority to one type of cognition over another: linguistic intelligence occupies no more important a place than musical intelligence when one considers the grey matter itself. In fact, Gardner cites many examples of cultures which place radically different values on the various intelligences than we do in Europe and North America. Of course, any culture can legitimately claim a hierarchy of intelligences within its own boundaries, but that hierarchy must be recognised as a cultural construction, not a human condition.

Assigning hierarchies to different intelligences is a dangerous business. As Gardner says,

> The story of the West is ... not a universal saga, and it is a grave mistake to assume that it should be. In my view, many of the most problematic aspects of modernization have resulted from an uncritical attempt to apply the model and the history of the West to alien traditions, with different histories, different traditions of education, and different favored blends of intelligence.[14]

Similarly, the story of the artworld is not a universal saga. The craftworld is a modern response to the unbalanced nature of the Western intellectual tradition. In their loyalty to medium, process and skill, the individuals who comprise craft culture elevate the bodily and spatial intelligences to a position of primary importance. Unluckily, the value of working with one's hands remains an esoteric wisdom in this world, evident only to initiates. Outside the craftworld it seems incomprehensible, and thus worthless. The artworld, predictably taking the imperialistic path so favoured by Western thought, continues to claim the primacy of verbal and logical intelligence, and to disparage any other 'favored blend of intelligence'. A cultural clash is inevitable.

I will offer one example here. Paul Smith (in his introduction to the American Craft Museum's *Poetry of the Physical* catalogue, 1986) remarked that 'Amid mass-production the craft experience can impart greater meaning to individual expression.' In response, the art critic Christopher Knight – who in the USA is regarded as something of a friend of craft – commented on Smith's assertion as follows:

> Surely that bit of charmingly old-fashioned nonsense was written circa 1886 by William Morris, the founder of the Arts-and-Crafts movement in England, and not 100 years later .... Smith left a few rather important words out of his exhortation, which ought to have gone like this: 'Amid mass-production, the craft experience can impart the *myth* of greater meaning to individual expression.'[15]

As representative of the artworld, Knight demonstrates his commitment to an atmosphere of artistic theory – linguistic and logical thought – as well as his incomprehension of (and disdain for) the remaining four intelligences. Taught that discourse is the only valid site for meaning, Knight arrogantly reduces the felt experiences of craftsmen to mere illusion. He cannot even imagine the meaning of bodily intelligence, much less respect it. Knight encapsulates the profound discontinuity between artworld and craftworld: meanings and experiences not officially endorsed by the artworld are denied the right to exist.

Under such conditions, it is very difficult to adequately compare craft and art. Each springs from a culture that assigns radically different hierarchies to Gardner's multiple intelligences. It is as if the two worlds spoke mutually incomprehensible languages, with no Rosetta Stone to establish a translation. The craftworld accepts the meanings of felt experience and the body, whereas the artworld remains dedicated to meanings embedded in texts and discourses. And, as Knight so clearly demonstrates, a world committed to such a narrow conception of thought and meaning will repudiate less 'rational' types of meaning, despite the compelling evidence that cognition is far more comprehensive than logical thought alone.

Perhaps the situation would be improved if every artworld professional were required to take up a craft, and they learned of bodily intelligence through intimate experience. I like to imagine the Director of the Whitney Museum weaving tablecloths or carving dovetail joints, but it isn't likely to happen. As long as Danto's thesis remains exclusively focused on text and discourse, the artworld will be unable to recognise the biological roots and the cultural values of twentieth-century crafts.

In this chapter, I have touched upon only one of the many complexes of biology and culture: the way bodily intelligence is transformed into an individual's dedication to his or her craft. But other such complexes exist. One could extend David Pye's meditation on workmanship. One could examine the way craft is incorporated into domestic life, especially as gifts. One could investigate the craftworld's comfortable (and selective) acceptance of tradition, especially in the light of the artworld's fascination with rupture and alienation. While the artworld concentrates on the philosophical, craft allows a more diffuse range of human capacity, cognition and emotion. Craft has a human face, and until the basis for comparing art and craft can accommodate the fullness, complexity and messiness of the human condition, it is unlikely that indiscriminately comparing craft and art will be productive.

Notes

1 For an argument against the formalist analysis of craft, see B. Metcalf, 'Replacing the Myth of Modernism', *American Craft*, February/March 1993.

2 A. Danto, *The Transfiguration of the Commonplace* (Cambridge, MA, Harvard University Press, 1981).

3 A. Danto, 'The Artworld', *Journal of Philosophy*, 61, 1964, p. 580.

4 G. Dickie, *Art and the Aesthetic: An Institutional Analysis* (Ithaca, Cornell University Press, 1975); and H. Becker, *Art Worlds* (Berkeley, University of California Press, 1982); among others.

5 For several broad, non-technical summations of recent research suggesting an immutable human nature, and the evolutionary theories that support this

evidence, see H. Gardner, *Frames of Mind: The Theory of Multiple Intelligences* (New York, Basic Books, 1985); J. Q. Wilson, *The Moral Sense* (New York, Pantheon Books, 1994); R. Wright, *The Moral Animal* (New York, Pantheon Books, 1994); and S. Pinker, *The Language Instinct* (New York, William Morrow & Co., 1994).

6 As cited in Pinker, *The Language Instinct*, ethnologist Donald E. Brown has characterised 'Universal People' in great detail. A few of his elements of human nature are gossip, lying, metaphor, words for emotions and sensations, binary distinctions (including male and female and natural and cultural), smiling as friendly greeting, decoration of artefacts, empathy, sexual jealousy, rape, and fondness for sweets. D. Brown, *Human Universals* (New York, McGraw-Hill, 1991).

7 P. Fuller, 'Art and Biology', in *The Naked Artist* (London, Writers and Readers Publishing Cooperative, 1983).

8 Fuller cites J. Benthal and T. Polhemus, *The Body as a Medium of Expression* (New York, Dutton, 1975), as one example.

9 Ellen Dissanayake, *What is Art For?* (Seattle, University of Washington Press, 1988), p. 92.

10 Gardner, *Frames of Mind*.

11 *Ibid.*, p. 206.

12 *Ibid.*, pp. 212–15.

13 See A. H. Maslow, *Motivation and Personality* (New York, Harper & Row, 1954).

14 Gardner, *Frames of Mind*, pp. 336–7.

15 C. Knight, 'American Craft Today', *Last Chance for Eden* (Los Angeles, Art Issues Press, 1995).

5 ✧ Craft within a consuming society

GLORIA HICKEY

Before language was written or money minted, humans exchanged gifts. Gift-giving is probably one of the oldest and most basic of human behaviours. To say that for centuries these gifts were handcrafted is a truism. However, to say that today, from the vast proliferation of market goods, craft objects are frequently selected as gifts *is* significant. It is not just because craftspeople must make a living that we find craft in our department stores, gift shops, speciality and museum shops, at craft fairs and, of course, for sale at the maker's studio. It is because people buy and give craft – motivated by some very revealing reasons.

Examining craft as giftware allows us to examine the variety of values and meanings assigned to the handcrafted object by contemporary society – by makers, retailers, buyers and recipients alike. Giving is potent communication – communication largely conveyed by the complex relationships the giver and recipient have with the gift object.

If anyone doubts the importance that objects play in our daily lives or that they reveal our values, they need only look to any densely populated residential building in a major city, such as London. Here you will find high-rise flats that offer its hundreds of residents largely the same features in each unit. Yet despite the uniform walls, counters and fixtures, each home is a different, private world created by a distinctive but fluid arrangement of market goods – craft included.

These worlds may focus on the dining-room table and entertaining, the television and solitary pursuits or on an abundance of children's toys. In addition to family status, ethnic background and degree of affluence we can determine interests – anything from exotic pets to travel – and tastes, which might vary from a pastiche of Victorian to 1970s funk. In short, the objects we select, and what we do with them, suggests everything from our daily routines to our ideals (Miller 1987: 9).

At an early age, we begin to project values on to objects and create powerful associations with them – as is indicated by the term 'security blanket', which conveys the talismanic, protective function of the blanket beyond mere warmth. We form likes and dislikes and experience an ever-widening scope of goods and associations until we learn to creatively use objects as tools of self-expression – we become consumers (Strathern 1991: 592). As evidence, consider the yearning of a youth in a Communist country for a pair of Levis.

Consumerism is not necessarily a 'shop till you drop' philosophy. It should not be confused with materialism, which preaches that the greatest satisfaction in life comes from the possession of goods. Consumerism is more benign, not based solely on acquisition but on differentiation and identity. However, the social and psychological links made with commodities have fuelled branding policies, design, targeting of goods and much company competition.

Increasingly since the 1960s, commerce has abandoned economies of scale aimed at selling to a huge homogeneous audience and attempted to accommodate the growing diversity of consumers (Miller 1987: 91). As such, commerce acknowledges the fragmentation of market interests and is willing to make a place for more limited and varied forms of production, such as craft. Meanwhile, it pays commerce to be finely tuned to the business of gift-giving. One-sixth of all retail sales in the United States are attributed to Christmas gift-shopping alone, which represents 4 per cent of all annual spending (Carrier 1993: 61).

Whether it is to give, to receive or to repay, gift-giving is about obligation (Mauss 1990: 68). When we give a gift we are responding to a felt obligation, or hoping to create one. This needn't be taken negatively, although bribes are a good example of the shadowy aspects. The engagement ring is an equally valid, although more acceptable, form of the same behaviour. Positive or negative, the obligation is about forging or maintaining a bond with the gift recipient.

Anthropologists have regarded gift-giving as a will to peace, allowing early and contemporary 'primitive' peoples to avoid war, isolation and economic stagnation.[1] Parents use gifts to reward or control children's behaviour, as is demonstrated by the clairvoyant abilities of the gift-bringer Santa, 'who knows whether you've been naughty or nice'.

Additionally, the gift serves to affirm the identity of the recipient, according to the giver, or mark its transformation – as in the cases of christenings, weddings, graduations, retirements and even inheritance (Schwartz 1967: 1). Still, with rites of passage, the prime focus is cementing the relationship between the recipient and the giver, and this is why it is universally regarded that the best form of gift-giving is to 'give of oneself' (Csikszentmihalyi 1981:38).

Ralph Waldo Emerson eulogised this view in his essay, 'Gifts': 'The only gift is a portion of thyself. ... Therefore the poet brings his poem; the shepherd, his lamb; the farmer, corn; the miner, a gem; the sailor, coral and shells; the painter, his picture; the girl, a handkerchief of her own sewing.' He concludes that 'a man's biography is conveyed in his gift' and contrasts it with the 'cold, lifeless business when you go to the shops' (Emerson 1903: 310).

Only giving cash could be regarded as more cold and anonymous. Money is suitable for bribes or for tips. Occasionally, it can be given by a superior to a subordinate, such as a bonus to an employee. Tipping is a gratuity rather than a service charge. It is a gift we give to those with whom we are forced into close but impersonal relationship: waiters, hairdressers, newspaper delivery boys (Visser 1994: 72). Money is at the opposite end of the spectrum from the handmade and the intimate.

The tension between the ideal of giving of yourself and the commercial world is lamented every year at Christmas time (Carrier 1993: 55). Supporters of the cause of craft might be led to think 'what a wonderful opportunity for craft – let's take advantage of the public's dissatisfaction with the commercial. Perhaps they will eschew the mass-produced and embrace the uniquely crafted as the best way to convey the heartfelt and genuine.'

In such a scenario, the handcrafted object might be promoted as possessing the following attributes that make it appropriate as a gift. It is 'special' or rare because it is handmade and perhaps customised; sophisticated because the making of the object required skill; it is precious due to materials or time invested in labour; it is expressive – in terms of subject-matter, function, traditional or historical reference; and is enduring.

85

At first glance, the attributes ring true to those familiar with craft and it would seem to be a superior choice as a gift because the attributes – unique, sophisticated, precious, expressive, enduring – are those we wish to impart to our relationships. It is the perfect raw material for creating the obligation of bonds and expression of identity. However, such a view of craft is limited to those professionally related to it or to connoisseurs and collectors of studio craft.

To be successful as a gift, those associations with craft would have to be shared by both giver and recipient. Craft stands out among market goods as being largely unadvertised, unpackaged and unpromoted. The result is a startling gap between insiders and outsiders of the craft world. The likelihood of an informed shared perception about craft is slim and limits its appropriateness as a gift to the most personal or predictable occasions.

Craft galleries in Ontario and Quebec report that most major purchases are by collectors for their own use and, in the case of gifts, exchanged between couples. A craftsperson's résumé, biography or point-of-purchase literature is usually consulted *after* a selection has been made. Information about the maker is used to confirm, not motivate, the purchase. It may be retained to show others as validation, and some craftspeople issue 'certificates of authenticity'.[2]

Less expensive but still significant purchases – such as wedding gifts – are more likely to be returned to craft shops or galleries in favour of more recognisable or brand-name goods. Craft is not a safe choice.[3]

Ironically, craft is most valued by those who believe that the ability to create is itself 'a gift'. Rather than a product of a marketable skill, some consumers express reverence towards handcrafted objects because they view them as products of inspiration. No amount of training, the consumer reasons, could enable them to create an equivalent object.

However, this reverence does not necessarily translate into higher prices for craft products. Craftspeople who exercise such 'given' talents are practising a vocation, not a lucrative profession. As a result, they have great difficulty pricing or marketing their products – as if it were a non-negotiable part of themselves or a child.[4] They are also reluctant to enter into dealings with the public who may not share their perspective. We do not usually bargain over what is inalienable.

Facing the public in retail contexts, without the buffer of a dealer, may challenge the self-image of the craftsperson. Monique Lajeunesse of Little

River Hotglass, based in Vermont, USA, relates an encounter at the display stand with a consumer who opened a conversation with 'I collect Lalique. Who are you?' Such experiences suggest that the craftsperson is not just marketing their product but him- or herself.

Nor is vocation the only alternative to profession in the public's mind. Awareness of craft is often based on exposure to it as a leisure activity. Whether practised by oneself, a relative or a colleague at work, most members of the the general public have had repeated contact with craft that is produced and sold through bazaars operated by community centres and churches. Consequently, craftspeople – especially at fairs – are at times confused with hobbyists. This confusion is unsavoury to crafts-people, who believe it undermines their professional status and the prices they can charge.

Karl Schantz, now glass master at the Ontario College of Art, still remembers an exchange overheard in a craft gallery in 1981. Marvelling over the intricately detailed objects, a husband remarked to his wife, 'God, these things are beautiful. I just don't know where these people get the time to make them.' And his wife said, 'Well, they don't work' (Flanders 1981: 93).

One ceramicist described his discomfort about selling his own vessels by saying that 'marketing was right up there with elective surgery'. Such vulnerability makes some craftspeople appear disdainful towards partici-pating in fairs and commercial opportunities, while others seem naive and self-defeating – like poker players holding their cards so as to show their hand to the table (Feschuk 1994: A5).

Finally, although complaints about commercialisation are common, craft is not the only means available to gift-givers hoping to create personal meaning with a distinctive object. Consider the ways gift-givers mitigate the impact of the mass-produced.

Does the grumbling over the 'hard work of Christmas shopping' sound familiar? Ever since the emergence of the modern form of Christ-mas gift-giving – not, coincidentally, about the time industrial capitalism flowered – intense shopping for the 'right' item has been the first way most people inject themselves into an otherwise anonymous process (Belk 1993: 90).

Once acquired, price-tags are removed from the selections. Next, they are gift-wrapped to further express the giver's personality and heighten the suspense. The wrapped presents are displayed in a special place – a mantelpiece or a Christmas tree – and exchanged in a ritualised fashion. If the presents are photographed it will be during the exchange or before, not afterwards, like a pile of loot or goods inventory. If all attempts fail there is recourse to expressions like 'It's the thought that counts.'

Retailers also do their share to make the factory-made more accept-able as gifts. In North America, the gradual shift from handmade Christmas presents to the factory-made can be traced in the newspaper advertise-ments of the 1870s. In Victorian America, charitable bazaar 'fancy fairs' promoting home-made gifts eventually gave way to factory-made merchan-dise expressly ordered for Christmas giving (Belk 1993: 90). Special displays, often in enlarged windows, lavishly featured the new stock – such as the display of $10,000-worth of imported dolls by Macy's depart-ment store in 1874.

So the factory-made product is recontextualised through advertising, display, packaging and giving, with the consequent 'special' shopping experience knitting together retailer and buyer. Not surprisingly, Canada's most successful craft-fair operator, the 'One of a Kind Canadian Craft Show & Sale', advertises its winter event as 'ten days of the best Christmas shopping in the city'. The Toronto Christmas fair attracts on average 100,000 shoppers. The spring fair, which attracts 60,000, is similarly aimed at the second most popular gift-giving season punctuated by Mother's Day, spring weddings and graduations. Shopping, rather than craft, is promoted.

This promotion is carefully managed through extensive advertising in both print and electronic media and the 'shopping experience' itself. When shoppers come to browse through close upon 600 stalls they can leave their coats, have parcels delivered to their cars, leave their children at a play area, sip free spring water and listen to live classical and traditional instrumental music or partake of espresso while watching an upbeat fashion show. Models wear One of a Kind clothing complete with fashion accessories and props from the craftspeople's stalls.

After each fair, studies are conducted to determine what kind of product sold and the appropriate 'mix' is determined for the following year. The number of potters' stalls may be reduced and the representation of glassworkers or metalsmiths increased. Annual telephone surveys update the profile of shoppers and non-shoppers, according to age, family status, income level and purchases. Modes of advertising are accordingly refined. Focus groups are also conducted to gauge response to key words and concepts.

Stephen Leavy and Martin Rumack, the entrepreneurs who have owned and managed One of a Kind for twenty-one years in Toronto, discovered early on that their English-speaking audience had 'a big problem with the word craft'. Leavy describes their perception of craft as largely being 'something pioneers did to survive'.

This is consistent with the image implied by the brand names of popular North American 'do-it-yourself' tools – American Craftsman and MasterCraft – and the dominance of cheery home-kits for what the mainstream press calls Country Crafts. Powerful and sophisticated advertising campaigns for these products – that are a world apart from studio craft – associate 'craft' with self-sufficiency, thrift, sanitised natural materials, happy childhoods and the comfort of hearth and home.[5]

Clearly, the general English-speaking public's perception of craft was more the stuff of church bazaars than that suited to the business goals of One of a Kind. Furthermore, if craft was going to be selected as giftware – the major focus of the two fairs – it needed more sex appeal. Rather than try and re-engineer the image of craft, Leavy and Rumack choose to promote shopping rather than craft. They also try to enforce professional appearance. Craftspeople's applications are accepted or rejected on the basis of product, stall presentation and professional conduct. Despite the large number of stalls, competition is fierce among those hoping to be accepted.

However, this pioneer perception of craft was not found among French-speaking Canadians. Apparently, 'métiers d'art' is understood as a broader cultural phenomenon and not necessarily associated with primitive, survival or domestic skills. This may account for a statistically higher percentage of the public, in Montreal, Quebec, who identified the purpose of their trip to the major craft fair as visiting rather than shopping, with 7.6 per cent expressly going to 'meet the artisan'.[6]

At the Toronto fairs there is clearly an effort to ensure that every member of the public who walks through the fair doors does not just visit, but buys something. And this is reflected in the 'something for every purse' range of goods; it is possible to spend anywhere from $10 to $1,000 on a single item.

But would you expect a shopper to spend $1,000 or more on

something they regard as quaint or pioneer-like? The difficulty is that craft as a generic term does not – according to the focus test results – encompass elite or highly-priced products. The values commonly associated with craft do not match the consumer's expectation or 'shopping experience' of buying a gift of exquisite silverware or woodwork. What, we may wonder, do they think they are buying?

Selections may hold some answers. The Canadian Museums Association's 1994 catalogue, subtitled *Gifts of Distinction from Canada's Cultural Centres*, contains a substantial number of craft items. For example, four of the six pieces on the cover are a celadon porcelain vase, an Indian beadwork container, a gold pendant and a handblown glass vessel. The remaining two items are a mineral sample and a pendant that may be factory-made.

The catalogue's welcoming letter from the president of the Canadian Museums Association, Michel Cheff, introduces potential shoppers not to craft but to 'a fascinating collection of jewellery, ornaments, objets d'art and special gifts'. He assures them that 'We've taken a great deal of care in selecting items that offer you outstanding artistic significance, character and value.' It is also noted that all purchases help support the respective cultural institutions.

Museum shops may sell craft but it is not their priority; craft is a means to an end. What the museums' marketing officers will explain to you is that the shops are designed to generate revenue to support the museum through the sale of merchandise, which reflects that particular museum's mandate.[7] What shoppers will tell you is that museum shops offer unusual goods or souvenir gifts that reflect their experience of visiting the museum or a recipient's interest or taste.

Craft articles may be seen as accentuating the regional character of an institution's collection – such as the carved fish toys by Michael Higgins at the Art Gallery of Nova Scotia – or they may be outright reproductions of specific artefacts – like the 'first century AD' Mediterranean oil lamps at the Royal Ontario Museum shop or the rococo looking-glasses at Upper Canada Village. For the museum, craftspeople are ideal suppliers for both the appropriate technical skills and the limited editions required for reproductions.

From the prospective of the gift-buyer, the fact that a reproduction is handmade makes it more authentic. It is closer to the original artefact, which is probably antique, and may have been executed with the same 'centuries-old' techniques and materials.

Authenticity is also a factor in another kind of craft object commonly bought as a gift – the souvenir. Here it is not just technique but location that is crucial. The craftsperson, the materials, the activity of making and consequently the object are regarded as characteristic of a place. However, don't be surprised if you find an Ontario potter's work in a Nova Scotia souvenir store. After all, Ontario still fulfils 'made in Canada' – especially if you are visiting from Japan.

The variety of objects and locations represented in a gift store remind us of the corresponding variety of tourists or gift-buyers looking for an appropriate object. For example, Grand Manan island off the coast of New Brunswick attracts visitors from within the province, across the country and from the nearby USA. On any given morning a gift shop may be visited by the whale-watching family from mainland New Brunswick, the lawyer from Toronto with his sea kayak, or a busload of senior citizens from the bird-watchers' club in Maine. Or as one retailer put it, 'Here come the Osh Kosh overalls, the Spandex and the all-weather Tilley hats.'

Although all of those tourists are visiting Grand Manan island they are respectively visiting 'Grand Manan', 'the Maritimes', and 'Canada'. The purchases – from the 'Cow Moon In', the 'Island Arts', or the general store – will reflect that experience along with specific tastes and gift-giving goals. The craft object deemed appropriate may range from a mug decorated with the lupins found in abundance on the island, to a glass sea-shell ornament, to a wooden dinosaur with a card attached saying, 'This simple form carved from red cedar is a reminder of Canada's heritage.'

Crafts, in all their variety, are considered suitable markers of cultural identity. Still, the craft objects of minority peoples seem to be especially favoured as cultural representations by developed countries. Canada borrows from its Eskimos and Cree Indians, the USA from the Iroquois, Thailand from its Karen minority, Russia from the Siberians, Norway from the Lapps, and so on (Graburn 1976: 29).

Likewise, craftspeople join the ranks of the aboriginals as minority peoples with a marketable ethnicity. The Nova Scotia tourist office, on the New Brunswick border, has a 'Crafts and Scenic Display' that links crafts-people with the land and its history. Gift items are displayed in cases against a backdrop of photographs of farm fields, fruit orchards and fishing villages. The tourist brochure lists galleries under 'shopping', along with malls, in a not-so-naive bid to satisfy consumers' demand for distinctive gifts with the cachet of travel, multiculturalism and nostalgia for the handmade.

Folklorists have attributed the commercial popularity of rural and traditional crafts as the taste for primitive art turned inwards. In much the same way as African art was at one time regarded as more viscerally charged or authentic than Western academic art, rural craft is regarded by some as engagingly naive, unspoilt and genuine. To an urban market, the rural craftsperson can be cast as a noble savage living in one's backyard.

Fuelled by romantic nationalism – we can be tourists without leaving home – the marketing of rural craft allows for rural economic development at the same time as glorifying the common man and heritage. It satisfies customers' taste for the old, dressed up as the new and personalised (Joyce 1986: 44). And before unemployment and drug abuse became higher priorities in the 1990s, it was also a way for politicans to gain popular support.[8]

Sponsored by West Virginia's Department of Culture and History, a crafts marketing programme was led with the very visible support of the state's First Lady, Sharon Percy Rockefeller, and Phyllis George Brown, wife of Kentucky Governor John Y. Brown. Crafts were marketed through Bloomingdale's, Marshall Field's and Neiman Marcus (Teske 1986: 76). Mrs Brown's photograph graced price-tags of articles in Bloomingdale's 'Oh Kentucky' boutiques, which spent $25 million on goods from 800 US craftspeople for a special two-month promotion in 1982.

According to David Long, the boutiques' head, the appeal of the crafts was that 'they offer traditional age-old techniques and mediums that people are very comfortable with'. However, Kentucky potters, for example, were encouraged to discard their dark, earth-toned glazes for pastels more to Bloomingdale's liking. Long explained, 'We felt that was a way to make traditional crafts fresh-looking' (Teske 1986: 80).

Marketing is the manipulation of the variables of product design, price, public relations and distribution. In asking for a change of glazes, Long probably felt he was well within his bounds as a buyer for a major department store. After all, if the 'fresher' colours resulted in higher pottery sales, wouldn't both the potters and Bloomingdale's benefit?

But the folklorist documenting the case, like many studio craftspeople, felt it was inappropriate intervention. Trendy, marketable colours on traditional forms was not an effective way of preserving traditional ways or fostering the self-worth and expression of rural makers. Still, other folklorists observing the case noted that throughout history crafts have existed in a market-place. Made for sale or commission, craft has usually been subject to the influence of its purchaser. This is true in situations of barter, a craft co-operative or a department store. It is doubtful whether a 'pure' craft, free from market influences, ever existed (Johnson 1986: 85).

The retail industry roughly divides gift shops into three kinds: table-ware, decorative and souvenir. Tableware shops are aimed at the wedding-gift trade. They must stock brand names and keep large stocks. Decorative shops are aimed at casual gift-giving and collectors; they are expected to follow trends and change stock frequently. By contrast, souvenir stores cater to a constantly changing flow of customers and consequently are not required to change stock to entice repeat visits. Nor are they expected to have brand names, as the appeal of the merchandise rests in featuring the regionally specific (Manitoba Industry Trade and Tourism 1992: 3).

The lack of brand names, trends and constant novelty makes souvenir stores appropriate outlets for craft. Still, the expectations of gift-shoppers can have a negative impact upon craft. The limitations of souvenir craft, or tourist art, as anthropologists call it, is that it must function as a pidgin language and bridge the cultural boundaries of the craftsperson and the consumer. As a result, it is often simple, preferably secular, frequently romantic, realistic or conversely grotesque and awe-inspiring (Graburn 1976: 17).

Souvenir craft must above all be accessible and as such is limited to the understanding of its buyers. At their lowest common denominator, souvenir gift objects can become visual clichés, conforming to the consumers' popular misconceptions. These clichés can vary from over-used representations of landmarks, wildlife and aboriginal peoples to assumptions about the appropriateness of materials and techniques. Perhaps most damaging to souvenir craft is the misconception that if something is handmade it must be obviously irregular, rustic or rudimentary – otherwise, 'it's too well made to be craft' (Graburn 1976: 20).

Marketing is most necessary when the gap between the buyer and the maker is the greatest (Eff 1986: 57). Advertising, packaging and brand-name associations fill the gap between the buyer of a bag of potato crisps and the factory that produces it. Galleries host receptions and strive to build first-name-basis relationships with collectors; department stores create special boutiques for the presentation of craft; tourist kiosks evoke a legitimating continuum of history and landscape to promote their region's crafts. Like the new pastels on the Kentucky pottery or the museum reproduction, each venue will directly or indirectly shape the craft object through marketing to meet its objectives.

However, there is one venue that places the craft object in its original context and where marketing is minimal because there is no gap between maker and buyer – the studio. The studio visit also provides a shopping experience enhanced by a tourist's sense of wonder or spectacle, consumption of the exotic and aesthetic appropriation (Kirshenblatt-Gimblett 1988: 68). Or, as one collector put it, 'when money is not an issue, the question becomes, "How do you want to spend your time?"'

What one buys, how, and where, are the basic freedoms in a culture of consumerism. It is the shopper's compensation for being powerless at the points of production and design (Wightman Fox 1983: x). It is the power of choice, and in the dynamic of gift-giving it is also an important way of investing one's self in the object, which is necessary whether it is factory- or studio-made.

A chief way in which the buyer of the crafted gift exercises his or her freedom is in choosing whether to buy at a craft shop, fair or directly from the studio. Each retail environment offers different levels of involvement for the consumer. Buying at a fair or shop, the consumer has access to information about the gift's maker and his or her techniques. However, it is rarely acquired. The focus is primarily on the object and its appropriateness according to the consumer.

By contrast, the studio shopping experience shifts the emphasis and makes the world of the object's origins unavoidable. In effect, the gift object is the last thing the consumer purchases. At the studio, the consumer first 'buys' the craftsperson, his or her life-style, the making process, perhaps a rural setting. Opting for experience instead of advertising, the buyer believes he or she is getting 'real life'.

Stated positively, the commitment of the craftsperson and the non-profit-making character of the work – the attributes that defined the 'vocation versus profession' distinction – are made to support the sales transaction. Rather than the craft object being commodified, marketing is inverted.

The studio visit is popular because it allows the consumer to participate vicariously in an alternative life-style, to rebel without risk. Like buying 'ecologically sensitive' products or punk fashion, the consumer can vote with his or her dollars against the mainstream while still being a part of the consuming culture. Buying becomes an effective way of validating alternative values.[9]

Objects purchased at the studio carry a social and ethical dimension consistent with the gift-giving process. Museum reproductions may define the gift-giver as a supporter of a cultural institution, but craft purchased from the studio declares the gift-giver to be patron, who champions the individualistic creative act. In this case, it is the studio craftsperson who is the endangered species being supported. The studio purchase is perceived by the giver and recipient as the gift that 'continues to give'.

Obtained without the help of an intermediary, the studio purchase is unquestionably authentic. Whereas the commercial venue usually obscures the maker behind the object, the studio visit responds to the need for verification (Kirshenblatt-Gimblett 1988: 61). Buyers can witness the process of the object's creation. In fact, glassblowers have lamented that they cannot sell the molten glass object because a buyer will often request 'the one on the pipe'.

If a visitor comments that a process looks easy they can be invited to try it for themselves. Trying to centre a handful of slippery clay on the potter's wheel is a sobering initiation for the unbeliever. Studio purchases are the ideal souvenir; they are evidence that 'I was really there'. And the gift purchased at the studio makes it possible for the gift-giver to share that experience – to say in essence, 'I wish you had been there – you would have enjoyed it, too.'

We live in a material world, a world in which objects – including those that are handcrafted – are more than just props. They are heirlooms, mementos, cultural markers and tools of self-expression. As the store clerk's claim, 'it's you!', of the dress, couch or car suggests, we seek objects that declare what groups we identify with or how we are different from others. Gifts are meant to strengthen relationships and reflect the identity of both the giver and the recipient. As a kind of super-object, the meanings associated with gift objects are crucial to a gift's success.

Through product design, branding and advertising, manufacturers try to harness that impulse for their benefit. Likewise, retailers use presentation and characteristic environments to create meaningful contexts that will appeal to the buyer's sense of 'life-style' and result in sales. Those contexts will highlight certain attributes of the objects for sale and can become synonymous with them. It can also leave other attributes in obscurity.

The success of the sale of craft – in the retail environments of the department store, the gift shops, the museum and speciality shop, the craft fair and studio visit – is evidence that craft is frequently selected as a desirable gift object. However, the values and meanings attached to craft objects that are given as gifts are very different for insiders and outsiders of the craft world. Makers, collectors and related professionals such as curators and craft instructors indeed see craft as 'special' and suitable for gifts. Yet the vast number of consumers, who are outsiders, regard a much wider selection of goods, both hand- and factory-made, as potentially 'special' gifts. Marketing both reflects and perpetuates this ambiguous status of craft.

The majority of craft in retail environments is more often promoted, sold and bought as a distinctive article, an *objet d'art* or collectable, than as craft. Sources of inspiration, delight in materials or the making process, technical skill, professional reputation or artistic aspirations are frequently lost or misplaced in retail contexts where the object is divorced from its origins.

As a result, many consumers of craft have become like urban children who say that milk comes from cartons rather than cows, or like adults who nebulously refer to rubbish being taken 'away'. The fact that there is an individual maker behind the object is overlooked as the object is recontextualised.

Marketing supports the producers' goals in so far as it manipulates the variables of design, distribution and promotion to generate sales and profit. Marketing attempts to match product with consumers' associations and expectations. Craft is seen as pre-industrial by these consumers – it comes from the past or is old-fashioned and rooted in a place and tradition. The lack of advertising, brand association or packaging confirms this limited view, as does the advertising by commodities, such as tools and kits, that have appropriated the word 'craft'. Consequently, craft is successfully marketed when the retail environment supports the notion of craft as pre-industrial – as museum reproductions, souvenirs or heritage and cultural markers.

The sale that takes place at the craftsperson's studio stands apart from other retail environments. The need for the intervention of marketing is minimised; the consumer forms his or her own associations with the craft product through direct experience. As a result, the object takes on enhanced significance and is valued as authentic. Like safari photographs, the studio acquisition is a politically correct trophy.

On one hand, the studio visit affords the ultimate shopping experience, providing an intimate knowledge of a distinctive object and a degree of personal attention normally associated with the most elite of retail environments. On the other hand, it takes place in a largely personal environment not commonly associated with profit motives. The possibility of a new status for craft emerges. It is ideally suited to the conflicting needs of today's gift-giver, who strives for the personal in a consumer culture. As such craft inhabits an ironic position: that of a commodity that rebels against the market-place.

Notes

I wish to thank the Canada Council and the Sheila Hugh Mackay Foundation for their financial assistance with my research on this chapter.

1 Marcel Mauss points out that gift-giving is a socially complete phenomenon, bridging the worlds of law, economics, ethics and aesthetics. There are still instances of this in corporate Canada, where cable companies – as part of licensing agreements – are required to donate a portion of profits to a fund for the creation of new programming in Canada.

2 That résumés are consulted *after* purchase decisions are made has been remarked upon to me by a number of dealers over a ten-year period. Most recently, it was mentioned by Victoria Henry, long-time owner of the Ufundi Gallery, who is now Head of Product Development and Marketing for the Canadian Museum of Civilization, and Elena Lee of Galerie Elena Lee Verre D'Art in Montreal.

3 From 1985 to 1990, I edited *Fusion*, a publication of the Ontario Clay and Glass Association, which also operated a shop. I made this observation then.

4 Lewis Hyde notes that bodily organs, brides and children may be donated or given away, but not sold. He could also have pointed out, in his comparison between artists and 'primitive' gift economies, that these peoples have a charged sense of the object – it has a name, a history, characteristics – not unlike the empowered view of objects possessed by some studio craftspeople.

5 Brian Moeran and Lise Skov, in 'Cinderella Christmas: Kitsch, Consumerism,

and Youth in Japan' (in Miller 1993: 124), document how Japanese buyers reacted to the downturn in the 1991 economy by promoting products associated with the key words – body warmth, authenticity, handmade – favoured by focus groups. The primary gift product was a bulky hand-knit sweater.

6 According to *Etude spéciale pour le projet de planification quinquennale*, p. 48: 'Profil des achats: but de la visite pour Montreal, 41.6% visiter, 33.7 acheter cadeaux de Noel, 15.5% acheter pour eux, 7.65 rencontrer les artisans.'

7 The relationship between museum mandate and marketing was first pointed out to me by Ute Okshevsky, Executive Director of the Museum Association of Newfoundland and Labrador.

8 Craft in Canada is still regarded in some provinces as rural economic development. Especially in Newfoundland, where the collapse of the fisheries has reached crisis proportions, craft, as an adjunct to tourism, is seen as a business alternative. It is estimated that between June and September 1994, 75 per cent of 83,400 visitors spent $2.7 million on souvenirs and crafts, or approximately 8.2 per cent of their total expenditure ('The Tourist Industry – Facts and Figures Auto Exit Survey', Newfoundland Department of Tourism, Culture and Recreation, Planning and Research Division, 1995).

9 Based on the rapid increase of charity Christmas-card sales in Britain, declaring one's values with gift purchases is a growing trend. According to the Oxfam Trading Office, charity Christmas-card sales rose from 17 per cent in 1980 to 30 per cent in 1991. For consumers in 'higher social groups' it is not uncommon for 70 per cent of all cards purchased to be of this type. They are perceived as being 'simultaneously a gift to the receiver, a recognition of a specific relationship, while at the same time being a small part of a collective gift to numerous unknown others. It indicates a sense of linkage with society at large' (Mary Searle-Chatterjee in Miller 1993: 181).

References

Belk, Russell W., 'Materialism and the Making of the Modern American Christmas' in Miller (ed.), *Unwrapping Christmas*.

Canadian Museum Selections: Gifts of Distinction From Canada's Cultural Centres (Orleans, Ontario, Canada: Canadian Museums Association, 1994).

Carrier, James G., 'The Rituals of Christmas Giving' in Miller (ed.), *Unwrapping Christmas*.

Csikszentmihalyi, Mihaly and Rochberg-Halton, Eugene, *The Meaning of Things: Domestic Symbols and the Self* (Cambridge, Cambridge University Press, 1981).

Eff, Elaine, 'Traditions for Sale: Marketing Mechanisms for Baltimore Screen Art, 1913–85', in *New York Folklore, Marketing Folk Art*, 12: 1–2, winter–spring, 1986.

Emerson, Ralph Waldo, 'Gifts' in *Essays* (New York, Carlton House, 1903).

Etude spéciale pour le projet de planification quinquennale, Tome 4 (Montreal, Quebec, MAC, 1975–78).

Feschuk, Scott, 'Inuit Carves Niche in Art of Street Sales', *Globe & Mail National News*, 24 July 1995.

Flanders, John, *The Craftsman's Way* (Toronto, University of Toronto Press, 1981).

Graburn, Nelson (ed.), *Ethnic and Tourist Arts: Cultural Expressions from the Fourth World* (Berkeley, University of California Press, 1976).

Hyde, Lewis, *The Gift, Imagination and the Erotic Life of Property* (New York, Random House, 1974).

Johnson, Geraldine, 'Commentary', *New York Folklore, Marketing Folk Art*, 12: 1–2, winter–spring, 1986.

Joyce, Rosemary O., 'Introduction by the Guest Editor', *New York Folklore, Marketing Folk Art*, 12: 1–2, winter–spring, 1986.

Kirshenblatt-Gimblett, B., 'Authenticity and Authority in the Representation of Culture: The Poetics and Politics of Tourist Production', *Kulturkontakt Kulturkonflikt*, 26 Deutscher Volkskundekongress in Frankfurt vom 28. September bis 2. Oktober 1987, Instituts für Kulturanthropologie und Europäische Ethnologie der Universität Frankfurt am Main, 1988.

Manitoba Industry Trade and Tourism, *Starting a Gift Store* (Winnipeg, Manitoba, Canada, Business Resource Center, 1993).

Mauss, Marcel, *The Gift: The Form and Reason for Exchange in Archaic Societies*, trans. W. D. Halls (London, W. W. Norton, 1990).

Miller, Daniel, *Material Culture and Mass Consumption* (Oxford, Blackwell, 1987).

—— (ed.), *Unwrapping Christmas* (Oxford, Clarendon, 1993).

Schwartz, Barry, 'The Social Psychology of the Gift', *The American Journal of Sociology*, 73: 1, July 1967.

Searle-Chatterjee, Mary, 'Christmas Cards and the Construction of Social Relations in Britain', in Miller (ed.), *Unwrapping Christmas*.

Strathern, Marilyn, 'Partners and Consumers: Making Relations Visible', *New Literary History: A Journal of Theory & Interpretation*, 22: 3, summer, 1991.

Teske, Robert Thomas, '"Crafts Assistance Programs" and Traditional Crafts', *New York Folklore, Marketing Folk Art*, 12: 1–2, winter–spring, 1986.

van Gennep, Arnold, *The Rites of Passage*, trans. Monika B. Vireddon and Gabrielle L. Coffee (Chicago, University of Chicago Press, 1960).

Visser, Margaret, *The Way We Are* (Toronto, Harper Perennial, 1994).

Wightman Fox, Richard and Lears, T. J. (eds), *The Culture of Consumption: Critical Essays in American History 1880–1980* (New York, Pantheon Books, 1983).

Willis, Susan, *A Primer For Daily Life: Is There More to Life Than Shopping?* (London, Routledge, 1991).

Mary Little's work demonstrates some of the contradictions of late-1990s design and craftsmanship. She neither neglects 'craft' nor does she worship it for the ideology and beliefs within which we have coddled the term. Nevertheless, she finds it difficult to get her single ideas produced in ranges. Many designers experience this difficulty, but then so do other professions – including authors.

THE CHALLENGE OF TECHNOLOGY

Modern technology has taken human skills away from the individual and redistributed these skills through machines, systems of production and systems of information. Technology, in all its diversity, is immensely powerful because it eludes the control of any one person or set of persons – no matter how rich they are or how much political power they think they yield. Power is diffused in technology because it is the continuous and changing product of a million decisions taken by anonymous individuals who add or subtract a small process here or make an improvement there.

Technology as we know it is rooted in craft but it is different from craft. To claim that one possesses a craft is to claim that one has autonomy in a field of knowledge: craft is something one can do for oneself. It does not mean that tools or other labour-saving and -enhancing devices are forbidden, on the contrary. But it does mean that the craftsperson remains the master or mistress of the craft. Whereas with technology, the craft of a process is diffused into the tools and into the systems of manufacture.

The power and attraction of technology is that it enables you to do things without understanding how they are done. The price you pay is a loss of autonomy: you are in the hands of the engineers, programmers and designers who give you the means but not the knowledge to perform certain acts. Yet modern life would be impossible if it were not for the redistribution of skills and diffusion of power that technology presents.

The irony for practitioners of 'the crafts' who claim that the one area of expertise that technology cannot take away is the unique aesthetic and emotional charge that only the human hand and brain can give to an object, is that gradually technology is successfully mimicking the appearance of craft. Even designers will have to strive hard to justify their existence in technology-led production, for their skills too will be mimicked successfully by computer programs. Devising an expert system that can generate innovations in style (together with suggestions for visual metaphor and irony) is far more readily conceivable today than the creation of artificial intelligence.

Helen Rees, whose chapter opens this part of the book, asks whether or not 'the nineteenth-century concept of craft, which prized the handmade precisely because it was the opposite of the factory-made, is either sustainable or useful today as a means of distinguishing between patterns of making.'

Among the other questions addressed by Neal French and Jeremy Myerson and myself are:

 (i) How does technology differ from craft?
 (ii) Do either artisanal or 'the studio crafts' have a contribution to make to the debate about aesthetics in design?
(iii) Can computing, our most advanced commonplace technological tool, be described as a craft?
(iv) Are there crafts which are naturally at ease with contemporary technology.

Perhaps in this section we are too bedazzled by the power of the computer. But suppose one were to write a European history of making, then one of the central themes would be just how much mental and physical effort has been put, in science as well as art, into mimicking aspects of the world. The computer, without in any way having to be intelligent, offers a means for mimicking the appearances of things we thought uniquely human, including the mark of the hand. This goes to the very heart of craft's justification for itself in the twentieth century.

6 ✧ The progress of Captain Ludd

PAUL GREENHALGH

Two hundred years ago Captain Ludd rallied his troops. This mythical leader of radical tradesmen in the Midlands and North of England guided the Luddites, as his army was known, on expeditions to smash the new machinery and factories they believed were destroying their way of working and living.[1]

On the whole, they have not had a good press these last two hundred years. They have been continuously depicted as a negative mob, standing against ideas of progress and civilisation. Whenever organised (or disorganised) groups attempt to resist change, they run the risk of being condemned as accomplices of Captain Ludd. The mentality has been made synonymous with ignorance: 'Luddites and anti-intellectuals do not master the differential equations of thermodynamics or the biochemical cures of illness. They stay in thatched huts and die young.'[2] To a considerable extent, craft has been seen as the cultural Luddism of our times. Throughout the twentieth century, it has been widely reported as a loosely structured response to the progress of technology and industrial culture. It has been so extensively characterised as the obverse of the phenomenon of industrialism, in fact, that many have come to understand it exclusively in this light. Consequently, in an age of mass communications and technology-driven positivism, it has been portrayed as a reactionary force and accordingly marginalised. A depressing scenario can be drawn:

> The crafts necessarily appear today as residual phenomena, anachronisms or survivals from the past. The less a society is developed industrially and technologically, the more it relies upon crafts in everyday

life, hence they continue to play an important role in third world countries. Within advanced societies, in sharp contrast, crafts tend to be part of the luxury and gift markets. First and third worlds come together in the craft products made by the poor for affluent foreign tourists, that is the so called 'ethnic', 'tourist' or 'airport arts'. It might seem that the destiny of the crafts is to vanish altogether.[3]

These perceptions of the craft world, as an under-funded respiratory unit, keeping alive practices which would naturally (deservedly?) have perished if left alone, as peopled with stubborn reactionaries, as a supporter of trinket-makers, as evidence of exotic poverty or as the material evidence of the ideology of nostalgia, need to be challenged. There can be no positive future for a set of practices which are understood to be artificially kept alive out of a sense of duty or false tradition.

Whilst it cannot be denied that craft as invented in the modern period has enjoyed a heritage of anti-industrial activity, this vision of it, in which it is deliberately made to play an oppositional, and therefore a peripheral, role to mass manufacturing, is based on a very particular historiographic and ideological reading. Both technology and craft are more complex than such a negative reductionism implies. The vision relies, in fact, on a falsification of the history of both.

In this short space I wish to outline objections to the notion of craft as a class based on negation and nostalgia, by briefly examining the heritage of anti-industrialism. I hope to show that it was not as wholly futile or reactionary as has often been suggested. I will also suggest that the philosophies of both machine pessimism and machine optimism have rarely been based on actual events and practices in the real world, but on moral prerogatives. From this point of view, in historical terms at least, they are both as mythical as Captain Ludd.

Machine pessimism has been a significant factor in most First World cultures for two centuries. Jacques Ellul sums up the phenomenon:

> It is said (and everyone agrees) that the machine has created an inhuman atmosphere. The machine, so characteristic of the nineteenth century, made an abrupt entrance into a society which, from the political, institutional, and human points of view, was not made to receive it; and man has had to put up with it as best he can. Men now live in conditions that

are less than human. Consider the concentration of our great cities, the slums, the lack of space, of air, of time, the gloomy streets and the sallow lights that confuse night and day. Think of our dehumanised factories, our unsatisfied senses, our working women, our estrangement from nature. Life in such an environment had no meaning. Consider our public transportation, in which man is less important than a parcel; our hospitals, in which he is only a number. Yet we call this progress .... And the noise, that monster boring into us at every hour of the night without respite.[4]

This eloquent passage actually describes more than one type of machine-induced chaos, and thus flags several quite distinct brands of technophobia. These fall into three main groups, which I will describe as *economic, psychological* and *aesthetic*. By 1850, all three were being used to promote handicraft in opposition to machine-based production.

The first type of objection, the *economic*, owes much to the original Luddites. The machine-breakers of Northern England had no intrinsic hatred of machinery in itself. Rather, they hated the politico-economic system that brought the machinery into being. They were fighting for their jobs and, in direct connection with this, the well-being of their communities. The cotton workers of Lancashire and the stockingers of Nottingham were among the first to feel the effects of unemployment due to the introduction of machinery. They also witnessed the reorganisation of their social spaces and had to endure a significant loss of control over their lives. As E. P. Thompson has explained, to imagine that this was due to machinery alone is to miss the point:

The conventional picture of ... Luddism as a blind opposition to machinery as such becomes less and less tenable. What was at issue was the 'freedom' of the capitalist to destroy the customs of the trade, whether by new machinery, by the factory system, or by unrestricted competition, beating down wages, under-cutting his rivals, and undermining standards of craftsmanship.[5]

Roger Coleman has summed up the position succinctly: 'The Luddite revolt was not a revolt against machinery itself, but against the machinery of enslavement.'[6] Had the conditions of existence of the work-force been maintained, the machines would not have been smashed. In this sense, Captain Ludd stood for the maintenance of culture and society, not its destruction.

The second type of opposition to machinery concerns its effects on the *psychological* condition of the population. This is in many ways the moot interesting, as it began so early that those expressing fears were talking about little more than the implications of a technologically orchestrated manufacturing industry rather than the reality of it, as the reality was not yet there. The Romantic poets and thinkers of the 1780s, for example, were already alerted to this threat to the spiritual well-being of mankind. It was Thomas Carlyle, however, who most decisively articulated the fears of his generation:

> For all earthly, and for some unearthly purposes, we have machines and mechanical furtherances; for mincing our cabbages; for casting us into magnetic sleep. We remove mountains, and make seas our smooth highway; nothing can resist us. We war with rude nature; and, by our resistless engines, come off always victorious, and loaded with spoils ....
>
> But leaving these matters for the present, let us observe how the mechanical genius of our time has diffused itself into quite other provinces. Not the external and physical alone is now managed by machinery, but the internal and spiritual also.[7]

Carlyle was centrally concerned with what is best described as the mechanisation of the human mind, with the increasing failure of people to demonstrate the ability to think in the absence of quasi-mechanistic structures. For him, society itself had become a machine and individual consciousness had fallen in line with an externally imposed pattern for cognitive activity. John Ruskin pushed this idea on, claiming that industrial processes 'unhumanised' people.[8] Following logically on from this, alienation theory, which is at the heart of most Marxist thought on production systems and society, has pushed the argument to its conclusion. The whole phenomenon of industrialism, as it apparently was and is practised, denudes the cognitive essence of humanity.

Looking at the unfolding of the psychological objection to machinery, we can perceive that essentially there are two arguments at work. The first articulates an objection to technology in a direct and simple sense as something which reduces the quality of the human mind and hence human society. For the most part, this is the Ruskinian position. The second is far more subtle, and suggests that it is not the machinery itself which affects the human mind, but the system of socio-political

107

organisation which the machine apparently spawns. Technology has been used, as it were, to make society, and by implication individuals, into mere mechanical contrivances. Herbert Marcuse:

> Society reproduced itself into a growing technical ensemble of things and relations which included the technical utilization of men – in other words, the struggle for existence and the exploitation of man and nature became ever more scientific and rational .... Scientific-technical rationality and manipulation are welded together into new forms of social control.[9]

This is technology at the service of political power, affecting the ability of humankind to think.

The third type of objection, the *aesthetic*, is a less dramatic but none the less ever-present force. It is based on the conviction that *a priori*, things made directly by the human hand are more beautiful than machine-generated produce:

> Wherever ornament is wholly affected by machinery, it is certainly the most degraded in style and execution; and the best workmanship and the best taste is invariably to be found in those manufactures and fabrics wherein handicraft is entirely or partially the means of producing the ornament.[10]

This opposition is explained partly from the need we have to assert the primacy of human dexterity over the machine in at least some areas of activity. Handmade things, of course, also enjoy the status of being unique pieces of art. Their exclusivity and expense are an encouragement for those of cultural status to prefer them to widely available manufactured goods.

The strength of the aesthetic position is revealed by the ongoing need to oppose it many authors felt. In 1911, for example, when William Burton asked an audience of design students to

> let me enter a respectful but emphatic protest against the widely prevalent idea that hand-work is so sacrosanct that all hand-work, whether ancient or modern, must be essentially artistic and superior to the best that can be done by modern machines

he was objecting to the powerful refusal on the part of many individuals and institutions to accept the possibility of a machine-based art.[11]

All of these views are dependent upon the belief in a dramatic transformation of industrial practices in our recent history. It is not only machine pessimism, but also machine optimism which is dependent on the idea of a rapidly transformed world. Neither pessimism nor optimism makes sense in the absence of machines, applied abrasively and universally to the practices of life over a discrete period.

There is a wide and generally accepted consensus as to what constituted the Industrial Revolution. Optimists and pessimists alike tend to accept its dates as being 1760–1830 and they seem to understand its causes and its results. They extract their visions of society from these givens.

Recent historians of this period, however, are far more ambivalent about the whole thing, to the point that many question whether it really happened at all in any meaningful sense:

> The idea …, of 'industrial revolution', has become a sort of turn-coat Vicar of Bray figure of scholarship, infinitely accommodating to the special interests of individual writers; it turns out to be more a part of myth than historical reality …. It is tempting to conclude that the idea of an industrial revolution turns out to be all things to all men.[12]

Thus the model of a sudden, technology- – *machine*- – driven transformation of culture and society has been widely rejected by the historical community. It has become clear that the world did not transform because of new technologies in the period 1760–1830. Machinery and new forms of work organisation were not systematically introduced across the face of the country. A machine-driven, factory-based work pattern transformed life in certain areas, but this was not a general experience. The majority of the wealth of Britain still resided in landownership and in finance, and the traditional class hierarchy of Britain was not seriously changed.[13] The original Luddites were responding to particular, local circumstances at particular times. This is not to deny that a process of modernisation has generally changed First World society, but to assert that the shift was not technologically determined. It was a result of a complex *mélange* of forces, unfolding over a considerably longer period of time. Thus the machine has been both praised and damned for changing our world, when in fact it was merely one cause among many. Alternative models for the process of modernisation have been offered, one of which, for example, concentrates on the idea of urban evolution:

109

Instead of experiencing an 'industrial revolution', England experienced an urban evolution, as part of an age-old process of a shift of population to the towns. This change was accompanied by changes in wealth, skill, commercial practices and transport facilities. It was part of a process which can first be observed to have occurred in the Sumerian cities of 3000 B.C., in which some people got much richer, and other people got poorer .... It is a mistake to take the idea of revolution over from political to economic and social history, in order to describe changes which are best thought of as cultural.[14]

Machine pessimists and optimists alike, therefore, have indulged in historical fantasy for considerable periods of time. The Romantics raged against machines virtually before there were any, in any sense we would understand, and technophiles saw needless labour alleviated everywhere they looked. There are some startling examples of this euphoria. H. G. Wells, for example, believed that technology had eliminated want and wage-slavery in his own time: 'The drudge, on whom all previous civilizations rested, the creature of mere obedience, the man whose brains were superfluous, had become unnecessary to the welfare of mankind.'[15] His incredible inability to see drudgery in work in the early modern period merely flags the uncomfortable truth that intellectuals on both sides rarely got close enough to assess the condition of real people engaged in actual industrialised employment. Indeed, models of human society are always more satisfying in the abstract, allowing one to elucidate a logical position. Both lobbies are, in this sense, little more than science fiction.

It is plain that the conditions of life for many in the later eighteenth and nineteenth centuries deteriorated, and that some areas of Britain were effectively destroyed in social and environmental terms. It is plain also that many were reduced to the point of slavery. However, the argument cannot be sustained that this was a result of new technology, or even of the introduction of the division of labour. Neither can we blame machines for alienating populations in areas where there weren't any.

People make the societies they live in. Machines, and I include here not only mechanical contrivances but also, following Carlyle's sense of the term, the machinations of organisational systems, are not invented in a vacuum; they do not fortuitously appear coincidentally with a perceived need for their functions. They are the result of specific motives and they require considerable material support before they can come into being:

capital, planning, organised research. New technologies only escape the prototype stage when appropriate powers decide they should. Political and economic decisions ultimately underpin the introduction of machinery into the workplace. Responses to machinery, therefore, whether positive or negative, will also be, at root, political and economic. In other words, people bring machines into existence and it is they, not the machines, who negate or enhance the conditions of existence.

Those who have been against the principle of organised labour since the eighteenth century have been quick to point to the negative aspects of the philosophy of Luddism. Especially after the development of the evolutionist ideas of society in the second half of the nineteenth century, Luddism was portrayed as the last struggle against inevitable and natural progress. New machines, the argument has gone, even if they inflicted ecological and economic misery in the short term, will nevertheless ultimately lead to a better form of civilisation. We now know that this is simply not true. Appropriate conditions for living are a matter of socio-political control and are not technologically determined. Thinkers such as William Morris realised this. He threw his energies not into the effort to negate technology – which factions within the Arts and Crafts movement did – but into the drive to change the system which controlled it. Oscar Wilde eloquently pointed to the use and misuse of the machine in his essay 'The Soul of Man under Socialism':

> Up to the present, man has been, to a certain extent, the slave of machinery, and there is something tragic in the fact that as soon as man had invented a machine to do his work he began to starve. This, however, is of course, the result of our property system and our system of competition.[16]

The main argument of my first chapter in this volume is that craft as we now understand it was largely an invention of the later nineteenth and twentieth centuries, and that this invention comprised three distinct elements. The *politics of work* gave it most of its intellectual structure and all of its ideological power, the *vernacular* gave it its ethnic credibility and its enduring tie to rural and traditional practices and the *decorative arts* were the age-old genres which had been collectivised as 'the arts not fine'.[17] The three elements came together in that particular context to create the concept of craft as we now have it.

It is instructive to look at the three elements from the standpoint of technology. We can immediately perceive that the *decorative arts* are not in negative tension with technology, and they never have been. As with all genres dependent on handwork, such as painting, sculpture and architecture, the age of mechanical reproduction has given rise to extraordinary complication in the way we see and consume unique, individually made objects, but there is no especial thesis driving the decorative artist with regard to technology. Individual makers produce high-quality objects, using a variety of hand and mechanised techniques. The decorative artist has always embraced any technology that allows him or her to achieve the end they seek.

The *vernacular* is premised on the pre- and non-industrial. It often entails the invention of legendary lands untouched by the world of industry and technology. It has provided the vision of craft as redundant technology, with its intellectual underpinning in unashamed nostalgia. To refer back to an earlier quotation, this is the element of craft that fills the airport and tourist shops of the world. It fulfils our need to remember where we have been and it satisfies our desire to believe in a world that is in some way more authentic than our own. Commemoration is an important role for objects to play, but it would be wholly wrong to categorise the whole of craft in this way.

At this time the *decorative arts* do not have an ideological or practical problem with technology. For quite different reasons, neither does the *vernacular*. This is because the vernacular now depends on technology for its existence. Its entire *raison d'être* is in appearing to be an opposition to the industrial world. Without technology there would be no need for it, and so it is not an opposition, but a natural corollary, a palliative.

These two relations are clear and simple. With the politics of work, however, we engage with the heart of the issue of craft and technology. As with the Luddites, the majority of craftsmen who adhere to the concept of work as the site of political struggle do not reject the machine per se, but rather are pitted against its misuse in the socio-economic sphere. Therefore, all of those who are suspicious of the motives of those who control the mass technologies of our times are, to a greater or lesser degree, Luddite. As was noted earlier, the Luddites had socio-economic motives.

Following this lead, I suggest we drop objections to technology on aesthetic grounds and that we also forget the contention that technology, machinery and/or industry, however one wishes to combine and define them, are somehow psychologically damaging in themselves. They are not. There is nothing *a priori* ugly or alienating about the machine. There is no historical evidence to show that there ever was.

I suggest that the *politics of work* is now most fruitfully discussed not in the context of the *vernacular* or the *decorative arts*, but in conjunction with the larger world of design and object production. Three of the most important issues which face the global community as we enter the new century are unemployment, the exploitation of labour and the environment. All three are to do with the way things are made and are bound up with the appropriate use of technology. Abuse of the work-force, either through its being rendered redundant or through its being brutalised, actively prevents many of us from enjoying an acceptable life-style. The destruction of the environment through the misapplication of technology could still be the end of us all. There is no reason why advances in science and technology should result in the impoverishment of large swathes of the world's populations. If the great thinkers and motivators of the Arts and Crafts movement were still with us, these are the issues they would focus on. So should we.

We should also remind ourselves of the larger goals of science and technology. In its pure form, science is an enquiry into the fabric and meaning of existence itself. It deals with issues that help us understand the human condition and it positions humanity more powerfully within the wider scheme of things than any art form could begin to contemplate. The landing of a man on the moon, for example, expanded our horizons in ways that can comfortably be described as poetic. Had this event occurred during the Renaissance, it would have been considered a work of art. Theories on the origins of the universe, on the formation of genes and on the behavioural systems of animals, among many others, are stretching the boundaries of knowledge and increasingly render boundaries between the humanities and sciences redundant.

It is important, therefore, that the unpleasant space between the arts and sciences be closed. At the moment it is alarmingly wide. Edward Wilson, an eminent biologist, recently lamented what he perceived to be an arrogant dismissal of scientists as non-intellectuals:

> In the United States intellectuals are virtually defined as those who work in the prevailing mode of the social sciences and humanities. Their

reflections are devoid of the idioms of chemistry and biology, as though humankind were still in some sense a numinous spectator of physical reality. In the pages of the *New York Review of Books, Commentary, The New Republic, Daedalus, National Review, Saturday Review* and other literary journals articles dominate that read as if most of basic science had halted during the nineteenth century.[18]

The artist's ignorance of science and the scientist's ignorance of art might well result in the final unravelling of our culture, into a fractionalised and impoverished concatenation of archaic customs and inhuman practices. It is be hoped that this will be avoided, but if we are to advance on from our present sorry state, we need to clarify the role of all our cultural forms, including the crafts. Captain Ludd could well have a role in all of this, not leading us to destroy machines this time, but helping us to integrate them into our way of making and thinking.

Notes

1 Captain Ludd was also known as King, Edward, Ned and General. See Thompson, n. 5 below.

2 Edward O. Wilson, *On Human Nature* (London, Penguin, 1995), p. 207.

3 J. A. Walker, *Design History and the History of Design* (London, Pluto, 1989), p. 39.

4 Jacques Ellul, *The Technological Society* (Paris, 1954), p. 5.

5 E. P. Thompson, *The Making of the English Working Class* (London, Penguin, 1963), p. 600.

6 Roger Coleman, *The Art of Work: An Epitaph to Skill* (London, Pluto, 1988), p. 149.

7 Thomas Carlyle, *Signs of the Times* (1829), quoted in Alasdair Clayre (ed.), *Nature and Industrialization* (Milton Keynes, Open University Press, 1977), p. 229.

8 See p. 33.

9 Herbert Marcuse, *One Dimensional Man* (London, Routledge & Kegan Paul, 1964), p. 146.

10 Richard Redgrave, *Manual of Design* (London, Chapman & Hall, 1876).

11 William Burton, *Designing for Machine Made Goods* (Manchester, Manchester School of Art, 1911).

12 Michael Fores, 'The Myth of a British Industrial Revolution', *History*, 66: 217, June 1981, pp. 183, 196.

13 See W. D. Rubinstein, 'Wealth, Elites and the Class Structure of Modern Britain', *Past and Present* 76, 1977, pp. 99–126.

14 Fores, *Myth*, p. 197.

15 H. G. Wells, *A Short History of the World* (London, 1933), p. 215.

16 1891. This edn, Osobel Murray (ed.), *Oscar Wilde, Plays, Prose and Poems* (London, Everyman, 1975), p. 250.

17 See p. 26.

18 Wilson, *On Human Nature*, p. 203.

HELEN REES

Introduction

I want to address the question of the nature of design by asking: what is it that designers do? My argument is that the absence of a single answer suggests that the relationship between design and craft is more complicated than is suggested by the traditional polarities of studio-craft production and the factory production-line. In this chapter I shall use the word 'craft' as shorthand for studio-craft, rather than in the older and wider sense of a trade or skill. The broad use of 'craft' embraced not only trades, such as carpentry, coopering, glass-blowing, leather-working and so on, but also those activities which we now call the 'fine arts' – painting, sculpting and drawing.

To avoid anachronistic confusion, therefore, I will confine my use of 'craft' to refer to the work of artist-craftspeople or designer-makers, whom I shall call simply 'craftspeople'. I am aware that I am adopting a narrow use of both 'craft' and 'craftspeople' and am not addressing the debates and different positions among contemporary craftspeople. It is, however, a recognisable and useful category and, as my primary concern is to explore definitions of design, I shall leave the controversies of 'craft' to other contributors to this book.

What is design today?

On 16 August 1995, *The Times* published an article entitled 'Six inventions that changed the world'.[1] They were the aerosol, the jumbo jet, the compact disc, the Mini, the biro, and the personal stereo. The context for the piece was that a seventh invention was about to be unveiled which, like these earlier inventions, had the capacity to revolutionise the way in which we work, play, communicate, and perceive ourselves and others However, the 'product' was Windows 95, which is not a product in the conventional sense at all, but a software environment for personal computers. Unlike the other six inventions, Windows 95 did not propose a new experience of the physical world, but a reorganisation of our cognitive toolbox – that is to say, the way in which we structure, manipulate and connect ideas. The marketing of Windows 95 as if it were a 'thing' deliberately subverted the categories that we apply in order to recognise and understand the material world.

The entrance of Windows 95 into the global world of goods and brands made the very idea of an 'industrial product designer' seem old-fashioned. The prefix 'industrial' reveals its origins in a production revolution which introduced the assembly line and the division of labour into the world. Although the era of Fordism, as both means of production and a model of industrial relations, has passed, the label 'industrial designer' survives. Designers, and also their teachers and employers, appear reluctant to abandon a term which signifies a particular way of viewing the world. The implication is that it is the production process which defines their work: that is to say that designers design for industry, rather than for the consumers of the products of industry. It is a way of thinking about the world which, by implication, denies the social, cultural and economic significance of consumption.

My starting-point, therefore, is that if we are to understand the ways in which designers work today, we must first jettison the misleading connotations of 'industrial' because designers do not ultimately design for producers, but for consumers. The corollary of this is that marketing, combined with the enabling power of technology, is the spur to innovation in design. The same is true for craft, albeit according to the logic of a market for luxury goods (or art goods) that derive high value from a close association with a creative individual. Thus a craftsperson is likely both to respond to demand and to try to stimulate it, with the aim of achieving an economically viable level of production to provide sufficient time, space and money to develop new ideas.

The difference is that innovation in design is often, but not always, market-led, whereas innovation in the crafts is likely to be maker-led. The craft object may thus reflect an exercise in personal choice, self-expression or an experiment with materials and techniques.

Commissions are, of course, an exception to the maker-led model of craft innovation. The direct relationship between a patron and crafts-person cannot exist in the mass market. Although I shall argue that one of the defining characteristics of designers is their understanding of and ability to predict consumer desires, they work at one remove. In industry, the desires of consumers are monitored, filtered and projected by market analysts and advertisers. The skill of the designer is first to abstract consumer needs and aspirations, and then to give them material form.

Who am I?

Given the backdrop of rapidly changing technologies against which designers work, it is not surprising that they are collectively preoccupied with definitions about what they do – and what they do not do. Designers in Britain have spent and continue to spend a lot of time worrying about whether or not they are being taken as seriously by government and commerce as they would like. Debates about design that take place at an institutional and political level are characteristically concerned with the status, purpose and value of design – usually in that order.

In this respect, designers share much in common with craftspeople who are similarly self-conscious about the terms in which they and others describe their work, and how it relates to other forms of visual production, especially (fine) art. Despite, or perhaps because of, the sense of history which inflects the work of many craftspeople, traditional labels may no longer feel adequate or appropriate. The boundary between art and craft is, for many makers, blurred, although the impetus is invariably to 'trade-up' in the visual hierarchy that confers greater cultural status on the non-functional objects of art. For designers as well, the debate about status and identity is not about technology, but culture.

In post-war Britain visual culture was neatly divided into design, craft and art, each of which had its own government-funded agency to promote its cause. The Council of Industrial Design (founded in 1944 and later renamed the Design Council) and the Crafts Council (founded in 1971) were each set up to educate consumers and to represent practitioners.[2] Each in their beginnings thought they were offering 'the housewife' a different, but complementary, lesson in taste, encouraging her simultaneously to buy the best of British manufactures, and also to purchase something rather different ... something handmade to mark her out as a little more discerning and adventurous.

The distinction between design and craft was thus publicly codified by the creation of separate councils, each of which pursued its own course, without being in direct competition with the other. Each was founded by a different government department: the Design Council came under the aegis of the Department of Trade and Industry, and the Crafts Council was funded by the Office of Arts and Libraries (since 1992, the Department of National Heritage). In the official mind, design promotion was perceived as a means to improve the performance of British manufacturing, while craft was regarded as an aspect of culture.

Over the years, both the Design Council and the Crafts Council gradually abandoned the cause of consumer education, having realised that it was an unattainable and unnecessary objective. Of the two, the Crafts Council has adapted to change with greater ease and success. Its focus is to promote the concept of craft and the work of craftspeople, and to encourage debate among practitioners and critics, albeit from its own purview of the studio-crafts. Through its activities, the Council implicitly defines – and sometimes explicitly defends – the idea of craft. An invisible exclusion zone surrounds its activities and no breach of the defence passes without protest. For example, the inclusion of the work of a non-craftsperson – say, a designer such as Jasper Morrison – in a Crafts Council show is guaranteed to provoke. Interestingly, many designers are just as keen to preserve their distance from the Crafts Council as some craftspeople are to keep them out.

By the 1980s, the Design Council was barely noticed by a sophisticated and indifferent public and it had long ceased to provide an effective rallying cry for designers. In 1994 large parts of the Council were shut down and replaced by a much smaller unit. The new, lean Council was reborn as a tool of government industrial policy. Few mourned the passing of the old Design Council; neither designers nor consumers needed the government to tell them what to make or what to buy.

Until 1994, as if embarrassed by the moral implications of materialism, the Design Council advocated that good design was good for the economy and for society, but strenuously avoided an analysis of the consumer

119

society as such. This was a fatal omission: to ignore the inescapable and never-ending process of consumption was to overlook the vital relationship at the heart of designers' work – and their justification.

That is to say, designers are distinguished by their critical engagement with consumers, which is manifest in their ability to give material expression to consumers' desires and perceived needs – sometimes before consumers themselves are even aware of them. This is one of the ways in which designers differ from, for example, engineers, notwithstanding their – sometimes considerable – professional understanding of manufacturing technologies and materials. Far from being superficial or meretricious, the terms of engagement between designers and consumers require specific and valuable understanding and skills.

In our society, consumption is a mechanism through which we construct individual identity and social relations. The social power of wealth, once only available to the leisure and possessing classes, is now available to the majority. Only the very poor are excluded from the games of conspicuous display. We construct meaning and communicate to one another through a complex hierarchy of goods. Many theorists have pointed out that there is no escape from this world of objects: it is complete and self-perpetuating.[3] The designer is, therefore, centre stage in the consumer society. By contrast, the craftsperson plays a relatively minor role in the theatre of consumption in economic terms, but an important one in symbolic and rhetorical terms. To many people the attraction of a craft object resides in its explicit identification with values which are as compelling today as they were in William Morris's time: social continuity, personal creativity, and fulfilment through making.

In their bid to be taken 'seriously', designers sometimes overlook the importance of their empathy with consumers. This is odd because designers are themselves highly discriminating consumers. In common with other makers, including sculptors and craftspeople, designers tend to derive above-average excitement from their relationship with the material world. Their understanding is intuitive. As British designer Ross Lovegrove comments: 'Memorable design does not always depend on a clever idea or advanced micro-electronics, but can be born out of an honest understanding of human sensitivity and values.'[4] One hundred years ago, the followers of Morris castigated factory-made goods for lacking precisely these values, but today even the most ardent champions of craft would agree that manufacturing is not necessarily a dehumanising process. Designers' collective preoccupation with their status and purpose is exacerbated by the media promotion of role models which are far removed from the reality which most experience. For example, student designers are taught how to work in teams because, they are told, that is how the world of making things works. For many of them, this will be true. But, like all of us, designers inhabit a cultural tradition which is obsessed with genius and a society which is captivated by fame. The lesson of working in teams is accompanied by the fantasy of becoming the individual signature on a designer label. And designers are no more immune to the lure of fame than anybody else.

Fame is the spur

The handful of celebrity designers who are fêted in each decade – Raymond Loewy in the 1930s and 1940s, Charles Eames in the 1950s, Dieter Rams in the 1970s, Philippe Starck in the 1980s and 1990s – are the heroes of a myth about the capacity of an autonomous individual to reshape the world. Stylistically their work is diverse, but the members of this Valhalla have more in common than they might care to admit. Each of them constructed a successful career on the idea that he is a charismatic visionary who single-handedly can make the world a more dynamic, intelligible, functional or enjoyable place. To argue that they provide an inappropriate role-model for the majority of young designers is not to deny their individual talents. Just as most art students will never be Damien Hirst, and most craftspeople will never be Hans Coper, so most design students will never be Philippe Starck.

The myth of the autonomous designer is a variation on the theme of the Romantic artist. Star designers are promoted as free spirits, unconstrained and inspired by their own boundless creativity. The designer label is the equivalent of the artist's signature. It confers value on a product which is unconnected to its functional worth. Like the market for old-master paintings, the market for signature design is global.

The craftsperson also needs a 'name' to achieve market success. The promotional apparatus of craft, including exhibitions, catalogues and gallery shops, is directly and deliberately copied from the art world, and is calculated to establish individual reputation in just the same way. Like

121

many young artists, some craftspeople are taking increasing control of their own self-promotion in exhibitions and publications.

The currency of success is self-perpetuating in craft, as in art. Once established, the artist and craftsperson must preserve the potential value of her/his work by not 'selling out' or appearing to be too 'commercial'. Of course, the reality is that successful artists and craftspeople are intensely aware of the market, and of the link between their commercial and cultural status. The pejorative connotations which 'commercial' carries in the art and craft worlds evaporate in the market-place for design, although the celebrity designer also needs to preserve the value of his signature by restricting its application to high-value, trend-setting goods. This kind of brand-control is highly visible in the fashion magazines which chronicle the retail development of a 'label', the inevitable diversification into cosmetics and accessories, and the intimate identification of designer with product (and vice versa).

Consumerism and style

Unlike artists and craftspeople, who are directly responsible for the process of making things, designers have to negotiate a relationship with the businesses that manufacture 'their' products. Even celebrity designers opt for either an 'employer' relationship – as in the case of Dieter Rams, who for many years was chief designer for the German electrical goods manufacturer Braun – or a 'client' relationship – as in the case of Philippe Starck, one of a stable of international designers who has worked for a range of companies, including the Italian firm Alessi. Whether as employee or consultant, all designers operate as part of a complex organisation. They are required to address quantifiable specifications – financial, technical and commercial. These specifications are called the 'brief', a concept which has assumed great significance in schools of design management. According to the 'science' of design management, 'good' design is not a beautiful or a useful product, but an efficient, well-managed process.

A craft object often reveals much about the skill and the technology used to make it. The relationship between craft process and product is likely to be, if not quite transparent, then at least relatively accessible to most of us. There is pleasure from wearing or using something whose creation we can both admire and understand. In a world where we have lost touch with the business of making things, the craft object restores for us the connection between making and using.

By contrast, design conceals. Not only do we not understand how designed objects are made, we do not understand how they work. Designers are skilled in abstracting consumer desire: I may think that I want a vacuum cleaner, but they know that I really want clean carpets. It is a cliché, but none the less true, that successful design is one step ahead of the customer.

In the 1930s, the absence of consumer desire was thought to be a cause of economic depression, and design was proclaimed as a means of rekindling demand. A flamboyant generation of designers emerged, including Norman Bel Geddes, Walter Dorwin Teague, Raymond Loewy and Henry Dreyfuss. Today, much of their work is dismissed as 'styling'. Their speciality was to encase mechanical or electrical contraptions – scales, duplicating machines, vacuum cleaners – in smooth curved shells of metal and plastic. The phenomenon was called 'streamlining', for their aesthetic had evolved from the emerging science of aerodynamics. Soon streamlining was being applied to static, as well as moving, goods. Sometimes, as in the case of Raymond Loewy's streamlined desktop pencil-sharpener of 1933, the effect was entirely decorative, having no functional gain at all. For the point about streamlining was not to increase ease and efficiency; goods were often heavier and more difficult to mend when they had been streamlined. The point was rather to make things look more dynamic and more modern.

Streamlining demonstrates that the designer's skill is to understand the value of product as metaphor. From the consumer's point of view, the streamlined curve was a symbol of smooth progress through modern technological society. From the designer's point of view, it was also a metaphor for the power of design to resist the inert forces of economic stagnation, to stimulate demand on the Main Street, and thus ease America out of a depression. A contemporary advertisement reads 'Streamlining a product and its methods of merchandising is bound to propel it quicker and more profitably through the channels of sales resistance.'

The American designer and advocate of streamlining, Egmont Arens, declared that he and his colleagues were engaged in 'consumer engineering'. He was right, and that is what designers have been doing ever since,

123

even though they do not describe their work in those terms today. For, despite its commercial success, streamlining had become vulnerable to criticism on ethical, rather than aesthetic, grounds. The argument against streamlining was that it was not an appropriate aesthetic for the modern age because, although it celebrated the machine, it actually disguised it. Thus, the external form of a product failed to express its function, and that was 'dishonest'.

It was not the first time this argument had been made. The architect Augustus Pugin had been one of the first critics of the products of nineteenth-century factories which, he claimed, exemplified

> the false notion of disguising instead of beautifying articles of utility. How many objects of ordinary use are rendered monstrous and ridiculous, simply because the artist, instead of seeking the most convenient form, and then decorating it, has embodied some extravagance to conceal the real purpose for which the article was made![5]

He advocated a return to an idealised Middle Ages, as a source not only of aesthetic but also of social regeneration. Pugin's intention was not to invent a new style, but rather to rediscover – and thus to re-establish – a visual grammar which could be commonly understood, and which was based on shared and explicit values.

Pugin was a major influence on the organisation of The Great Exhibition of the Industry of All Nations in 1851, as was the civil servant Henry Cole. The impact of the Exhibition on Victorian taste was profound, and its success led directly to the founding of the Museum of Manufactures in Pall Mall the following year, under the control of Cole. Here he famously castigated the products of Victorian factories, which were dressed up to look like something which they were not. Lack of transparency and clarity in the form of a product was, according to Cole, a sign of dishonesty. It was an argument about style – and a lesson in morality. With characteristic certainty, Cole identified the following as 'false principles of design': lack of symmetry; disregard for structural form; formless confusion; and concentration on superficial aspects of design.

Some years later, the American architect Louis Sullivan expressed the same design ideal rather more succinctly, when he coined the famous maxim 'form follows function'. This was to become the credo for a new theory of design: functionalism. Functionalists sought to replace arbitrary decoration with rational objectivity. Although Sullivan himself believed that ornament had a valid role in an aesthetic appropriate to the modern world, functionalists subsequently argued that decoration was superfluous to design that was truly rational. The theory was that there is a logical design for every object, which is revealed by a true understanding of the product in question. The correct form of a product therefore emerges from a disinterested analysis of its primary function and ergonomic requirements.

This kind of thinking fell neatly into the paradigm of design as 'problem-solving'. It was based on the premise that a universally recognised 'problem' was always susceptible to rational 'solution'. Design could be described as the pursuit of ideal forms, which were self-evident if you approached the design problem in a logical way. Designers liked to believe that the question that they were answering was not how to sell more chairs, but how to design a better chair. The Bauhaus school of art and design (which was based in Weimar from 1919 to 1925, then moved to Dessau until 1932, and finally relocated to Berlin for a year before it was closed in 1933) represented the high-water mark of functionalist theory. Walter Gropius, director of the Bauhaus from 1919 to 1928, rallied designers for 'the creation of type-forms for all practical commodities of everyday use'.[6]

Students and teachers at the Bauhaus advocated the theory that good or true design is 'styleless' inasmuch as the only thing it expresses is its purpose, and the construction necessary to achieve that. They also aimed to raise the status of design and craft, so as to unite the visual arts into a cohesive whole. Gropius argued that 'There is no essential difference between the artist and the craftsman .... The artist is an exalted craftsman.'[7]

Functionalist design theory simultaneously converges towards and diverges from craft practice. The process of making by hand can be a tight discipline, but it can also permit wonderful flamboyance. Craft objects may be functionally expressive, but not necessarily at the expense of the expression of other values, including the personality of the maker. Functionalist design does, however, reflect Morris's craft ethos in its emphasis on the inseparability of process and product. Like Morris, functionalists believed that the ethical, as well as the aesthetic, value of an object is derived from the way in which it is made.

Students and teachers at the Bauhaus were craftspeople who made their own designs, at least in the sense of building models and prototypes, and no one troubled very much about the commercial application of their ideas. After all, it was a school, not a business. Other designers could not afford the luxury of Bauhaus theory for its own sake. One way of making functionalism fit the market was to analyse the needs (significantly, not the desires) of consumers in terms of quantifiable physical dimensions. Ergonomics, or the science of human measurements, was thus invoked to support the functionalists' claim for rational design. The application of ergonomics in the design process was intended to ensure increased comfort and efficiency in the resulting product. (Yet objects made by hand frequently achieve the same effect, simply because human factors are integrated into every part of the process, from conception to realisation.)

By contrast with the intuitive, holistic approach of many craftspeople, functionalist theoreticians emphasised the scientific foundation of ergonomics, at the expense of the historical and cultural construction of comfort. Comfort is a modern phenomenon. In the past, it was so unattainable as to be irrelevant for most people, while for the rich and leisured minority, dignity and elegance appeared more important than they do today. The argument for efficiency alone has not generally been sufficiently persuasive to change deeply-held expectations. If it had, this essay would not be typed on a conventional QWERTY keyboard, but on a layout which is demonstrably more comfortable for both the hand and eye.

For all their denial of the emotional, aspirational, social aspects of consumption, functionalist designers still produced products with strong symbolic and metaphorical appeal. In the 1950s, the German company Braun introduced a new style of household goods, beginning with radios and moving on to other products. Designed on a proportional system and enveloped in discreet white, grey and black boxes, Braun products were punctuated by only the minimum of controls and the company logo. They embodied the functionalist ideal of formal purity, and were highly suggestive of values of hygiene and efficiency. The most famous of the Braun designers is Dieter Rams, whose design philosophy had crystallised during his years as a teacher at the Hochschule für Gestaltung at Ulm, a design school famous for its insistence on the possibility of pure and rational design solutions.

Before he even started working for Braun, Rams said that products 'should be there, ready to perform effortlessly well when they are needed, but keep out of the way when they are not, just like an English butler'.[8] Whether or not he was conscious of it, Rams's analogy with a servant echoed a much older marketing fashion for giving maids' names such as 'Daisy' and 'Betty' to household products such as vacuum cleaners. The difference was that Rams tried to suppress the metaphor by invoking the supposedly invisible presence of the discreet and silent butler.

The fashion for understatement in design could also be interpreted as a visual and symbolic response to a growing unease among some designers, critics and consumers about the heedless use of resources necessary to sustain the consumer society. In 1960, Vance Packard published *The Waste Makers* (London, Longman), which attacked the cycle of inbuilt obsolescence on which mass consumption is constructed, on the grounds that it was both exploitative and wasteful. Packard pointed out that in the forty years since the end of the First World War, America had used up more of the world's resources than the whole of mankind during the previous 400 years. Products such as Rams's were not necessarily less extravagant in their use of resources, but they did not look so wasteful. But appearances are deceptive: minimalism may be just as costly as flamboyance.

Unlike craft objects, which are often designed to last for a long time and, if needs be, to be repaired, it is virtually impossible to mend the majority of manufactured goods. Often component parts are unavailable and, when they are, even the smallest modification to a product is enough to ensure that a customer is forced to buy a full replacement, even if just a part of one component has broken. Most of us are familiar with the experience of breaking, say, the lid of a coffee-grinder, only to discover that you have to buy a new grinder as well as a new lid, because a modified lid design no longer fits the previous generation of grinders.

The British theorist Reyner Banham (1920–88) introduced a more sophisticated argument into the debate about planned obsolescence. He undermined the claims of functional absolutism by arguing that once a product is technically outmoded, it is necessarily visually out of date. Banham described this as the 'expendable aesthetic'. Far from believing that styling was a bad thing *per se*, he suggested that it had a specific and valid role, particularly for products with a short life-span. Arguing that it is absurd to treat all objects as if they could or should have eternal validity, Banham concluded that successful products should be understood in terms of the relationship between styling, symbolism and the consumer.

The success of many craft objects could be judged by the same criteria, although this is not to say that they have a short life-span. Often the opposite is the case: craft objects are not only made to last, they are made to look as though they are going to last. A large part of their appeal lies in their resistance to fashion and their appearance of timelessness. In the luxury market outside the mainstream, craft objects are sold on the basis of their symbolic value.

Designing, not making

Where does Banham's view of design position the designer? Is she or he necessarily relegated to the role of stylist, with its connotations of superficiality? There is no single answer to this, because designers work in such different ways, but most do combine both visual and technological skills. Nowadays an unashamed stylist such as Raymond Loewy is mocked for flitting from the design of a cigarette packet to the design of a car, from the design of a teapot to the design of a NASA space-station. Certainly it is difficult to believe that he could have had more than a perfunctory understanding of the materials and technology used in such diverse production processes. But that was not the point. Loewy's role was to add an inspirational flourish, not to become deeply involved in a multi-discplinary process of product development. He was also the head of a studio of assistants.

The contemporary counterpart to Loewy is the French designer Philippe Starck. Explaining how he designed one of his most commercially successful chairs, the *Dr Glob*, Starck says,

> I designed it on a flight to Tokyo between sitting down and fastening my seat belt … Fortunately, I have a faithful tribe who help me in spite of everything, and transform my ideas into reality. I can't do that. The more the object develops towards its final form, the less I like it.[9]

That is an extreme position. Other designers specialise, and certain studios are known for a particular area of expertise. Queensbury Hunt Levien combine craft skills and computer technology to design ceramics, DCA (David Carter Associates) specialise in the design-engineering of transport systems, and PID (Product Identity Design) develop plastic coathangers for retail display. Teams in these consultancies work closely and over a number of years with manufacturers and suppliers. Their knowledge of materials and processes is integral to their work. Their degree of specialisation rivals that of the industry insiders. Designers who work for manufacturers, work in teams not of other designers, but of engineers, production managers, marketing managers, and even accountants.

Most designers cannot help but work speculatively, to generate their own ideas in private in order to 'stay fresh' and remind themselves of horizons beyond the next phone call which may – or may not – bring an offer of work. In this respect, they are, of course, like craftspeople. Many also enjoy – and are good at – the process of making things themselves. Three-dimensional modelling on computers has not yet entirely replaced older methods of making models and prototypes from clay or foam, and so long as the physical activity of modelling is both satisfying and informative, it probably never will. Designers are usually interested in the most effective means of communicating and developing their ideas, and that often involves the skill of making, as well as drawing.

Sometimes a designer succeeds in selling an idea to a manufacturer, but this is rarely an easy path. It can be costly in terms of both time and money. For example, in 1990, the designer Ross Lovegrove developed an idea for a coloured glass-fibre one-piece shell resting on a low-cost tubular steel frame. The idea grew out of Lovegrove's paper-folding 'doodles': he folded a loop of paper into a circle, pinched its centre and bent the shape to an angle of 105 degrees to create a comfortable sitting profile. He called it *FO8*, standing for 'figure of eight', which was the shape of the seat and back.

Lovegrove built a prototype, which was exhibited in the new product section of the Design Museum, and persuaded the Italian company Cappellini to manufacture it. The retail price would be about £150, which was within Lovegrove's definition of 'affordability'. Everything was set for a launch at the 1991 Milan Furniture Fair, but problems and delays ensued. It was not until 1994 that *FO8* appeared on the market. For Lovegrove the production of *F08* had been a labour of love, which had taken years to realise.

The genesis of *FO8* is unusual because it is rare for a designer, unlike a craftsperson, to combine the roles of inventor and entrepreneur. The resulting product has much in common with a craft object. It was not a response to a commercial brief, and a single creative personality guided the process from beginning to end. The resulting chair is not unique, but neither it is produced for a mass market. Its production involved manufacturing technology, but so does the production of some ceramic or glass objects which are generally recognised as craft. Perhaps the boundary between design and craft – or, specifically, the boundary between designed object and craft object – is also porous. A designer such as Ross Lovegrove frequently works at the end of the design spectrum closest to craft. For example, a commission for a company such as Louis Vuitton involves working with traditional leather-workers, who are very skilled craftspeople of the non-artistic kind. Is a Louis Vuitton bag, highly-wrought for a global luxury market, craft or design? The answer is both: it is, like haute-couture fashion, the product of both design and craft skills. It is uniquely identified with Paris, yet is a global status symbol, which simultaneously signals unchanging values and up-to-the-minute style.

Design and craft: two different arguments in two different languages?

Every designed object incorporates and expresses a set of assumptions and values about the way we live. Design is an argument, and so is craft. In fact, given the marginal status of the craft economy, its power is almost entirely rhetorical and symbolic. It is easy to overlook the arguments presented by design, because they constitute the mainstream and represent the dominant mode of production. Only at the edges (of fashion, price or taste) does a design 'statement' become impossible to ignore. On the other hand, all craft represents a counter-culture, and thus the production or purchase of a craft object is a form of dissent. The choice of a craft object is always self-conscious.

Today the design of the most banal product has acquired the character of a craft object. For example, a mass-manufactured jug will pour my milk just as well as a hand-thrown one, and for a fraction of the cost. Yet still I may choose to associate myself with the process of individual skill and creativity which produced the handmade jug. In the same way, although a standard lemon-squeezer from the hardware shop extracts juice perfectly efficiently, I may spend twenty times as much on one which looks like something from a science fiction film and which bears a designer label.[10]

Such an object derives its intellectual imprimatur from the school of postmodernism which stresses the playful and narrative potential of the most mundane things. These products force their attentions on you, never letting you forget that ownership is a badge of identity. They deliberately look like the antithesis of Rams's English butler.

Nothing, it seems, is too humble for the attentions of Philippe Starck: *ID* magazine in New York described his *Fluocaril* toothbrush, which uses three times more plastic than conventional toothbrushes, as walking 'a thin line between the collectible and the contemptible'.[11] Andrea Branzi, the Italian designer, who, like Starck, has designed a number of pieces for the manufacturer Alessi, drew a parallel between the domestication of animals, and the domestication of technology. The latter, he says, has yet to be fully achieved:

> For many years now appliances and furniture have been entering the home as extraneous presences, out of step with man's cultural outlook, technical instruments devoid of grace and valued only for their utility.

Branzi adds: 'Increasingly the objects found in the home will … have more of a literary value than a functional one.'[12] Products by a company such as Alessi break down the old polarity between mass-market design and luxury-market craft. Alessi produces for a limited market high-quality products that are closely identified with the designer who conceived them. There are few constraints on the design process; designers have a high degree of autonomy and are encouraged to take creative risks. The model for the working environment is the artist's or craftsperson's studio. There is a recognition that the language of irony and humour is cultural, and one that is shared by artists, craftspeople and designers alike.

Some designers have used the newly invigorated language of 'product semantics' – a deliberate appropriation from the discourse of linguistics – to develop an alternative to the white/black-box aesthetic of functionalism. It was called 'soft-tech', a phrase coined by British designers Richard Seymour and Dick Powell.[13] Designers such as Seymour and Powell recognised that in the electronic age, form was no longer at the mercy of function and that micro-technology permitted many products to look like anything at all. Moreover, accustomed to the power of technology, consumers took performance for granted and did not need to be reassured by overtly functional design. Designers felt free to experiment with shapes which were organic rather than angular, playful rather than serious, and friendly rather than functional.

In other countries, notably Japan and the USA, the impact of micro-technology on both production and consumption has stimulated a deeper reappraisal of the role of design, and of the designer. One context for new American thinking is in academic institutions where design practitioners and teachers exchange ideas. Katherine and Michael McCoy, co-chairmen of the design department at Cranbrook Academy of Art, encourage product design students to explore the use of irony, complexity, layering, and quotation from both vernacular and classical sources. The parallel with the currency of contemporary art and craft is striking and, of course, intentional. The McCoys say that they 'are looking for design that is connective, but that does not require decoding to make connections'.[14] For them, the idea of 'universal design' is both rigid and outmoded. At Cranbrook there is not one visual language, but many.

Katherine and Michael McCoy reject the possibility of a self-evident, rational solution to every design problem, in favour of an approach which embraces culture and psychology, as well as ergonomics. Corporate Japan has reached the same conclusion via the market rather than the seminar room. As society has become more fragmented, marketing analysts have abandoned rigid socio-economic categories as markers of taste and life-style. Instead they talk in terms of 'modes' which relate to specific occasions or aspects of our lives. Going to the airport may stimulate 'panic mode', whereas listening to music at home induces 'relaxing mode'. 'Modes' recognise the multiplication of roles in any individual's life as she or he crosses boundaries between work, home, education, family, friends and so on.[15]

Flexible manufacturing systems enable designers and manufacturers to respond to the complexity and fluidity of people's lives. The old divisions between bespoke and off-the-shelf, and between mass-produced and limited editions, are breaking down. The Japanese have already made cars for niche-markets, which would have been unthinkably small by the old standards of mass production. The Nissan 'S-Cargo' van (1989) and 'Figaro' car (1991) were manufactured in editions of tens, rather than hundreds, of thousands. Each was designed to appeal to a very tight market of urban young men and women, with high disposable incomes and the willingness to spend their money on cliquey status symbols.

Today the Japanese describe design as being 'dreamlike'. The idea is deliberately ambiguous. It means both that that design can make your dreams come true, and also that the design process is dreamlike in the sense of allowing the imagination to roam unrestrained. In corporate Japan design can be an unpredictable, exploratory process. Compared with Western models of product development, the design process in Japan can seem amorphous, even chaotic. Designers are given time and freedom to develop ideas which may not have any commercial application. Young women are actively recruited to work in Japanese design studios, because companies believe that women produce intuitive solutions to problems which are 'right' for the design of products for work and leisure. While cost remains a factor, it is no longer decisive for either producers or consumers. Function is taken for granted: all that remains is desire.

The problem is that we know that desire, if unchecked, can destroy our world. Many designers feel that their work makes them especially responsible for the development of environmentally sustainable products and materials. Over the last decade, it is a theme which has come to dominate debates about design. For example, at the beginning of the 1990s, 'de-designing' became a new buzz-word and the signal for a mood of restraint. Many of the arguments put forward for environmentally responsible design had their roots in the philosophy of craft. Ideas such as the benefit of using local materials to make things which grow old gracefully and which last longer, may be radical in industry, but had always underpinned craft practice.

Design turns ideas into fashion, and soon design students began to use what they called 'post-consumer waste' to create limited-edition furniture, such as tables from railway sleepers, storage units from washing-machine drums, screens woven from processed 35mm film, garden benches from the aluminium tail-flaps of old aeroplanes. But recycling is not necessarily as friendly to the environment as it might appear: the choice of such materials is aesthetic, as much as ethical or economic. Some materials are hard to obtain and expensive. Edward Teasdale, an environmental specialist in the furniture department at the Royal College of Art, London, makes finely crafted chests out of driftwood and says, 'Mass production generally requires a standard raw material and industry finds it easier and cheaper to buy new materials without faults or blemishes.'[16]   Recycled chic may have appropriated the look of the handmade, but not the values of craft.

June Atfield, an English designer-maker who trained at the Royal College of Art, makes simple, angular furniture made from sheets of recycled plastic. Her pieces are intended to make a strong statement about recycling, but at first she was obliged to import the processed waste she wanted to use from the USA. Subsequently, Atfield and Colin Williamson, Chairman of the British Plastics Federation Recycling Council, have established 'Made of Waste', an agency that sources, distributes and promotes recycled material. Atfield works independently and has a high degree of control over her work, which straddles the design–craft divide.

The majority of designers do not and cannot detach themselves from the values of the companies for which they work. The extent to which designers can make use of their knowledge of, say, environmental issues varies greatly according to their patterns and structures of work. But if consumers demand change, then designers will play their part in providing it. Although their ability to effect change in large organisations is, of course, limited, designers are peculiarly capable of articulating the interests of both consumer and producer in a dialogue which is becoming increasingly sophisticated. For example, ethical consumption is often invisible, but market research shows that 50 per cent of British shoppers are operating some kind of consumer boycott. The most common concerns are depletion of the ozone layer, animal rights and the dangers of beef, and unacceptable governments in countries of origin. Some people still avoid goods from Germany and Japan because of the actions of those countries in the Second World War. According to the magazine *The Ethical Consumer*, 'Ethical consumerism ... argues that the marketplace is a vast untapped resource that people can use to express their ethical and political beliefs in a non-violent manner.'[17]

Conclusion

Design and craft used to be explicable by the dichotomy of values which separated them: machine-made vs. handmade; mass-market vs. luxury-market; urban vs. rural; innovative vs. traditional; sophisticated vs. vernacular; male vs. female. Today, the distance between these spheres of making is not so wide nor so fixed: new technology has reinvented the economics of scale in manufacturing, and designers and craftspeople share the language of postmodernism. The boundary between design and craft (and also between craft and art) is porous. In a changing world of work, technology and consumption, some practitioners may want, and be able, to exploit this porosity, while others will continue to work within recognisable traditions.

Former polarities have become a spectrum, and the moral dichotomy between the factory and the studio lost its content and meaning long ago. Each craftsperson and each designer is responsible for the values which they bring to and express through their work. Neither has a monopoly of virtue, nor does a higher degree of creative autonomy constitute greater moral freedom or responsibility.

Notes

1 As part of the promotion of the global launch of Windows 95, *The Times* was given away free of charge on 16 August 1995. The launch was, of course, front-page news in an article headlined 'Tills ring at midnight as Windows 95 opens'.

2 The Society of Industrial Artists and Designers (SIAD), founded in 1930, was granted a Royal Charter in 1976. It was subsequently renamed the Chartered Society of Designers.

3 See, for example, Jean Baudrillard's developing analysis of consumption in *Le Système des Objets* (Paris, Gallimard, 1968) and *Société de Consommation* (Paris, Gallimard, 1970).

4 Quoted in P. Thompson (ed.), *Review 1* (London, The Design Museum, 1989).

5 A. Pugin, *The True Principles of Christian Architecture* (London, H. G. Bohn, 1853).

6 Quoted in F. Whitford, *Bauhaus* (London, Thames & Hudson, 1984).

7 *Ibid.*

8 Quoted in *Styling Study Notes* (London, The Design Museum, 1989).

9 Quoted in *Casa Vogue* (Milan, November 1992).

10 In 1989 the Italian manufacturer Alessi launched a lemon-squeezer called *Juicy Salif*, the first of range of kitchen products commissioned from Philippe Starck. As much ornament as functional object, *Juicy Salif* quickly came to symbolise the conspicuous consumption of the 1980s, as well as the influence of postmodernism on product design.

11 From 'Taking a stand against Mr Starck', *ID* magazine, New York, October 1993.

12 A. Branzi, *Domestic Animals* (London, Academy Editions, 1987).

13 Richard Seymour and Dick Powell formed the consultancy Seymour Powell in 1984. See Thompson (ed.), *Review,* for a discussion of the phenomenon of 'soft-tech'.

14 See K. and M. McCoy *et al.*, *Cranbrook Design: The New Discourse* (New York, Rizzoli, 1990).

15 For a discussion of this idea, see   J. Woudhuysen, 'In defence of the Enlightenment', in J. Myerson (ed.), *Design Renaissance*, selected papers from the International Design Congress (Horsham, Open Eye Publishing, 1993).

16 Quoted in Paul Forster, 'They have designs on your rubbish', *The Weekend Telegraph*, 15 April 1995.

17 *The Ethical Consumer*, 12, February/March 1994.

PETER DORMER

This chapter is an examination of the studio crafts in the context of machine and computer technology. Computer technology now provides craft with its most serious philosophical and practical challenges. A hint of this challenge was provided by Oliver Morton, editor-in-chief of *Wired* magazine (Europe), when he lectured at the 'Doors of Perception' conference in Amsterdam (9–11 November 1995). He pointed out that computers, coupled to the very latest multi-armed 'lathes', were now producing objects that had never before been seen on earth. Human choice was involved, but no 'hands-on' making. He also said, however, that the only way to understand how a thing works is to make it. These two observations alone provide us with a wealth of possibilities and contradictions for the crafts. On the one hand our very notion of what it is to *make* something is being transformed; on the other, the importance of hands-on making is not thereby removed by computer technology's ability to 'make' everything. For it is conceivable that different kinds of making provide different kinds of understanding, and so my chapter ends with a discussion of why intelligent people continue to make things in a 'craft' fashion in an intellectual culture that seems indifferent to their presence.

Craft in the context of technology

When, in his book *The Nature and Art of Workmanship* (Cambridge, Cambridge University Press, 1968), the designer, craftsman and writer David Pye set out to answer the question, 'Is anything done by hand?', he

137

showed us how very confused we can be about the nature of craft. He argued that very few things can properly be said to have been made by hand. The activity we call craft does not, he said, mean 'made by hand'. Most things that are made by craft workers require tools, and some of these tools are elaborate, time-saving machines. In fact Pye could think of very little pure handwork beyond such examples as basket-weaving and coiling pots.

Pye preferred to write about workmanship rather than craft. And when he examined what workmanship meant as a concept and as an activity he concluded that there were two sorts of workmanship. He called these 'the workmanship of risk' and 'the workmanship of certainty'. These definitions have had a considerable influence upon the way many of us who are interested in craft and technology generally view the notion of workmanship.

The workmanship of certainty refers to mass or serial production. You design, you prototype, you test your prototype and you try to iron out all the production problems before you set production into being. You set the lathes, the cutting tools and the assembling teams in such a way that you can predict the outcome and the quality of each and every object that is to flow from your final prototype. Once production begins the manufacturing process is supposed to provide you with certainty. It was this goal that Japanese car-makers had in mind in the 1980s. They set out to attain it and, in the process, achieved almost 100 per cent certainty in production, which meant that, unlike their European rivals, there were few if any defective cars requiring further quality checks and consuming valuable labour. The workmanship of certainty is the product of testing and planning a design, a series of prototypes, and the system of manufacture that is to produce the design. As far as production is concerned, it is a system, not an individual, who produces.

In the workmanship of risk we are in the realm where individuals, rather than a process of manufacture, hold the key to success. The crafted product may or may not be the product of a single person; it may be the product of several skilled persons, but each of them at any moment could ruin the product with a mistake. Here, in a sense, every fresh object is a new beginning rather than a continuation of one beginning. Every new beginning is a risk.

There is another way of looking at the distinction between craft and non-craft production. We can look at it in terms of the difference between *personal know-how* and *distributed knowledge*.

The concept of personal know-how is plain enough. It is knowledge of a 'how to' kind which you have and can call upon whenever the need arises. You not only know that you know but you feel that you know. To know how to throw a pot is to feel how to throw. Such personal know-how is a characteristic of experts that novices do not have – it comes with experience.

Distributed knowledge is a messier concept and it refers to two linked ideas. First, we live in an age in which the majority of objects exist only because of the coming-together of a variety of disciplines and industries. For example, whilst many people could learn to *assemble* a television set, the idea of any one person *making* a television set is absurd. You would need to be a metallurgist, an expert in plastics, and much else besides. Or, to take another example, there are no handmade cars. There are cars that are hand-assembled with panels beaten by men wielding mallets, but the electronics, the lights and the light bulbs are bought in. The knowledge needed to make any piece of product design is spread over many systems of production and thought.

The second, related idea contained in the concept of distributed knowledge concerns the notion of tools, jigs and, indeed, computer software. For there is a category of tool and artefact that allows us to make things without ourselves possessing the know-how to make them. This category contains a range of tools: some, such as 'instant cameras', are an example where you need know nothing of the skill involved (photography) in order to take some pictures. Other examples are more equivocal. Desktop publishing and graphics software packages can be used in an uninspired way which allows every editor of a parish newsletter to become an instant graphic designer by assembling images from a menu of images and typefaces. However, someone who has an interest in and knowledge of graphic design can take that same menu and make designs from it that have quality. It is rather like the difference between someone who buys instant food from a supermarket and eats it as it comes and another individual who uses instant foods as the foundation for something more palatable. The critical ingredient is the possession of knowledge that can supplement or override that which you have bought as a package.

Long before such sophisticated tools as software packages there were (and remain) simple but powerful means of distributing knowledge. Moulds are a good example. A mould enables someone to make more than one of something. It might be a clay bowl or a clay figure. Moreover, having made your original model and made a mould of it, you can hire someone else to produce more of your original model using the mould.

The beauty of this system is that the user of moulds need not be very skilled or knowledgeable. Pressing clay into moulds is probably one of the most basic senses in which practical knowledge is distributed from a skilled to an unskilled producer.

However, the mould user may not in fact be unskilled or unknowledgeable. He or she may have different skills. And thus, though unable to model a figure, she or he may be a superb colourist and decorator. In this case one set of skills (the modeller's/sculptor's) is distributed in order to be the foundation for another set of skills (the colourist's).

Most contemporary technology has embedded within it knowledge that is not and cannot be ours to possess, but it does not follow necessarily that technology removes the need for personal know-how. For example, a potter, whether he or she is a professional or an amateur, may rely on an electric wheel and an electric kiln, but the technology is quite useless without the potter's personal know-how of how to throw pots and what different sorts of firing to adopt for different sorts of clays and glazes. The same is true of a great many (although not all) tools. The metal- or woodworking lathe, the electric drill or router, are of no use unless you know how to use them and have some use to which to put them.

Which leads to the conclusion that craftspeople can be defined generally as people engaged in a practical activity where they are seen to be in control of their work. They are in control by virtue of possessing personal know-how that allows them to be masters or mistresses of the available technology, irrespective of whether it is a mould, a hand tool, an electrically driven machine or a computer. It is not craft as 'handcraft' that defines contemporary craftsmanship: it is craft as knowledge that empowers a maker to take charge of technology.

The relationship that has just been outlined between personal know-how and knowledge distributed through technology sounds very benign. Without the potter, the electric wheel is dumb and so we can rest with the assurance that humans remain forever in control. But we know that the relationship between personal know-how and technology need not be as accommodating to individual human talents as the potter and his or her wheel suggests. We are aware that one of the common effects of distributed knowledge is to do away, as far as possible, with the need for personal know-how. Indeed, this doing-away with individual know-how, and the risks and uncertainties that accompany it, is one of the goals of the users of contemporary technology.

One of the features of late-twentieth-century technology as applied both to the manufacture of objects and to the provision of services is the refinement of the concept of a system in which all risks, especially those produced by human error, are removed.

Consider architecture. Modern buildings are complex objects and they are shaped by complex planning and health and safety laws, as well as by the expectations of developers, bankers and pension-fund managers. There is, among everyone concerned with a new building, a desire, often driven by fear, not to make mistakes because mistakes have financial penalties. Consequently there has been a surge in the development of systems that give predictable, guaranteed outcomes of quality. In particular there has been a pronounced development in the idea of a building as a kit of parts whose individual functions are tested and known, whose cost and performance has been set and whose use can be specified in one country and used in another and everyone concerns knows what to expect. Such a 'kit' approach to building components is paralleled by the designs covering the management of the labour forces erecting the building and fast-track, time and motion study analyses governing the performance of all contractors and subcontractors. Wherever possible, methods of building are employed in which the know-how is embedded in the system rather than in individuals, in order to exchange the workmanship of risk for that of certainty.

Among the ingredients that give technology its organising and mould-making power appear to be the following:
(i) simplicity;
(ii) distribution of knowledge through systems and organisations;
(iii) ubiquity.

Simplicity. When two or more people pool different skills that allow each of them to do together more than any one of them can accomplish on their own, then there is a price to be paid: none of them may any longer

141

fully comprehend all that is involved in their joint production. Consequently, the concept of simplicity becomes desirable.

Keeping things simple does not mean that the objective is only to make simple things. The objective is to make complicated things with procedures that are as simple as possible.

Systems. Kits or collections of prefabricated components exemplify technology's ability to create systems that rely on distributed knowledge and are not subverted by a local lack of know-how. Systems also aid clear communication: if you have a kit of parts, as you have in the building or the print industry, for example, then designers can specify their design by numbers and have some guarantee that wherever in the world their designs are to be made they will be made accurately. However, this does suggest that designers and architects could be replaced by managers whose job is not to invent but to manage the use of existing systems.

Ubiquity. The commonest feature about technology, with its distributed knowledge, is that everything begins to look the same. If all over the country the same building technology or computer or graphics software is applied to the variety of architectural, graphic or industrial design commissions, then each of these individual jobs and commissions receives the same underlying thought. Consistency and predictability of outcome are almost guaranteed, but the price is uniformity.

Mimicking machines

At this point, taking simplicity, systems and ubiquity as the cue, it would be easy to argue that what gives 'craft' its distinctiveness from technology is that technology has become so predictable that its aesthetic is predictable, even boring. Meanwhile, the familiar argument in favour of supporting craft is its potential to provide variety and an unexpected diversity of form and texture.

To some extent the path of 'looking different' is the one that many practitioners, advocates and curators of craft have chosen to take as the platform for 'why craft matters'. But it is important to recognise that looking different is a choice for the crafts, it is not a necessity. There is no essential reason why the products produced by a process of the workmanship of risk should look different from those produced by the workmanship of certainty.

Contrary to expectations, the appearance of the product of the workmanship of risk and that of certainty is often so similar it is hard to tell them apart. Consider a minor example. Anyone who has ever dented his or her car is pleasantly surprised by how neat and machine-like the finish created by the panel-beater and paint-sprayer can be. Indeed, there are many examples of handcraft or craft producers mimicking machine-produced wares. More recently, machines have begun to produce objects that mimic handcraft and craft ware.

The elusiveness of 'craft' versus 'machine-made' appearance is illustrated by George H. Marcus in his book *Functionalist Design* (Berlin, Prestel Verlag, 1995), in which he discusses the Bauhaus in terms of handcraftsmanship applied to the production of prototypes for industry. He describes two teapots made by Marianne Brandt in 1924 in the Bauhaus metal workshop:

> one, made of silver, clearly reveals its handcrafted nature in the repeated marks of the hammer that cover the surface of its spherical bowl, witness to the arduous process of its creation. The second, in brass, takes the same shape, but its bowl is smooth and reflective, masking all evidence of its hand manufacture under a highly finished surface, implying that it could have been made by machine.

I like this example because here we have the same craftsperson working the same product by hand in two separate idioms – crafted and machined – and it reminds us that the model of perfection that technology delivers is not set by machines but by humans. We set up machine technology to achieve more efficiently that which we can nevertheless and with great effort achieve without machine technology. The standards of 'perfection' that are so often ascribed to the example of machine production were set first by human imagination and craft achievement.

This idea has interesting consequences for the way in which we divide objects into those that have 'humanity' and those that do not. There is a tendency, for example, to see regularity, neatness and 'perfection' as cold, and irregularity as 'warm'. But regularity is as much a human desire as irregularity and some people feel warmly emotional towards the precision of a motor vehicle, an aircraft component or a machine tool as others do towards carved stone or textured pots.

But from the point of view of appearances, and especially from the

143

point of view of the craftsperson, the central issue is no longer 'Can I create perfection?' but 'Is technology robbing me of my unique claim to diversity?' From the contemporary studio craftsperson's point of view, the most destabilising effect of technology is how effectively technology can *mimic* craft in its randomness, accidental quirks and less than perfect condition. Or, in other words, how many consumers can now tell the difference between handmade and machine-made lace?

The harnessing of computer technology to machine tools and the use of software that includes 'fuzzy logic' makes it possible to loosen up perfection and give an appearance of the differentiation of pattern and surface that we have hitherto associated with crafted work. The ability of machines to mimic craft may not yet be very widespread or deep but it might already be significant. For it may be that whilst the world of computing science has not made as much headway as it wished to in the world of artificial conceptual intelligence, it is perhaps further down the road with regard to artificial practical 'intelligence'.

Consider the famous Turing Test. Alan Turing, one of the people credited with imagining and defining what artificial intelligence would look like, believed that computers would one day operate in a manner virtually indistinguishable from human thought. He proposed what is now known as the Turing Test. A Turing Test calls for a person to interact with a computer for an hour or so, the results of the conversation being printed out. If, from a reading of the transcript, an outsider is unable to determine that one of the participants is a machine, then the machine has passed the test.

Suppose one adapted the Turing Test to cover practical thinking. Suppose one cannot tell among a group of similar objects which one is the product of personal know-how and handcraft and which was produced by machine (or through the system of distributed knowledge): then one of the foundations of the status of craft – that it produces things that machines cannot imitate – becomes wobbly.

I accept that it is a moot point as to whether or not computer-organised production yet possesses this ability to defeat the connoisseur when it comes to differentiating between the products of personal know-how and the products of the computer, but in some fields, especially textiles, the differences are becoming harder to distinguish. I suspect that another area of craftwork that is vulnerable to the ever improving mimicking capabilities of computer software is calligraphy and lettering.

Such developments do bring into contention many of the accepted beliefs that make up the ideology of studio craft: that the hand of the maker is necessarily special, that craft objects are poetic objects, that craft objects reveal aspects of the personality (some say the 'soul') of the maker. But the Turing Test for Personal Know-How in Crafts would call all this into question. If you cannot tell whether a piece of machined textile is hand-done or machined, then either the much-vaunted poetry of the handcraft aesthetic is a myth, or the same poetic aesthetic claimed for handcraft is also achievable through technology, and consequently what technology distributes is not only knowledge but also 'poetry'. Either way, the special status of craft would collapse.

Woven textiles are the single most natural candidate for computerisation. Ann Sutton, weaver, textile designer and textile artist, has made the following comments:

> Life can now be very different for the handweaver, whether weaving art works, craft products, or designs for industrial production. Dobby looms are now available with an interface to a computer. I have one. I still have ideas in the bath, work them out on the back of an envelope, then sort my brain out on some graph paper. But then it's straight to the computer and with the help of my favourite software I am able to see, more or less, the result of my ideas on screen. I still have to set up the warp and thread it through the loom, but there the chores stop. I press two buttons and my loom is programmed and ready to weave. No pangs if a mistake shows up: a second's tweak and we're off again accurately. It's magic. It's given me twenty years' extra weaving life. (interview with author, 7.11.95)

Middle-aged wisdom

The introduction of Ann Sutton's experience into the discussion raises another question about the relationship between craft and technology. As a person with a craft and with experience of making things by hand she has, like many people who trained in a design profession during the 1950s or 1960s, achieved a situation in which she has two sorts of knowledge. She has the personal know-how of craft experience and she now has the possibilities of computerised, distributed knowledge at her disposal.

Many middle-aged designers in a similar position to hers (they may be weavers, engineers or architects) argue that you get the best out of the computer and its software if you are able to drive the tool rather than being driven by it.

Consider Neal French's chapter in this book, where he discusses CADCAM in the ceramics industry, an industry he worked in as a designer for twenty years. His conclusion is that CADCAM is here to stay in the ceramics industry and that it will become more central to the industry and more refined. His more tentative conclusion, based on his own experience, is that those who use CADCAM as a modelling tool will be better able to exploit its potential and the potential of clay as a material if they have the tacit knowledge of modelling by hand and by eye.

In principle the argument that one needs a variety of personal know-how in order to take control of such powerful tools as computer software packages is cogent. The cogency of the argument rests on this logic: (a) design software is very powerful, and although it does not do the designer's thinking it has, embedded within its own design structure, a style, a way of procedure, and limitations on refinement that will impose themselves upon the designer's work. (b) Therefore, in order to be alert to the biases within the design software the designer needs alternative knowledge of his or her own by which to compare and contrast and form the basis of individual discrimination. (c) Consequently, one may argue that a person who has worked real materials as well the virtual materials of CAD will have an advantage over a person who has knowledge of CAD only. QED – it is the triumph of the middle-aged over the young.

However, it is not a foregone conclusion that a craft background is a necessary condition for being a successful 'modeller', graphic designer, or any other sort of designer using CADCAM. After all, young designers, in graphics, for example, are under no compulsion to be able to draw or paint, let alone do calligraphy or cut letters in stone or wood. Their design education is as likely now to be directly on to the computer software. Their favourite resource is the scanner, which enables them to take any existing image they want, load it into the computer and then 'play' with it.

Yet Neal French has made the point in conversation that the big difference between craft and CADCAM is that in craft the relationship is between a person, a tool and real material. In CADCAM the relationship is only between the person and the tool.

There is more to this issue of the idealism of virtual making than may at first meet the eye. In real making with real materials one comes up against gravity and physics. One also comes up against the unexpected in the materials themselves. Materials have flaws, and in real life these flaws have to be worked on or worked around but on computer the material remains imaginary and flawless. Now it may be that the response from the materials industries in respect of the fact that CADCAM designers will be specifying flawless materials, will be to perfect metals, alloys, composites and plastics in order to make them ideal. In which case there is no necessity for designers to gain practical experience of 'real' materials because what is 'real' and what is 'virtual' will have been made one and the same thing: the materials technologists will meet the standards set by the computer.

This may, however, leave a niche for the craftsperson or designer who is able to design for and work with flawed materials, including the natural ones of wood and stone. In a world of easily achieved perfection flaws may become rather special.

What is the nature of craft?

Craft relies on tacit knowledge. Tacit knowledge is acquired through experience and it is the knowledge that enables you to do things as distinct from talking or writing about them. That in itself is an apparently odd thing to say, because one might assume that if you know something well enough to write explicitly about it then you can do it. But it does not follow. One may write fairly vivid descriptions without being able to enact those descriptions for real. For example, a scientist with no practical ability can describe an experiment, a crime novelist can describe the perfect murder without being in the least able to wield the carving knife in an efficient manner, and a theatre critic can describe how an actor *should* play Cleopatra without herself being able to act.

Tacit knowledge is practical know-how, and it exists in people. Consequently tacit knowledge is learned and absorbed by individuals through practice and from other people; it cannot usually be learned from books. Books (and videos, CD-ROMs and models) are effective sources in helping a student to understand the principles of practice, but the actual business of learning is usually best done by face-to-face teaching or apprenticeship with people who are already themselves practically knowledgeable. Students or apprentices need to be shown how to make things.

However, different sorts of tacit knowledge have different sorts of relationships with explicit knowledge. For example, whilst it seems unlikely that someone who wanted to learn to throw pots on the wheel could get very much help from a book, someone who wants to learn to draw can find 'how to draw' books informative and instructive.

If knowledgeable people fail to pass on their tacit knowledge then that knowledge will disappear. When practical knowledge disappears it is hard and time-consuming to rediscover it. One of the reasons why tacit knowledge, once lost, is difficult to regain is explained by the fact that when a body of knowledge disappears the institutions (collections of like-minded persons) that helped to sustain it – academies, guilds, workshops, unions – also disappear.

There are circumstances where we might want to encourage the loss of tacit knowledge. In the July 1995 issue of the *American Journal of Science*, and subsequently reported in *The Independent* (London, 1 August 1995), two social scientists, Donald Mackenzie and Graham Spinardi, both at the University of Edinburgh, stated that whilst the theoretical knowledge of atomic weapons is unlikely to be lost, we could lose the skills, the tacit knowledge, needed to make them since the number of people who now know how to build a weapon is dwindling. The two scientists wrote,

> To the extent that nuclear weapons depend on highly specific tacit knowledge, they can be uninvented. Tacit knowledge is, quite literally, embodied in the people who possess it. If these people die without a new generation of nuclear-weapons designers to pass it on to, their knowledge dies with them. It could be recreated only by going through a process of learning akin to the original invention of nuclear weapons. Nuclear weapons could be reinvented after a period of nuclear disarmament, but the task would be much harder than commonly thought. (p. 22)

As has been stated, the nature of tacit knowledge is that it is personal know-how – you must know 'x' in order to do it, as distinct from knowing about 'x' in order to write about it. However, tacit knowledge is also, as has already been suggested, institutional or communal knowledge. Any craft of any complexity is always greater in content and range than any one individual; hence the importance to the health of a craft that many rather than a few, people practise it. Moreover, these people need to get together from time to time in guilds, demonstrations and conferences, whilst working together consistently through institutions such as art schools or university engineering departments. In technology, knowledge is distributed especially among systems of people and hardware; in craft, knowledge is also distributed but through people alone.

The possession and practice of practical know-how has, like the acquisition of other forms of knowledge, the potential to be open-ended – you keep finding new ways of doing things and new applications for the things that you do. Yet, and this is one of the contradictions about 'the crafts', a number of studio craft practitioners do not build themselves careers based on continuous invention.

Within the studio crafts the pattern tends to be that a person will find a form or a limited series of forms, and work year after year mining the same vein of possibilities, by extending the form or the methods of shaping or decorating the form cautiously and incrementally. The practical lives of many craftspeople really do fall under the heading of 'The diary of a snail'. Why is this?

One answer to the question of specialisation rests in the nature of individual crafts. Setting aside the fact that you can get by on a little knowledge (slabbing, coiling and thumb pots, for example) it is a fact that if a craft is to be pursued in any depth then it can take years to acquire. The British calligrapher Ann Hechle, for example, believes that the disappearance of calligraphy as a major subject in British art-school education was partly the consequence of its taking a long time to learn, and also that it was expensive in terms of intensive teaching.

Moreover, one of the lessons that a novice learns is quite how long it takes to make any single object, be it of art, craft, design or engineering. Dr Tom Bligh, of the Cambridge University Engineering Department, a teacher on the Manufacturing Engineering Tripos, explained why an experience of prototyping in design was important for his students. He said,

> The advantages of prototyping lie in the experience of making or getting something made, and in recognising the gap between theory and practice. … Making things yourself takes a long time and making anything takes longer than most inexperienced people imagine. (interview with author, 16.5.95)

(However, it was ironic to discover that – despite the formidably impressive work of the Engineering Manufacturing Department at Cambridge – whilst the tutors espoused the need for hands-on knowledge, their students did not have time for it. Most if not all design and 'making' was done using CAD systems.)

Yet if single objects take so long, why not go for variety rather than continuity? Life is short and the imagination is fertile. But the investment of time and the almost inevitable feeling that one might have done better than one actually did apparently have the opposite effect upon makers. Having seen where they went wrong, their desire is to go back and do it again. The studio crafts seem to be populated by people who are searching for their ideal forms.

Interestingly, it is this very search for an ideal form that has driven some craftsmen and craftswomen towards CAD. The attraction is that, provided they are content with virtual rather than actual objects, they can be spared the frustrations and disappointments of real making. And they can make so many more virtual objects than ever they could produce real ones. One such craftsman is the American metalsmith Professor Stanley Lechtzin of the Tyler School of Art, Temple University, USA.

He has given up making things. He creates virtual object after virtual object on his computer. He is experimenting with computer-aided manufacture and rapid prototyping but, meanwhile, the ability to quickly create objects in full rendering and three dimensions on screen allows him to

> keep up with my ideas. I am free to follow ideas now in a way that making by hand did not permit. I can, using CAD, refine and refine until I get each design right. The computer gives me the time to do this because virtual making is quicker than actual making and when computer-aided lathes or tools do the actual making for me I will be back at the computer creating the next object in the series whilst the machines labour away. (interview with author, 21.3.95)

'Why do you make things?'

There is a difference between 'craft' and 'the crafts'. Craft, or the workmanship of risk, or the knowledge of personal know-how, cuts across the design and making of all kinds of objects, from hand-thrown pots, sculpture and painting, to the making of vessels which contain the fuel rods in nuclear reactors (there is a lot of craft there). But 'the crafts' refers to a wide range of objects made with craft but which are identified as art-craft, design-craft and studio craft. Each category has different ambitions and aspires to a different status from the others. Each has a different relationship to the dominant culture of technology.

So, to take a subject such as weaving, one may find a weaver creating installation artworks using woven fibres as the basic material; another weaver will use a loom connected to a computer to create designs and samples for use by industry; and yet another weaver will be creating shawls or scarves of great complexity or subtlety on a one-off basis.

For the time being – the reach of the computer's power is not yet godlike – each of these people can justify the use of craft procedures for apparently good logical reasons. The installation artist will want to create environments that have a reality whose sensuousness cannot be captured on computer; the craft-designer will argue that working small samples for industry is good because each real sample gives the factory more information than a computer print-out can provide (although that is changing); and the studio-weaver using a handloom can still argue there are techniques and effects that cannot be obtained using the computer-driven power loom.

And similar arguments can be used with greater or lesser degrees of strength for other activities including lettering, furniture production, pottery, glass, jewellery and metalwork. Indeed, ceramicists, glass artists, and jewellery artists will point out they are making things that only the human hand can make, because the technology to replicate handwork does not exist or because it is far too expensive for a small one- or two-person business.

But although such reasoning for the continuance of craft and 'the crafts' is logical, it is also secondary in importance to many craftspeople. The primary reasons for wanting to make things for oneself have little to do with good accounting or the availability of appropriate technology.

If you ask a craftsperson 'Why do you make things?' the majority respond predictably: 'I have always liked making things.' It is a basic liking, a fundamental preference which, like first causes, beggars further justification. This passion goes hand-in-hand with a passion for objects. Sue Halls, a ceramicist and figurative sculptor whose works owe a lot to pottery techniques of slabbing and folding clay as well as the more traditional modelling approach of the sculpture studio, says,

As a child I loved objects – things. I used to spend hours rummaging through cupboards and turning out the contents of drawers. And I've always loved ceramics. I can remember the plates and cups we used when I was five or six … and not just the stuff in our house! At the same time I was very attracted to sculpture … Lord Kitchener was the most mesmerising local example. (letter to author, 29.10.95)

Sue Halls's remarks are endorsed in different ways by other correspondents, all of whom in their different ways are struck by the 'eloquence' of objects. Objects communicate to some people as powerfully as written texts or musical scores or mathematical equations do for others.

The receptiveness to the knowledge and achievement that an object represents and demonstrates is quite often not communicable in words but it is communicable by making some stuff of one's own. Which is why people who like objects appear to like making similar objects of their own. It seems that craftspeople make things out of homage to the objects that already exist – and this is also still true of some artists. They make things partly to articulate to the rest of us their passion for a genre and partly to understand and extend that genre for themselves.

For along with a passion for objects and as a part of wanting to make work of one's own in 'homage' to these objects there is the desire to gain understanding through making. Making is a form of intellectual and imaginative possession. For example, children who have an obsession – be it horses, aircraft, racing cars – like to draw pictures or make models of these things. Making things is a way of anchoring one's obsession in one's imagination. (Making by craft is not the only way of gaining the understanding of and possessing the objects of one's desire, but it is a powerful one.)

This is what Sue Halls says:

Two things dominated my life from very early on (pre-school), Art and Animals. Not 'Art' in the grandiose sense – I didn't know about the Great Masters, etc., until much later. What I mean by 'Art' is pushing a pencil around – image-making. And the images that predominated were those of animals. Not figures, ANIMALS. It wasn't just that I found them easy to draw. I had a great desire to be near them and own them, obtain them in any way possible, and so drawing was a means of doing that … My attitude to animals is still as powerful, if not more so. When I see an animal, and it doesn't matter if it's in a picture or a stuffed specimen in a museum, or the real thing there in front of me, the response is always the same. I am overwhelmed … I'm very lucky really as I'm never stuck for ideas. As you have said, 'I have a subject', but it's not as though I chose it … In many ways my subject is my downfall. Animal artists are never taken very seriously … And you can't get much lower than making them in clay. At least bronze has some kind of status! (letter to author, 29.10.95)

Sue Halls presents a particularly clear example of an obsession and a desire to understand it through making because animals are an especially tangible subject. But other sorts of makers illustrate a similar pleasure in making and a similar desire to understand through making, but with less tangible subject-matter.

Consider Richard La Trobe-Bateman, furniture and bridge designer and maker. This is what he says about two simple structures:

Four sticks joined together in a square are not rigid but three sticks joined in a triangle are. Most people know this (although it is surprising how many 'educated' people don't) but they do not stop to wonder; they merely accept it, they probably have other things, more interesting to them, to think about. There is nothing to be said about the physical fact; it just is; it's the result of the geometry; it doesn't mean anything – but it can be exploited, this simple shape phenomenon. That is one sort of 'beauty'. (letter to author, 20.10.95)

Another sort of beauty that matters to him is:

the material, the stuff itself that the world is made of … stone is strong in compression but weak in tension, hard but heavy. In contrast, wood is strong in tension, not so strong in compression, locally soft but light. These two characteristics in just two materials account for the appearance of a huge proportion of man's artefacts. (letter to author, 20.10.95)

Much of the making of his work, especially footbridges for crossing streams or small rivers, is just hard physical labour. Yet the labour involved in each piece he constructs, be it a bridge, a chair or a table, contributes to his tacit understanding of the physics of that object. The making of one piece contributes to the foundation of the thinking of another. This also coincides with Professor French's remarks concerning the difference between working with CADCAM and the more traditional design-tools–material relationship. La Trobe-Bateman is working a material as well as a design.

La Trobe-Bateman says he must make purposeful objects.

> My work seeks, as simply as possible, to demonstrate, to exemplify, to clarify, these physical characteristics and devices. The choice of utilitarian objects as a vehicle is then obvious because a required performance and its mode of achievement (support, shelter, span, lift and so on) is the way we see it. An art object would not do, as it does not provide a measure of performance. (letter to author, 20.10.95)

The performance that La Trobe-Bateman is concerned with has also to demonstrate the passion he feels for what an object can communicate about function and physics and material. For example, he writes, 'Forces travel in straight lines. When the object expresses this, or is seen to resolve a curve, it will be that much clearer (and therefore visually satisfying to me).' And, he adds, 'If the device is made of more than one piece of material then how those pieces are joined is important, so I seek to show it.' In any case the demonstration of how things are successfully put together is a part of the point of making things – it is a part of the craftsperson's exploration and pleasure in making things.

Making – craft, skill, and the realisation of the object through craft labour – is not a trivial issue for craftspeople. Making is both the means through which the craftsperson explores their obsession or idea and an end in itself.

Sue Halls wrote,

> The physical act of making things is very traumatic … There's nothing frenzied about it … I carry my work around with me all the time and wherever I go I'm constantly translating form, pattern and colour into subjects for my work. (letter to author, 29.10.95)

Or consider the following points raised by Dorothy Hogg, metalsmith and jeweller, in her letter to me of 3 October 1995.

> When I left the Royal College of Art I took a design job for industry. Working through design ideas mainly on paper does not satisfy me entirely, although I found it easy. I discovered that I need to make, because I need the challenge of working three-dimensionally. I do not find it easy to visualise objects in three dimensions.
>
> The step following the exploration of an idea on paper is one of attempting to come near to it in mock-up form and then to move it into

a finished statement with the correct edges, surface finish, proportions made as well as I can and with a dynamic relationship to the body.

When making something in metal it is NEVER easy, always a challenge. When you are soldering something difficult you have to tread the tightrope between overheating and therefore melting and correct soldering and a good join. You use all your skills, concentration, intuition and intelligence … That feeling of being totally stretched must form a major part of the satisfaction.

However, people can grow out of their desire to make things. Michael Harvey is a letterer and a type-designer. As a carver of letters his most public work is probably the lettering he carved for the Sainsbury Wing of the National Gallery, London.

Relating how he was described as an 'artistic child', Michael Harvey explains that he missed a lot of schooling because of air raids and he left school having taken no exams (letter to author, 3.10.95). He spent six years doing engineering drawing but he did not like the fact that his drawings were only a part of the manufacturing process and not the final product.

In his early twenties he came across Eric Gill's *Autobiography*, which he thought contained the answer to his future: 'I would become the new Eric Gill, so I set about learning to carve letters in wood and stone.' He got himself a job with Reynolds Stone, letterer and wood-engraver, and in 1955 he exchanged his engineering drawing-office for Stone's workshop.

Eventually he became bored with executing Stone's designs and found he had a talent for creating book-jackets, which allowed him to develop all kinds of freely-drawn lettering. Harvey left Stone's workshop when he was able to live from designing book-jackets, although he also did some carving of inscriptions and part-time teaching. In 1966 he designed his first typeface. Today he has almost stopped teaching, he no longer does book-jackets, and designing typefaces on the computer is his main activity.

'Craft is now a dirty word to me', he says. And he adds that he has come to dislike 'one-offs' and the world of the connoisseur. He has misgivings about craft because of its connotations of preciousness and its aspiration to be seen as art; he much prefers the straightforward anonymity of artisans.

However, he does entertain seriously the notion that the variety of craft experience has shaped his understanding of lettering and that his tacit knowledge so acquired is an important foundation for his current work with the computer. He says that carving, painting and drawing letters gave him an understanding of letterforms and how letters go together without which he could not design typefaces. The question that remains, of course, is whether 'understanding through craft making' is a necessary part of a designer's education or not. It is a subject worthy of research because it may have consequences for future design training or, conceivably, the design of the software that designers will use in the future.

Most craftspeople do not stop making, however. And I think it fair to give the last word to Mick Casson, the well-known British studio potter who has made pots for fifty years. The letter is dated 14 October 1995.

> When you 'phoned I said I had just unpacked a kiln – actually I had been all day unpacking it – a salt kiln – an emotionally draining job. I sorted them (the pots) into good (a few), not so good and awful (smashed). I attempted to evaluate them, get some vibes from some, sort out the trials (there are always many of these, most fail but they are the future).
>
> So, you asked me what am I doing? Well, I'm earning a living from what I make and I've always liked that fact and this time again I quickly added up the kiln load, roughly. It was all right and I was pleased. But the other, the real preoccupation always takes over – quality. Why are some pots better than others? I'm making pots that I hope people will use even if the word 'use' has to be interpreted differently by different people. I mean them to be functional.
>
> What am I doing? I'm taking 'raw' materials – clays, rocks, minerals – and I'm putting them together to make clay bodies, colours, slips and washes. I try to keep these technical aspects with me when I think about the forming method – throwing – and the firing process – high fired salt glaze and often wood fired.
>
> Michael Cardew said it years ago. 'The materials and processes the potter uses are not a category separate and distinct from the expression the artist makes with them.' I read that in 1950. I was 25 and I did not understand it. Now with my own slight variations it is my creed.
>
> What else is there to say? What else would I wish to underline as being of importance to me? Yes, it must be something about the use of the senses. The physical sense of throwing, for me a wonderful amalgam of power and delicacy. The sense of touch on a pot, smooth or craggy; the

sense of sight – colour and visual texture (these are why salt is so good) and the sense of sound a pot makes when struck which tells much about form and materials and firing. Last but not least a sense of weight – apparently there is an African word that means 'good to pick up and feel right in the hand' – a good pot to lift. This speaks of form?

Any last thoughts? Yes, what do I want to do? I want to make pots that have that compelling significance that many 'old' pots have that were so much a part of life – I'll never do it of course but that's what I aspire to!

So strong is the urge to make things in the fashion that Mick Casson has described that it seems likely that making will endure in the teeth of its apparent cultural or technological irrelevance. For some people the method of exploring ideas through making is the best route to understanding those ideas or responding to a class of objects that already exist. For others there is the control provided by directing their life through their work and making a living from it. These two reasons often overlap. Regardless of the status of craft or 'the crafts' and regardless also of the apparent irrelevance of some crafts to mainstream culture, craft making is unlikely to disappear. It gives some individuals so much intellectual, imaginative and sensory pleasure to make things and acquire the complexities of know-how for themselves that craft making will continue even when the Turing Test for practical thinking has been satisfied in every conceivable craft discipline.

9 ✧ CADCAM
and the British ceramics tableware industry

NEAL FRENCH

Early in the nineteenth century, press-moulding replaced throwing as the main method for making ceramic holloware in the developing tableware and giftware industry. This brought the craft of modelling to the fore because the press-moulds were initially designed and made by craftsmen modellers, and later in the century designed by designers and then made by craftsmen.

Modelling has been an essential craft in the pottery industry, but since the early 1980s its importance has been diluted by the introduction of computer-aided design and computer-aided manufacture (CADCAM) systems. This chapter explores the implications of this change and the nature of the challenge posed by CADCAM to 'traditional' modelling skills.

However, although CADCAM is central to this chapter, it is only one element in a larger process of change in the industry. Other changes include the driving-out of hand-based craft skills in general by mechanisation and automation; another change concerns the way the evolution of style in ceramic design has become market-driven. This has led to what some people perceive as 'conservatism' or even 'timidity' in design.

In the 1960s the fine china companies began reducing their product ranges, introducing time and motion studies and organising themselves around the twin principles of 'ease of production' and 'perceived public demand'. These companies concentrated increasingly on mass markets where profit margins were small, competition fierce but the opportunities great.

They ranged themselves against large, efficient European, North American and Japanese firms who, by and large, were ten years ahead in terms of automation and efficiency. Craft processes were among the early casualties of rationalisation; this was a loss because these processes were flexible and allowed a great breadth of richness in the product ranges.

Pottery manufacturers that were once highly conscious and proud of their house style now focused on market research. Market research inevitably gave all companies the same advice, and with all using increasingly similar production methods there were bound to be fewer distinctive differences between competitors. Today there seems almost to be a desire for anonymity, a feeling that the only way one should be able to tell the origin of a piece of their china is by the back stamp.

This then is the background to the introduction of CADCAM but before discussing CADCAM I need to describe the nature of 'traditional' modelling and the relationship between the modelling shop and the design studio.

A hundred years of modelling

Before CADCAM, modelling methods were rooted in three basic techniques which had remained virtually unchanged for over 100 years. These were turning, profiling and hand modelling. The material used was usually plaster of Paris, although there were modelling shops which used clay or wood. All three techniques could be used in a very inventive way to create all manner of components.

For example, round shapes were turned on a lathe, or a machine known as a vertical whirler, from a cylinder of hard plaster. If a piece was to be fluted then it would first be turned as a plain, round shape and then fluted by hand. Regular oval shapes would be made on an oval jolley, a whirler with an eccentric spindle which, in combination with a stationary metal profile and a revolving block of half-set plaster, would produce elliptical shapes.

Irregular ovals, oblongs, diamond shapes and their like would be formed using a hand-held profile, which, as on the oval jolley, gave the vertical section. A block of soft plaster would be set on a base which gave the plan section. Spouts, handles, knobs and decorative modelling would be made by eye, either carved in plaster or modelled in clay. When all the components of a piece were modelled they were passed to the mould-making department.

159

Clearly the modeller was highly skilled and the skills ranged from the manual through to the manipulative, organisational and judgemental. Co-ordination between hand and eye was an essential skill and it was used with an extraordinary degree of precision. Consider, for example, that the modeller had to be capable of centring a model accurately to within hundredths of an inch on a revolving turntable or whirler by tapping the model by hand.

Modelling requires work on both positive and negative shapes. Moreover, complex shapes are arrived at by working backwards and forwards on a sequence of slowly developing models and moulds. This requires the modeller to be capable of thinking 'inside out'. Knowing how to sequence a piece of modelling and being able to decide which tasks should be done on the model and which in the mould are also crucial. Thus one may appreciate that the 'mechanical' skills of a modeller are also conceptual; it is an intelligent craft.

The modeller faces several complications in his work. For instance, clay shrinks when it is fired; worse still, it shrinks by different amounts according to the nature of the clay used, the temperature at which it is fired, and the method of its making. Now obviously, in many cases the size of a finished piece is important: cups, jugs and teapots have a specific capacity. Consequently the modeller has to be able to judge the size of his model to allow for the shrinkage of the clay at the right making method and give the correct capacity.

In essence, then, the modeller's skills are difficult to learn; the person must have an aptitude for the work. And although experience is a great teacher, the modeller can never let up his concentration and watchfulness.

Designers and modellers

Until the 1960s when many of the hundreds of small, ruggedly indepen-dent companies began to consolidate into larger companies, few factories employed designers. However, those that did employ designers had a set of procedures for generating design briefs for the design department which would then produce drawings of the required shapes from which the modeller would work. Companies without designers instructed the modeller in some other way.

The first task of the designer and modeller was to produce a response to the design brief in such a form that the company's executive could make a decision whether or not to proceed with the idea. Only when this hurdle was cleared would the modeller begin to make models for mould-making.

As one may imagine, a crucial part of this sequence of events was the transition from the designer's two-dimensional drawing to the three-dimensional model. The first attempts at an 'interpretation' by the modeller were usually unsatisfactory to the designer.

If the brief was for a complete range of tableware work would start by taking a key piece such as a teapot or a coffee-pot, because it was items such as these which most obviously expressed the character of the range. The designer would have a clear idea about the character of the shape and his or her drawings would have attempted to express this character as well as setting down factual and dimensional information. The designer and the modeller would also talk to one another about the design before attempting the first sketch model. But, of course, it is difficult to convey complex and subtle ideas about, say, tactility, and the first attempts at an 'interpretation' by the modeller were usually unsatisfactory to the designer. Further models would be made until a compromise was reached.

In other words, the designer would come to realise that while the first few attempts would show a gradual improvement, the law of diminishing returns would operate thereafter and the modeller's patience would become stretched.

These problems could be avoided by the designer learning how to model, but apart from the friction that this could cause, designers seldom had the time or the skill to go beyond lathe-turning and handle- and spout-carving. But styles change, and what was popular in the 1860s was long out of fashion in the 1960s. In the 1960s tableware shapes were round in section and simple in profile and therefore within the designer's abilities to model. Designers were thus able to work directly in three dimensions and fine-tune the shapes to their own satisfaction.

Designers did not have the power to say 'yes' or 'no' to production. Approval of the design lay with the company directors who were usually unskilled in 'reading' a drawing or a sketch model. To the uninitiated drawings do not convey three-dimensionality, and solid models with glued-on spouts, handles and knobs did little to convey to the layperson the visual or tactile qualities of finished glazed ware. And so, in order to convince the directors and help them make a decision on the best available evidence, the plaster sketch models would be hollowed out and painted to resemble as closely as possible the actual ware. Or if time and resources allowed, a key piece would be moulded, cast, fired and glazed. It was an enormous expenditure of time and effort.

Unsurprisingly, when CADCAM became practically and economically viable, the largest ceramic companies took notice.

CADCAM

Only the largest ceramic companies can currently operate CADCAM in house, although CADCAM facilities are offered as a service by specialist firms and smaller ceramic factories can rent time from them.

The 'idea to production' sequence for CADCAM is similar to that which relies on traditional design/modelling. The design department is given a brief and outline drawings of the proposed pieces are made. These are passed to the modelling department, and re-created on the computer on the visual display unit (VDU) using an 'object-oriented' drawing system. These plans and elevations are converted into three-dimensional drawings on screen. They look like three-dimensional wire models. Hence they are called 'wire models' even though they only exist in computer space.

It is possible to produce not only the body shape of, say, a teapot, but also its handle, spout, lid and knob, and for all of them to be assembled in a convincing relationship to one another in wire-model form on screen.

Wire models can be rotated, viewed from any angle, and modified in any way; this includes dimension, proportion, interval, angle and the character of the curves. The modeller and the designer have control over every aspect of the shape: there is no call for the time-consuming production of plaster models.

Wire models do not, however, look like the real thing, but advanced CAD systems now have rendering facilities that show the shapes in convincing three-dimensional form, complete with reflections and shadows.

Definitive shapes can be created quickly using the wire-modelling and rendering system and these on-screen simulations are easier to read than drawings or plaster models. They are also very persuasive. Decisions can be taken by the company's executive on the potential of any shape much earlier than would have been possible in the past.

Nevertheless, there is still a need for actual three dimensional models that one can hold in the hand, and here the technology of rapid prototyping comes into its own. This technology enables the designer to get a hollow sketch model of the design from the data held in the computer. The process is fully automated; no hands-on craftsmanship is required. The prototypes that are produced give a surface that is good enough to enable the designer to assess the ergonomic, functional and visual aspects of the shape before proceeding to the block moulding stage.

CADCAM also offers advantages in the final stage of modelling for mould-making. The data held in the computer can be fed directly to a milling machine which produces a wax model from which the block mould can be made. Moreover, the calculations necessary to take account of shrinkage in firing are simple to do on the computer. Thus CADCAM offers a relatively fast form of modelling that is faultlessly accurate and light on human labour.

Accuracy is as important as speed. Before the computer, much of a modeller's time would be taken up with changing the size and shape of models to cope with a different shrinkage caused by a change in making methods or eccentric shrinkage caused by the nature of the shape itself. Scaling up or down, or adjusting proportion is easy for a computer, but difficult for the modeller.

Digital and laser technology has brought both accuracy and speed to other aspects of the ceramic industry. For example, relief modelling, digitised on computer, can be brought up on screen where it can be enlarged, shrunk, stretched, made deeper or more shallow and finally transmitted to the milling machine which will produce the modified relief in whatever form is required. At the moment some final hand modelling is needed to sharpen up the detail and remove the milling marks. But the saving in time and hand-skilled labour is huge.

Finally, the CAD system is adept at showing tableware patterns wrapped around appropriate holloware: positions, proportions and ways of using the decoration can be readily manipulated and weeks of arduous work are avoided.

Comparisons

Before the computer (BC?) it took two years to develop a tableware range; now it takes twelve weeks. So CADCAM provides speed. But what are the advantages of this speed? After all, there are only just so many new tableware ranges that the market-place can accommodate. Moreover, compressing the development time into twelve weeks also entails a compression of thinking time: it allows the modeller and designer much less opportunity to reflect upon what they are creating. When time is of the essence the best becomes the enemy of the good and the quest for the 'perfect' shape must be curtailed.

Traditional modelling is the slowest part of ceramic product development and the time it takes has irritated company directors and sales managers alike who want to respond quickly to market needs and changes. New products are wanted immediately in order to steal a march on rivals. CADCAM offers this quickness of response.

As it happens, this quickness of response is less to do with the introduction of whole new ranges, but rather remodelling of existing shapes where, for example, instant correction of faults on current ware is needed to keep the production-line going. And in decorative ware and giftware, the changes in market demand are frequent and sudden and, once again, CADCAM is invaluable because of its quickness and accuracy.

Where the consolidation of small potteries into larger groupings has led to one design and modelling shop serving several factories, CADCAM makes it possible for this shop to cope with the greatly increased workload.

So quickness is one considerable difference between the old and the new in design and modelling. There is, however, an equally considerable but less obvious difference between the two approaches: one relies heavily on hand drawing and real three-dimensional modelling, the other does not. For although one 'draws' on screen, it is a different way of drawing to that of pencil and paper, and although the CAD and rapid prototyping processes offer three-dimensionality, in practice CAD is used to work in two dimensions rather than three. Does this matter?

Here we enter a debate which is difficult to resolve and it relies on opinion, taste and connoisseurship – on both sides.

The traditional approach, as has been discussed, was slower and a good deal less accurate than the new, but it allowed a certain liveliness to enter into the design and modelling process. For example, the drawings that preceded the modelling *sometimes* took the form of measured elevations, but, as often as not, they were lively freehand sketches intended to show the character of the piece. Even the measured drawings sometimes showed this vitality, and this affected the way the modeller interpreted the drawing. And if the modeller was good then he too made a contribution because what he was doing was an act of *interpretation*.

Drawings made on the computer seem to lack the spontaneity of hand drawing even if they are created with a stylus rather than a mouse. There is inevitably a difference between hand drawing and computer drawing because the computer does not create drawings in a manner that is analogous to the method used by a human being.

CADCAM uses what is known as an 'object-oriented' system of drawing: here a line is expressed by a number of points and the angle of the line to the vertical at each of these points. The line is controlled by varying the intervals between the points and the angles, and the curves between are governed by formulae. Since the profile line determines everything about the computer modelling then something of this lack of vitality is likely to transmit itself to the quality of the final product.

We need to think a little about what 'quality' in a piece of tableware means. There is the feel and function of a piece, there is the look of a piece, and there is the question of 'truth to material'.

Feel and function involves how comfortable a piece is to use. Is the handle an effective lever for lifting the cup? Is it suitable for holding the cup to the lips? Does the teapot's spout pour well?

Then there is the appearance of a piece. Do the components relate happily together, and does a single piece of work have the look of an integrated, satisfying 'abstract' sculpture? Does that single piece relate well to the other pieces in the range?

Finally, there is the matter of clay. Ceramic ware, however produced, is made from clay. It ought to show this and not look as if it is made from some other material such as metal or plastic.

Regarding these three elements there are both advantages and disadvantages on both sides of the CADCAM versus 'traditional' debate. A wire model on a computer will not provide sufficient tactile information about the feel and function of a handle; a plaster model will. On the other hand, rapid prototyping will produce models that will compete with plaster ones; the trouble is that rapid prototyping is only used a long way down the process of design, and radical changes may then be uneconomic – it may be easier and quicker to compromise.

Regarding appearance, however, a fully rendered three-dimensional model on screen that can be viewed from any angle can give you all the visual information you need to make a decision to proceed to production.

But in considering that elusive 'clay' quality it should be said that neither plaster models, nor wire or fully rendered models can capture the texture, vitality and uniqueness of clay. A sensitivity to clay and its qualities has to be acquired by the individual modeller, be he or she a traditionalist or a computer specialist. It may be just that bit harder for someone whose experience is exclusively computer-orientated to acquire that sensitivity.

Yet, weighing all things in the balance, it seems that CADCAM has to be the future for the ceramics industry, except that factories with CADCAM still run traditional modelling shops using clay and plaster. This is because CADCAM is expensive and it makes sense to use it on the complex jobs, leaving the simpler modelling jobs to other methods. Not all tasks can be done using new technology. For example, as discussed earlier, using digital technology it is easy to modify and alter relief modelling but the *initial* modelling has to be done by hand.

Running traditional and CADCAM workshops together allows interaction of information between the two modelling methods. One chief modeller in charge of CADCAM believes that experience in plaster modelling is necessary before a modeller can use the potential of the computer. This is not necessarily nostalgia, but a recognition that perhaps one needs to learn to think in three dimensions in the real world before one can get the best out of the computer's 'virtual' world.

Inferences and implications

The craft of pottery modelling will undoubtedly change: there will be fewer modellers skilled in using plaster. And there are some crafts whose demise is to be welcomed, not least because they were deadly boring for the modeller. But not all the 'traditional' crafts will disappear. There are two reasons: CADCAM is, and will probably remain, expensive and some potteries will have to rely on hand modellin; secondly, there are kinds of modelling that CADCAM cannot do.

There are very obvious distinctions between the two technologies, but the intriguing question is what, conceptually, distinguishes computer skills from handcraft skills? There is one answer and that is there are no limitations to the kinds of shape that can be produced on the computer. This licence or freedom to be creative is a liberation for the designer/modeller tempered only by the knowledge, awareness and creativity of the operator. There are limitations to CAD modelling that I mentioned above relating to the quality of line and its effect upon the final product; there are limitations also regarding how much tactile information CAD and rapid prototyping provides. But it is probable that these deficiencies will be corrected in the next generation of CAD – if, that is, there is a client recognition and hence demand for correcting such deficiencies.

The irony is that, at least currently, most manufacturers do not want to use the creative potential of CAD; they are using CADCAM as a slave to model inoffensive, undemanding shapes that are easy to decorate. To break this stylistic monotony it is necessary for shape designers to work with computer modellers to explore together what the computer can do. CAD should be capable of producing exciting shapes unobtainable by the old methods; at the moment it is not doing so. But whether or not both designers and computer modellers should have some experience of real, hands-on modelling in clay and plaster in order to aid them in their creative control over the computer is a very interesting and moot point. It is still being debated.

10 ✧ *Textiles and technology*

PETER DORMER

Of the craft areas, textiles, especially woven cloth, is most at ease with the demands of technology and design of contemporary Western culture. Craft textiles are arguably not only the least marginal of the crafts but have a centrality unique among crafts. There are two broad reasons for this: one rests in the basic technology of textile craft, the other resides in the continuity that exists between the 'craftsperson', 'production designer', 'amateur' and the 'professional'.

There is a fluidity in the practice, design and art of woven textiles that enables textiles to fit easily with contemporary technology. A textile maker or designer who works at a small craft-shop level producing one-off pieces can, from the same conceptual base and using the same equipment, produce samples that industry can convert without fuss for factory production.

Textiles are at the centre of several mainstream areas of contemporary material culture and research. Woven structures feature in the design and construction of military aircraft; they have been central to the search for new products for the petro-chemical industry; and new forms of engineering, based on tension structures familiar to weavers, have been used to develop new forms of architecture, especially sports stadiums.

Finally there is a natural affinity between weaving and mathematics, and the loom and the digital computer.

Although the fortunes of hand-weaving have vacillated in Britain since the First World War, worldwide the twentieth century has seen handcraft and industrial craft more often than not working together. In the 1930s Ethel Mairet, a twentieth-century pioneer in making links between hand-weaving and textiles, wrote of the work by Scandinavian weavers in experimenting with the new fibres then being introduced by the chemical industry. Many Scandinavian designers left Europe to settle in America and some of them obtained work as teachers or instructors at Cranbrook Academy of Art. As a result Cranbrook became a leader in textile craft, design and art.

In the 1940s, a generation of American students, building on the knowledge of their European mentors, quickly made the connection between experimentation, 'art' and industry in textiles. In the late 1940s Robert D. Sailors, a Cranbrook graduate, began working with woven textures and structures. He wove together anything that could be woven and was especially drawn to the interplay of contradictory materials: Cellophane and paper or wool and metal gauze. In 1950 his experiments bore fruit in his successful range of furnishing fabrics for industry that had delicate, complex textures. For example, Sailors combined rayon warp and a lurex weft because such a structure used light to make the surface shimmer.

The apparent ease with which textile craftspeople and designers use new materials is notable. It is a tradition within the craft that contradictory or complementary materials be woven together. For example, Ann Sutton and Diane Sheehan's book *Ideas in Weaving* (London, Batsford, 1989) shows a sample of sixteenth-century brocade with a paper strip weft from Japan and a sample of cut and uncut velvet of metal and silk from fifteenth-century Italy.

But then the nature of *weaving* encourages a natural incorporation of diverse materials. Indeed the term 'weaving' and the activity it represents is often used as a metaphor for the combining of disparate materials or ideas. Not for nothing have the workings of the human brain been described as 'weaving' and the brain itself been called 'the magic loom'.

Nevertheless, the aesthetic incorporation of new materials took time to get right. Ethel Mairet wrote in her book *Hand Weaving Today* (London, Faber & Faber, 1939),

> Synthetic yarns are dangerous to play with. They can be used in an utterly unaesthetic way more easily than any other yarns. They can deceive and be pretentious, they can go very far wrong in colour and texture. They are very easy to use and because of this they need the greater artist to use them. (pp. 76–7)

169

Other crafts have incorporated new materials but with less ease and less consistent success. In jewellery in the late 1960s onwards there were many attempts to use acrylics as a replacement for precious metal and stone. For a long while the use of these materials was unsophisticated. Much of the avant-garde jewellery in Britain, the Netherlands and the USA during the 1970s used acrylics, rubber, found objects and industrial debris in an obvious manner: merely tying the stuff together and hanging it round the neck, wrist or waist. The material itself was often left unworked.

Designers and artists have found it even harder to embrace new materials in other crafts. In furniture-making the main material remains timber, and in pottery, although the chemical industry has contributed ready-made glazes to the potters' studios, no place has been found in these workshops for the new, high-performance ceramic materials used in engineering.

Then there is the relationship with the computer. The small-scale or studio jeweller, potter, glass- or furniture-maker has a struggle with the computer because as yet the *link* between the design process and the manufacturing process is either expensive to computerise or it is technically unfeasible (for the moment). The potter cannot currently go from her Apple Mac to the finished pot in a seamless, computerised hands-off process (assuming that is what she *wants* to do). Woven textiles are different. For example, the British weaver Ann Sutton links a basic Apple Mac to her loom to produce samples of what she designs on computer.

Chloe Colchester, author of *The New Textiles* (London, Thames & Hudson, 1991), observed:

> There is a neat, circular logic to using digital computers to design woven cloth, given that electronic digital processing in the 1940s was originally developed from punch cards that had themselves been designed to manipulate threads in Jaquard weaving in the very early 19th century. [Joseph-Marie Jacquard introduced his revolutionary loom in France in 1805.] (unpublished essay, 1995)

The interconnectedness between craft and high technology in woven textiles has been pursued by some practitioners with zeal. One such person is the Japanese designer and craftsman Junichi Arai. Chloe Colchester comments,

> Arai's story is interesting because the fabrics that result from his industrial

collaborations are fabulous and inspiring, and because his story has become a contemporary legend which encapsulates the Post-Modern fantasy that computer technologies will ensure the continuity of a regionally specific artisanal heritage whilst linking it to new developments in synthetics. (*ibid.*)

Junichi Arai, born in 1932, has made the handcraft/traditional craft/new design/new technology link appear stylish (as well as natural). Arai's textiles are used by fashion designers such as Issey Miyake, and such fashionable connections secure a high profile and an acceptable provenance for the craft.

Arai's father was a weaver, his grandfather was a spinner, and Arai grew up in Kiryu, a small town north of Tokyo which is a centre of Japanese craft weaving and jacquard weaving in particular. Arai's awareness of the potential of these processes led him to enlist computers into the process in order to produce more complex jacquard punch-cards than were used traditionally. At the same time Arai has also introduced elements of risk and chance into his designs by, for example, destabilising the structures of the woven textiles. Colchester explains in *The New Textiles*, 'All woven fabrics are tension structures of a sort ... Arai's designs are based on destabilising fabrics and releasing rather than controlling tension.'

Colchester thinks that rather than making designs for manufacture, Arai designs *with* the many manufacturing processes employed by craft-based producers. He also involves the skills and knowledge of people who specialise in synthetic materials and those whose work is centred upon *finishing* textiles – a discipline in its own right.

There is a conceptual core to woven textiles based on the physical structure of weaving that holds the elements of craft, art, design and manufacturing together in a unity: woven structures and woven designs are based on rule-directed processes. The unity provided by these rules encourages rather than closes down innovation; and, indeed, the sense of the 'capricious', so dear to the modern conception of creativity, is only visible against the background of rules (see also, for example, modern dance or listen to free jazz). It is because all the creative possibilities are played with or against a common collection of rules, and also because these rules can be used and played with using our most advanced technology, that there is a continuity of thought between the most basic and the most sophisticated of looms. Computers and looms share a similar class of rules. The craftsperson can play merry hell with these rules in the search for new ideas and she or he can do it at any level of weaving technology.

All crafts possess rules although, with the probable exception of lettering, in no craft other than woven textiles are the rules so transparent or so easy to clarify. In ceramics, for example, there are rules that guide processes but they are not easily clarified – they do not form a 'choreography'.

The book *Ideas in Weaving* by Ann Sutton and Diane Sheehan makes the rule-orientated, conceptual core quite clear. The book demonstrates how numerous are the possibilities for innovation. The authors observe that, very broadly, we in the West have divided thinking into two schools: Classical, which relies on reason, logic and order, and Romantic, which relies on intuition and emotion. Sutton and Sheehan believe that woven works require a classical approach. Both authors believe that weaving attracts those whose affinity is for logic and restraint. They explain that those textile artists who have sought to make more organic, perhaps 'sculptural' textiles of a non-functional kind, have found it necessary to work off the loom (to rid themselves of all the rules).

One chapter in *Ideas in Weaving* is called 'Using Chance' and it introduces the idea of 'The Design Game'. It reads like an analogy of those computer experiments which demonstrate how complexity arises from simple conditions. This educational game has seven categories: technique, colour, yarn, fibre, finishing, general design and weave. In each category there are up to thirty possibilities. By writing each of these possibilities on to separate cards, shuffling these and playing the game like Pontoon or Blackjack many design combinations are thrown up. Not all the combinations make sense because they give rise to impossible fabrics, but the game is a good way of exploring the conceptual and structural base of woven textiles.

On the other hand one can throw such games of reason and chance to the wind, adopt the Arai approach and devise briefs for oneself or others such as 'make a textile that is like a cloud or like poison'.

In considering the centrality of woven textile craft to contemporary culture it is important not to overlook the 'amateur' who, whilst not producing cloth, uses cloth to make clothes for the family or furnishings for the home. (The term 'amateur' here is used in the sense of 'without payment'.) The tradition of textiles as a domestic design and craft activity has continued in the twentieth century in spite of the competition offered by the manufacturers and retailers of good clothing. Domestic textile craft has been bolstered, rather than usurped, by advances in technology: thus the current generation of electronic knitting or sewing machines for the home market are sophisticated and programmable and enable the amateur to do more things than she (or he) would otherwise have the time or the ability to produce. (Semi-computerised knitting or sewing machines are good examples of the concept of 'distributed knowledge' replacing or enhancing personal knowledge – see chapter 8.)

With the exception of 'Do-it-Yourself' (an industry for the amateur maker which began in Britain in the mid-1950s and which is wholly led by the development of new technology and new materials), no craft other than textiles has such a widespread domestic presence. A few people make furniture for their homes but very few would make glassware, crockery, cutlery or any of the other staple tools of domestic life. The technology is not amenable for domestic use and also, whilst the home producer of clothing can match the quality of the factory product, the home producer in other crafts cannot.

There is also another strand of continuity between the domestic making of textile items and the highest level of professionally designed clothing. For instance, anyone so inclined can buy patterns and instructions for a design, say, by Issey Miyake, and make it up for themselves. Such continuity is rare between the amateur and the professional in other crafts, although sometimes the amateur woodcraft or furniture craft magazines do commission well-known designers to produce designs for their readers.

All-in-all the status and centrality of craft textiles in terms of design and utility cannot reasonably be queried but there is an uncertainty among art critics, contemporary art curators and others of this ilk about the status of textile art, some of which is woven and some of it fabricated, printed or embroidered. Yet this uncertainty about status is not necessarily felt by the practitioners themselves.

For example, in the USA there is a society called The Surface Design Association which publishes a quarterly journal called *Surface*. In Volume 20, No. 3(1966) of this publication, which is devoted to the 'art quilt', the editorial asserts that the arrival of the 'art quilt' as an art form at home in galleries and museums is a *fait accompli*. This is an interesting claim, especially from a European perspective, where few of the prestigious contemporary art museums consider themselves to be a home for quilts or any other kind of textile art.

That there is a large art textile or Fiber Art movement, as it is known in the USA, is beyond question and this movement, looked at impartially, has a family resemblance to most other contemporary visual art practices. That is to say there is a great concern about 'meaning' and about how the work of the textile artist is written about and evaluated. For example, in the art-quilt issue of *Surface* it was interesting to see articles with titles such as 'Beyond Aesthetics' or 'Material Matters: Three Artists Look Beyond Fabric for Meaning'. The work discussed deals with issues as diverse as 'race' and the 'superiority of the hand over technology' – this latter issue is sometimes expressed as a female/male opposition. As an example of how such an issue is discussed, here, from the review in *Surface*, is a description and interpretation of a mixed-media quilt:

> Over the course of a year, the relative visual importance of the compo-nents has shifted: the faxes – men's work – have faded, allowing the women's red marks to become more prominent. The meaning, however, extends beyond visual fact. What also are set against each other, on a subliminal level, are the non-material immediacy of the faxing process, a parallel to the flash of intellect, and the time-consuming process of making marks by hand, which has the final say. (p. 2)

In essence, contemporary art textiles share two dominant strategies with other areas of visual-art practice, namely an interest in exploring visual metaphor in order to make comment upon or allude to social or political issues, and an interest in using textile art to comment on the nature of the art itself.

However, what differentiates art textiles from other forms of visual art practice is the use of craft as a medium for creating meaning. Craft – handmaking – is not important in other art practices. This difference is one of the features that accounts for some of art textiles' energy but it is also its undoing. For craft is not an issue of debate in the art world as a whole: craft simply does not figure in the art magazines or the serious art reviews in newspapers as a subject to discuss.

This is a great pity. Textile practitioners have not only not renounced handwork or craft as a means of making art, they positively explore and exploit that craft. There is therefore a genuine opposition between much textile art and other forms of 'conceptualised' art that ought to be the focus of general art debate and attention – but it isn't. For wherever one cares to dip into a current 'fine art' magazine or visit a 'fine art' museum – in Europe at any rate – or looks at any of the books or television documentaries that essay a history of contemporary art, textiles are not there; their *craft* argument is absent. This absence is intellectually perverse but it remains real. The claim that *Surface* magazine makes of a *fait accompli* is surely disingenuous? Art textiles are not yet 'at home' in the wider art debate.

However, this exclusion may not be too important because the 'wider art debate' itself is not seen by everyone as central to contemporary culture. More to the point, the number of people who are interested in all textiles is in itself large. It is confirmed by curators of textile exhibitions that any textile show – be it of historical works, contemporary design or avant-garde art – is well attended and that the viewers tend to be both knowledgeable and catholic in their tastes. More women than men look at textiles and they form an audience of connoisseurs. Consequently, a large part of the population feels no uncertainty about viewing textiles as art (or craft or design). The uncertainty rests with others elsewhere.

These 'others' (not all of them are men) are those who feel themselves to be the leaders or at least the guardians of a certain way of looking at, talking about and selecting contemporary art. They could be ignored by textile artists were it not for one thing: textile artists, like most artists, want to get their work shown. Moreover, they want it presented with proper space, lighting and professional presentation. These facilities are found mostly in the fine art galleries and museums. In Europe, at any rate, these spaces are not run by people with a welcoming attitude towards textiles. This lack of access to public exhibition space is frustrating to the artists and, given the audience for their work, may be regarded as undemocratic.

JEREMY MYERSON

Hollywood, early 1996. Executives of Warner Brothers are awaiting word on the progress of a major new film being directed by the Dutchman Jan de Bont. Its title is *Twister* and its subject is the tornadoes of the American Midwest. As the background rushes come in from Oklahoma, where filming is taking place, they are sent directly to a young British art director in a northern Californian special-effects studio whose job it is to design the dark, swirling eye of the hurricane entirely on computer. This is a creative project which will make or break the movie, as this is a film without major box-office stars.

I make no apology for starting this essay in Hollywood. As more and more people suggest that virtual computer-based design is the new craft of the late twentieth century, the dream factory of the American film industry is the obvious – indeed the *only* – place to start to test the proposition.

The young art director is Guy Dyas and his employer is Industrial Light and Magic, the world-renowned special-effects studio established by George Lucas who directed Star Wars. There are few places on earth more keenly in touch with the influence of the computer on our design sensibilities and cultural expectations than Industrial Light and Magic, which created the computer-generated dinosaurs in Jurassic Park and made them utterly believable. Every day Guy Dyas sits down at his computer and uses the Photoshop graphics software programme to create the clouds, chaos, debris and falling masonry that will signal the destructive impact of a tornado on newly-minted background plates sent from Oklahoma.

To create the right look for the tornado, Dyas has been studying reams of amateur footage of this mysterious meteorological phenomenon. A weather expert has also been invited in to give advice. *Twister*, released in Britain in summer 1996, tells the chilling story of a group of weird Midwestern 'geeks' who chase around after tornadoes with homemade weather instruments – and the disastrous consequences which follow. 'My role is to convey the mystery of the tornado, to let the cinemagoer see right up into its eye', explains Dyas.[1] Like the dinosaurs roaming around *Jurassic Park*, live footage is out of the question. Creative and effective computer simulation will be the only thing that counts in turning the screenwriter's ideas into a commercially-exploitable form of 'reality'.

Guy Dyas is a product of neither film school nor computer science. He is an industrial designer, a graduate of Chelsea Art College, London, and the Royal College of Art, who trained in the traditional way as a designer, bending metal, shaving wood, building models and prototypes in the workshop. Such skills were good enough to take him to Sony's design department in Tokyo for a couple of years, after such powerful RCA student projects as a vacuum cleaner shaped like a demon king (with glowing red eyes that light up when the machine is switched on) and a circular bubble-top microwave oven brought him to international attention. From Sony, Dyas crossed the Pacific to enter the virtual world of Industrial Light and Magic, but he is emphatic that the computer-based creativity of *Twister* relies entirely on the virtues of his previous design background. 'I see a lot of people using the graphic tools of Photoshop and Freehand on computer', says Dyas.

> Those without a traditional design background don't do as well as those with one. People who can draw well do better on Photoshop. It may sound simplistic but in terms of lighting, colour and composition, the basic studio and workshop skills of rendering and model-making, working with line and materials, make all the difference.

Aged twenty-seven, Guy Dyas can hardly be put in the category of those middle-aged typographers who dismiss the new generation of Apple Mac-based designers because they haven't handled hot-metal type. With a seat at the table of George Lucas, who is planning a futuristic new *Star Wars* trilogy, he is as close to the leading edge as it is possible to be. And yet he insists that using a computer is not a craft in itself, it is a utilisation of a tool, no matter how creative the outcome; the real skill in utilising that tool is derived from traditional design knowledge.

177

Such a seemingly reactionary observation from a young art director, at a time of increasingly ubiquitous technology, will be reassuring to those British design educationalists who have long fought a rearguard action to protect the traditional studio environment and workshop practice from the modernisers and streamliners of the new universities, for whom the accelerating use of the computer as a design tool has become a convenient excuse to shut down expensive craft workshops and sack hands-on technicians.

At the start of this decade, a major UK study[2] of the effects of technological change on industrial and product design courses in higher education concluded that although computing had become part of a technological 'core' of course content, this was in addition to – not as a replacement for – more traditional subject areas. The potential of the computer as an organisational and presentation tool, and the growing importance of two-dimensional draughting, three-dimensional modelling and design, and computer-aided design and manufacture (CADCAM), were all duly given recognition – but not at the expense of other factors commonly understood to mould the contemporary designer.

The study, commissioned by Britain's Council for National Academic Awards, identified a technological core under five main headings, one of which was materials and another of which was workshop practice; processes, human factors and computing made up the core. The defence of workshop practice, under attack for appearing anachronistic in the 1990s, raised strong emotions. Teaching staff argued that whilst workshop machinery no longer enabled students to simulate the increasingly sophisticated manufacturing process (except in such instances as batch-produced furniture), workshop practice and model-making skills were taking on another role – as part of the exploratory design process, providing an insight into form, shape and materials, and assisting in problem-solving and decision-making.

As one head of department described it,

> We know our students won't physically make things when they leave … but their decisions will be based on the experience of making things and they'll know what's good, bad and indifferent. For instance, you know precisely how metal bends when you've actually bent it yourself.[3]

He was talking about the act of specification as a designer, as opposed to making an object as a craftsperson, but he could just as easily have been talking about the act of virtual design on computer.

This lack of a tactile or physical encounter with materials as the basis for decision-making in design is cited by many as a reason why computing cannot yet be regarded as a craft in its own right. Even on the Royal College of Art's Computer-Related Design course – which is widely regarded as an educational flagship in exploring the new technologies of computing, electronics and telecommunications – course director Professor Gillian Crampton Smith has some serious reservations about computers in their current form. She is also a somewhat unlikely supporter of the basic know-how-it-feels workshop idea.

'I'm actually a believer in people learning how to draw type', she explains.

> I taught myself the basic construction of letterforms. We've not got time to do that with our students at the RCA, but it is a good thing because it gives you a different perspective. That is why I have some sympathy with the workshop argument about experience through prototyping. I am deeply sceptical about the computers that we currently use. With the computer, you have to envisage what you want it to do. You can't 'work into' your material in the same way as with traditional design methods. The computer always responds, offers options and alternatives, and it stops you thinking things through. We're all lazy so we try different options instead of working it out. And there is always the same level of finish on computer, whereas sketches are more suggestive of different possibilities.

These observations are borne out by a piece of research carried out by Alison Black, a psychologist with a special interest in cognitive ergonomics and information design, while research fellow in the Department of Typography and Graphic Communication at the University of Reading. Black studied a group of novice typographers working on screen and on paper in the studio. Those relying on the computer felt better about it while doing it and generally thought they were doing well. But on reflection afterwards, they were dissatisfied. Those not working on the computer experienced more of a struggle but felt more pleased with the results later. According to Black, 'Students had been deflected from thinking about the design problem fully by the finished veneer of the solutions that they had produced on screen.'

Alison Black and Gillian Crampton Smith are both prominent figures in the current surge of interest in the discipline of interface or interaction design. Crampton Smith describes six key iterative stages in designing a computer interface: research; observation of people; concept development (what it should do and be); how it should be represented to the user; detailed design; and evaluation. Only the fifth stage – detailed design of the surface which the user perceives – does she describe as a craft. 'Of course, it is more cerebral, it is more disembodied, but it is a craft the same as any other', she explains.

> If you are making jewellery, you can instinctively scratch a nice surface. On the computer, you have to decide and do it. There is a lot of selecting and deciding, rather than moulding. Traditionally, designers worked with head, hand and heart. On computer, the hand is less important.

Restricted scope for the kinaesthetic and tactile sensitivity of hand skills on the computer is what makes the new technology so frustrating for so many designers, especially those with craft leanings. Gillian Crampton Smith recognises this:

> It is difficult to catch ideas on computer the way you sketch notes to yourself – a pencil in the hand is like an extension of the brain. But at the moment the computer mouse can't be like that. You can't luxuriate in a material like you do in shaping clay or bending wood. You have to stop thinking to click on an icon or piece of text and it interrupts your creative flow.

That viewpoint finds echoes in others who want the computer interface to be more organic, intuitive and human – and less mechanistic. According to Nicholas Negraponte, the founder of MediaLab at MIT and the author of *Being Digital* (London, Hodder & Stoughton, 1995), computers won't really progress in creative terms until they get beyond point-and-press functions and start to integrate human skills. Negraponte, who raised the money for *Wired* magazine, envisages a digital near-future of gloves and clothing embedded with sensors. These will make computers less like plug-in boxes and more like biological extensions of the user. One can immediately see an enhanced role for the computer in both the self-expression of art and the human factors of industrial design.

Negraponte's message is that designing on computer is not yet a craft, but computers could move a lot closer to the conditions in which a craft could be developed.

Amid visions such as these, a key objective of the Computer-Related Design course at the RCA is not just to refine the use of computers as a design tool but to redesign the computers themselves. Professor Crampton Smith explains: 'The course began five years ago as part of industrial design and a key starting point was: why is working with computers so horrid? By not being passive towards the computer, we knew we could make it better.' As an example, she describes her efforts to design a graphics layout programme using the left hand, leaving the right hand free as if you had a sketching pencil in it. 'We need more "playing the piano" in computing', she suggests.

> At the moment programmes are designed for everyone to use. But there should be programmes for virtuoso players. There are parallels with playing a musical instrument so that it takes you a long time to learn and practise and get there, but when you play you don't think about it.

The RCA Computer-Related Design course takes ten postgraduate students a year into its laboratories, plus a handful of Ph.D. researchers. Staff and students come from a variety of different disciplines, including architecture, software engineering, music, product design, graphic design, fine art and electronic engineering. The course is project-based, with a highly-structured first term devoted to short week-long projects which explore a range of interaction 'languages': three-dimensional form, sound, movement, space, graphic image and film. Thereafter projects become lengthier and more complex, involving a range of external companies at the leading age of the new technologies.

Significantly students create things on paper, solder pieces of metal and build installations in space as well as work on screen – although the ultimate results are computer-related. They also study the broader cultural effects of technology in a democratic society. They go on placements and find jobs in such high-tech corporations as Apple, Philips and Microsoft, in design consultancies such as IDEO, and in entertainment companies such as the Geffen–Spielberg outfit, Dreamworks. 'The language of film design can be applied to interactive IT products of all kinds', insists Crampton Smith.

If there is any sense of using computer technology as a new craft, then it is only in a very thin slice of the activity. 'In one sense, we are crafting the user experience, which is why we should draw so much from the language of film', suggests Gillian Crampton Smith. 'But it is mental craft, not a hand craft. One of our student projects is to redesign the calculator on the Apple computer and it is exactly like crafting graphic design.'

Bill Moggridge, a pioneer of interface design, takes another perspective. He is a founding director of IDEO, the international design and engineering consultancy, and a Visiting Professor in the RCA's School of Design for Industry where the Computer-Related Design course is based. 'If the nature of craft', he explains, 'is that in the process of designing something, you produce an object, then a multimedia design for CD-ROM is a craft but interaction design is not.'

Whether you can discuss designing on computer in the same context as older design methods is a moot point, even though thus far the computer as a tool has mainly been a much faster extension of what has been done before – tasks such as lettering and preparing artwork for print. 'One can imagine the Internet as basically a long strip of paper', says Gillian Crampton Smith in reference to the idea of the computer as a communications medium and not just a communications tool. But it is clear that a new generation of graphic designers schooled entirely in digital techniques would take little comfort or meaning from such an analogy, and would see little relevance in applying the traditional notion of craft to their work.

Me Company is an entirely digital design studio based in London and run by two young designers, Alistair Beattie and Paul White. Their work for such clients as the pop star Bjork and the running-shoe company Nike is visually arresting, what one might call 'computer baroque'. It is overt in its use of three-dimensional modelling and scanned and manipulated computer images. If 'craft' means the practical application of a skill, says the partners in Me Company, then computing is a contemporary craft. Certainly the computer is a means of realising all their thoughts and experiences – there is no design 'process' prior to going on screen – but they are hesitant to ascribe a significance to this craft. 'The craft of designers in our markets is to create compelling images', explains Alistair Beattie. 'For us, the computer is a favoured tool but we wouldn't want to draw any conclusions in relation to our own work or anyone else's.'

The feeling among Me Company and their peers is that new technology makes the creation of new typography and imagery inevitable. Young designers will always push the creative boundaries of the computer because 'it would be profoundly boring not to', says Beattie. More pertinently, however, there is the critical issue of the time it takes to do things, a point raised by Katherine McCoy, the American graphic designer who trained many young designers during her years running the innovative design department at Cranbrook Academy of Art near Detroit. McCoy believes that those with previous experience of hand-drawing may have a more intimate knowledge of type but would face great sacrifices if they eschewed today's technologies.

She also believes the Apple Mac is greatly underestimated as an introductory type-teaching tool. 'Every tiny nuance becomes *instantly* visible, with no waiting required', she explains.

> Conceptualising and experimentation becomes genuinely possible much sooner. New forms become more possible. This is not better or worse than the slower, more intimate method of typography, just its evolution. What both methods are fulfilling is the fundamental human urge to make things.

If the urge to make things is essentially a craft activity, then for McCoy the wordprocessing of a letter on a computer is as much a craft as designing a poster on one. For her, any communication that displays 'intentionality' is connected with craft. To the argument that information is manipulated and transferred around Net and Web without any end product, she quotes Charles Eames on the lines that, just because computers number-crunch, this does not discount what they can effect. Bits connect to form data which connect to form information which connects to create communication. In this context, even the effect of the wordprocessor on writing skills and language is relevant to the idea of craft as involving the change of matter from one form to another.

The computer has already realised at least some of its potential to transform matter swiftly and dramatically. 'There are now people so fluent with Photoshop', says Gillian Crampton Smith, 'that they don't have to think about what they're doing, it is their medium, and they get exactly the same sensation as a potter or woodcarver. It is possible to learn to do things in different ways, to challenge the computer without relying on a traditional design background.' Yet there is also a great resistance to these digital tools taking over the terrain of design thinking entirely. In television channel identity, where computer animation created all those mindless revolving globes and flying girders we see on our television screens every night, it is ironic that the most influential design in Britain of the 1980s – the computer-generated ident for British television's Channel 4 – has been replaced as the state of the art by the witty and humanistic ident for BBC 2, a figure made of balsa wood and splattered with paint, among other things.

Both the Channel 4 and BBC 2 identities are the work of the same designer, Martin Lambie-Nairn, the most experienced design consultant working in British television today. He produced the award-winning Channel 4 identity in 1982 at a time when computer graphics was still in its infancy; he was forced to go to Los Angeles and to the makers of the movie *Tron* to source the solid-modelling technique he required to make his design idea work. By the time Lambie-Nairn worked on BBC 2's new onscreen identity nearly a decade later, computer graphics had lost its novelty and had become just another technique. Live-action filming and traditional model-making were back in vogue. In any case Lambie-Nairn, who received a traditional training in design skills as a teenager at Canterbury School of Art and in the BBC graphic design department, had never been seduced by the computer. He had always regarded it as a means to an end, and because of union restrictions on who twiddled which knobs in television, he had never really learnt how to use one. Lambie-Nairn recalls:

> On Channel 4, it didn't matter to me in the slightest whether what we were doing was technologically state of the art or not. That was because the technology itself didn't matter. What mattered was that I was developing a design idea – and the tool was simply there to express it. That has always been my motto.

According to computer graphics pioneer John Vince, who first introduced Martin Lambie-Nairn to the computer at Middlesex Polytechnic in the late 1970s, 'What I think the computer did was release his imagination. It enabled him to go into fantasy worlds and create things that would have been impossible to do using any other tool or technique.' Lambie-Nairn's famous unwillingness to accept the limitations of the computer and his powerful desire to challenge its conventions certainly resulted in some spectacular work in television advertising. Yet the British designer once more closely associated with computer graphics than any other has distanced himself from a genre he regards not as a craft but as a tool – and an over-used one at that.

There is nothing in Martin Lambie-Nairn's experiences with the computer to suggest the craft fulfilment he experienced in painting Chinese willow patterns on to plates at art college or cutting out cardboard captions at the BBC. Clearly, for most designers, working on computer lacks the intuitive flow of ideas inherent in, say, silversmithing or furniture-making. 'You really need to sketch and model and decide what you want to do *before* you go on screen', says Gillian Crampton Smith of the RCA. And yet there is a creative dimension to realising an idea that cannot be realised using any other means, whether that idea is to create a Tyrannosaurus Rex chasing a carload of tourists or a tornado blowing up a storm in Oklahoma.

In the studios of Industrial Light and Magic, Guy Dyas reflects on his *Twister* assignment: 'You can't learn to be more artistic through using Photoshop, you can only learn to be more artistic and *then* apply that artistry using Photoshop', he suggests. Until the computer becomes less of a machine and more of a biological extension of its user, then ascribing craftlike qualities to its process will be like looking into the proverbial eye of the hurricane.

Notes

1 Unless otherwise indicated, all references are to interviews carried out by the author between November 1995 and January 1996.

2 *Technological Change and Industrial Design Education* (London, CNAA, 1991).

3 *Ibid.*

Rosemary Hill, a writer with many interests in contemporary applied art and crafts, is a biographer of A. W. Pugin. Judging from this portrait, we may acknowledge her as a seasoned decorator in her own right. The contribution to clear writing and criticism in the crafts made by her and several other writers of her generation – Margot Coatts, Tanya Harrod, Pamela Johnson, Alan Powers and Martina Margetts – has not been sufficiently recognised by 'academic scholarship'. Academics prefer to write in *lingua obscura*: what they are hiding from is unclear.

WRITING ABOUT THE CRAFTS

It is a commonplace observation that the studio crafts are a 'new' category of art activity, not as new as video or installation art but, in the late 1990s, more precarious than either in terms of art-world acceptability. Administrators and practitioners in the studio crafts world believe that what has eased other new art forms into acceptability has been the development of appropriate art theory and the nurturing of specialist writers. Naturally the inference has been made that what 'the crafts need' are its own theories and writers of similar status and stature.

Yet, as Rosemary Hill points out in her chapter, there has been no shortage of perfectly sound writing. It is simply the case that almost none of it has had any effect upon the wider debates in the visual arts. This is true even of exceptionally good craft books such as E. H. Gombrich's *A Sense of Order*: many copies may have been sold, but few appear to have been read.

But those who are interested in the crafts want to discuss what is good and what is bad, and within the constituency of craft interest all manner of persons, including many makers, have contributed criticism and practical theory. Yet for those many visual arts writers for whom craft is of no interest 'the studio crafts' are as puzzling a subject to write about as the artefacts of alien, non-Western cultures. For one thing, quite a lot of craft production is repetitious and fairly traditional in its form. This lack of 'originality' in an art world which prizes originality beyond all other values is a puzzle to the uninitiated art critic.

'Originality' and 'creativity' are the great orthodoxies of contemporary art, but both concepts cause difficulties in the crafts, which rely on the conservation and handing-on of shared knowledge accumulated over generations. Jonathan Meuli discusses both these orthodoxies in the context of writing about non-Western art and does so in a way that sheds light on some of the difficulties of writing about Western studio crafts.

Rosemary Hill discusses the development and the practicalities of writing about contemporary studio crafts. Although her examples are drawn from the last fifteen years of British experience, it is reasonable to argue that the development she has traced in Britain over the last few years has many parallels and overlaps with Western writing on the crafts generally.

My own chapter discusses the idea of craft as a practical philosophy and how resistant its central values are to being described in language.

12 ✧ *Writing about the studio crafts*

ROSEMARY HILL

Writing about the studio crafts, as we understand them today, begins with Bernard Leach, who established the intellectual and artistic status of pottery in a single octavo page. Anyone who doubts the value of critical writing about the crafts might look again in some detail at the first page of *A Potter's Book* (London, Faber & Faber, 1940). We pass from the chapter heading, 'Towards a Standard', by way of the first sentence, 'Very few people in this country think of the making of pottery as an art', to the elaboration of the third paragraph:

> Here at the very beginning it should be made clear that the work of the individual potter or potter-artist, who performs all or nearly all the processes of production with his own hands, belongs to one aesthetic category, and the finished result of the operations of industrialized manufacture, or mass-production to another and quite different category.

By a series of elegant sleights of hand we are brought, at the end of this page, to an acceptance of several, by no means unarguable, points. The title, 'Towards a Standard', assumes the standard is definable, assumes, in other words, that studio pottery is amenable to a system of intellectual criticism comparable to some degree at least with music, for example, or tragedy as defined by Aristotle. What is more, we are not required to look for this standard: we are already, in Leach's company, moving 'towards' it. Lodged within the modest assertion of the opening sentence, that only a few people in England think of pottery as art, there is a little barb. The English, we infer, are somewhat insular. It is correct to think of pottery as an art. The reader is allied with the more sophisticated minority.

By the time we reach paragraph three, in which Leach 'makes clear' the aesthetic position of studio pottery, we hardly notice that his supposed clarification is in fact an unsupported assertion. As the chapter continues, the position is amplified, but the language is always that of explanation, rather than assertion or argument.

These are the facts, the author's role merely to elucidate. By page two we have, most of us, accepted studio ceramics as a branch of art, amenable to critical analysis, expressive of the undivided personality of its creator. This position, while it grows out of an Arts and Crafts view, represents a development.

Leach's text is, in the ways I have suggested, deceptive. But it is not deceitful. Indeed it succeeds not by argument but through the integrity of language and subject. The prose is well modulated without being showy, sensitive but not emotional, the idiom lucid and unspecialised. His style is that of the educated Englishman of his day, not so far from a *Times* third leader. It is Leach the writer who is the proof of his assertion that Leach the artist-potter – and hence the artist-potter as species – inhabits the higher cultural ground.

Leach's prose repays close reading, for it was he, more than anyone else, who established the studio craftsman as an artist moving naturally within the artistic and intellectual mainstream. His writing was at least as important as his pottery and his powerful personality in achieving this.

It worked by offering a philosophical context – albeit rather a vague one – and a series of undaunting critical and technical terms that did much to make discussion, and hence recognition and refinement of the idea, possible. It is writing in this tradition that I want to discuss.

What I mean by the Leach tradition of criticism is not (necessarily) writing by practitioners, but writing that works from within the accepted cultural and linguistic conventions of a broad section of society: journalism, certain kinds of essay, popular history. Criticism that looks at the crafts from a theoretical point of view such as Marxism or deconstructionism has important insights to offer but it annexes the crafts to an existing intellectual system. The writer without such a position, addressing a non-specialist reader, must, like Leach, create their own critical point of view and terms of reference.

In looking at some of the best of this writing over the last fifteen years I have chosen to deal at some length with specific examples, thereby creating a picture which, while I hope it is representative, inevitably omits more than it includes. I begin with the journalism, moving on to essays and then to the writing of history, because this sequence reflects the order in which writing about the crafts has, largely, developed since 1980, each phase building the foundations for the next.

Since Leach's day the quantity of writing has increased enormously; so, I believe, has the standard. As journalism it is spread over a wider range of publications, reflecting the greater diversity of the studio crafts themselves. And yet this can be seen as both an advance and a retreat. From the middle of the cultural upper ground, as it might be called, from the in-tray of the arts editor on a national newspaper, this variety appears as diffuseness. There is not thought to be sufficient interest or financial investment in any one area to justify dropping a theatre review a week to cover craft. Hence a review such as Abigail Frost's of Linda Gunn-Russell in *Crafts*, Number 72 (January/February 1985), would be unlikely to appear in a broadsheet, although, in terms of style, it easily could.

> [the pots] are angular, visually punning and come in an extraordinary range of colours, surface qualities and patterns … she is clearly a technical wizard. The pots are also shallow – if she can pun then so can I … they seem to me to be almost cynically devoid of any emotional qualities. A mental comparison between these pots and those of … Elizabeth Fritsch is like looking at a poster and trying to remember a painting.

Thought-provoking, economical, entertaining, Frost engages the reader on familiar ground in order to draw them into new territory, without going too far or too fast. She accords status to the work, as Leach does, implicitly by moving from colour, surface, form, to an interpretation that allows for ceramics as expressive of emotion and of different degrees of emotional depth and sincerity. This is to take the studio crafts seriously indeed, to rate them as high art, capable of offering a critique of human experience.

This, however, is not a view that pertains widely and so it is not one that can easily be expressed outside the pages of special-interest publications. Some, such as *Crafts* magazine, are subsidised. *Crafts*, which became the focus of critical debate under the editorship of Martina Margetts from 1979, offered, as it still does, a unique platform. It has, too, some of the inevitable disadvantages of the backwater.

The readership of the British weekly magazine *The Spectator* is larger and non-specialist. The urbane catholicity of the magazine, which runs craft reviews variously under 'Crafts', 'Design' or 'Fine Art', allows its critic, Tanya Harrod, to take a similarly broad view. Of an exhibition of work by the woodworker Jim Partridge in 1989 she wrote:

> It is hard to know to what extent his work is rooted in surviving skills and to what extent he has reinvented ... but what he has done is to go back to essential simplicities. His bowls, benches and tables manage to look as if they are the first of their kind – Ur-tables and Ur-bowls. The finest pieces develop, Brancusi-like, from a series of spheres and cubes. At Grizedale Forest in the Lake District and at other sites he has further proved himself with a series of practical interventions in the form of bridges, seats and a walkway that already look rooted in the landscape. (2 September, p. 37)

The play of references between traditional craft, studio craft and sculpture is unforced. Elsewhere in the review Harrod takes the Crafts Council mildly to task for eschewing rural crafts. The article itself demonstrates how the aspirations of craft towards the condition of art is in no way mitigated by association with function or tradition. By comparison, Harrod implies, the Council's efforts to insist on the status of craft by promoting work allied to the avant-garde in art are sometimes counter-productive.

Once again, as with Leach, the point is made by the style of the prose as much as the content. Like Frost, Harrod builds on the readers' perceptions to enlarge them, rather than trying to knock them down. It is one of the great advantages of writing journalism about craft – as opposed to, say, modern opera – that however 'non-specialist' readers may be they will feel, with some reason, that they know a fair amount about tables, pots and earrings.

Writing that seeks to elevate the status of craft by overloading it with significance, until the reader feels they no longer understand their own furniture, provokes nothing but irritation. Neologisms work best when used sparingly. 'Vessel', 'maker', 'craftsperson' sound more self-important than important in many contexts.

Tanya Harrod takes her subject as seriously as Frost, albeit from a different, more aesthetic point of view. The critical account is usually developed, along the lines of academic art history, in terms of styles, schools, influences. This gives the reader the necessary sense of a broader picture from which the detail represented by the review is taken.

Her writing does appear, sometimes, on the arts pages of newspapers. But in the mass media the crafts cling by their fingernails. Other developments – fashion, recession, advertising or a change of editor – determine their fate. Nothing could have demonstrated this more effectively than the 'Architecture' page in the London newspaper *The Independent*. Its arrival was prompted in part by the Prince of Wales's onslaught on modern architecture and the wider debate that that generated, and opened up spaces between arts and design in which, perhaps because of some race memory of the role of architecture in the Arts and Crafts movement, it seemed acceptable at times to feature craft. Recently, however, the format of the page has changed. It is now a tabloid and there is, literally, less room for the shorter articles that were sometimes given over to craft. It is a salutary example. As Philip Larkin so economically expressed it when he called his collected journalism 'Required Writing', the journalist has all the advantages and all the limitations of contingency.

When no longer required, journalism – unlike pottery or poetry – ceases to exist. We can only, in other words, start from where we are wanted, or at least accepted.

Where we are, in terms of press coverage of the crafts in popular print, is usually either on what used to be called the Women's Page or in the ever-multiplying supplements, most of them aimed at women, though they no longer openly admit it: Shopping, Collecting, Life-style, Gardening, Interiors, Fashion and – baffling but popular – You. These reflect the most widely-held views of the crafts which are, in varying combinations, decorative, domestic, rural, nostalgic, brown, culturally marginal, something to do at evening classes. Occasionally there is a feature on 'the new crafts' with a witty headline like 'Smocks Away'. Having, however, written this article several times myself, I conclude that it results more from the editorial need for an alternative view every eighteen months than a desire to take the higher aspirations of the studio crafts seriously.

It is common for critics and craftspeople alike to bemoan this state of affairs. Up to a point this is reasonable. A weekly review, of the quality of the examples quoted, would enhance most arts sections and interest, I believe, more readers than editors imagine. But, on the whole, the mass perception of the majority of craft work is correct. As a contributing editor to *Crafts* it does not seem that there are so many more exhibitions worth reviewing or makers worth interviewing than a bi-monthly magazine can accommodate. It would be a pity if a desire to insist on the status of the studio crafts led writers to collude with the received disdain for the decorative and domestic by eschewing the life-style pages.

A great deal of studio craft work is well served by the kind of illustrated features that run in supplements and monthly magazines: basket-making, many kinds of weaving and textile printing, jewellery and functional pottery. They advance the status and appreciation of the work by making it better known and by introducing it to an audience, such as those who read *House and Garden*, who can afford to buy it. In some cases the subject would be further illuminated by the more analytic kind of criticism I have discussed, but not always. Not all studio craft work aims at the aesthetic intensity of sculpture or to be a critique of the human condition.

In so far as the studio crafts are radical or subversive they are so because they challenge notions of hierarchy in the arts and hence other, social and philosophical assumptions about value. The Arts and Crafts movement fought – with mixed results – mainly on the home front to bring beauty and good design within the reach of as many people as possible. Post-war crafts have been more preoccupied with the art side, with makers hammering on the doors of the galleries while the critics inserted themselves into the universities. The pleasing result for the craft writer is that we now occupy a situation in which we can write on aspects of the same subject for a magazine such as *Country Living* or a book of academic essays like this. It is not a question of which is better, but what is possible, or appropriate in different contexts.

The critic must, then, be adaptable, but not dishonest. The difficulty with magazine/life-style features, the point at which they begin to do a disservice to both readers and makers, is where the popular preconceptions are directly at odds with the facts.

The muddied legacy of Morris misunderstood still washes through the media and many an artist-craftsman finds himself bouncing queasily across the wake. Typical of this was the regular craft feature, run for some years by *Interiors* magazine, which was known to the staff as the 'little men' slot, as in 'I know a marvellous little man who makes the most wonderful pots/spoons/bagpipes', etc.

In this sort of article the picture sets the tone. The 'little man' is characteristically shown at work, the hands – wonderfully sensitive and/or gnarled – highly-lit, the face obscured. The text is often in the passive mood ('the straw is plaited', etc.), a small but significant shift of textual gear which renders the activity more generic, the individual maker less significant – anonymous, an artisan, if possible the last of a dying line. This is Morris's nostalgia stripped of its radicalism, his socialism turned on its head.

In at least four popular books on 'traditional craft' you may find a picture in this style of David Drew, who grew up in the Home Counties, trained as an engineer and then decided to live in Somerset and make baskets, as a way of living consistently with his political and ecological views. In all cases the caption is, more or less, 'basket-making in the West Country'. The implication, that this is a typical example of a continuous, unselfconscious rural tradition, could hardly be more misleading.

Glossy, friendly, but dishonest, the books and magazines that peddle this view of the studio crafts – and to which in my time I have contributed – are the worst kind of writing on the subject. There is no need to dwell at length on the difference between writing in this vein in magazines and other, more extended forms.

Elsewhere, however, the relationship between journalism and more extended writing, essays and books, is worth examining. Most of the important publications of the last fifteen years to deal with the studio crafts have grown directly out of magazine articles and reviews. Peter Dormer's series including *The New Jewellery* (with Ralph Turner; London, Thames & Hudson, 1986), *The New Ceramics* (London, Thames & Hudson, 1985), etc., the section on the crafts in Peter Fuller's *Images of God* (London, Chatto & Windus, 1985), the essays in the catalogue *Craft Matters* (1985, for an exhibition at the John Hansard Gallery, Southampton) and Oliver Watson's *British Studio Pottery* (Oxford, Phaidon, 1990) provide a variety of distinguished, but not isolated, examples of the way in which this dialogue has grown up, illustrating what is possible when the writer can develop ideas over a longer distance.

In *Craft Matters* Christopher Reid, who worked on *Crafts*, was given the opportunity, with two other selectors, to choose a group of objects and write a companion piece of some length. He called his essay 'Function and Symbolism', thereby grasping a handful of the nettles with which the magazine had been wrestling for some time.

Debates about function in the 1980s had reached such a Jansenist level of introspection that, no matter what the subject of a lecture, the first question afterwards was always, 'What use is a teapot if it doesn't work?' There was even an exhibition called 'Does it Pour?'

Reid starts at a good distance – historically and aesthetically – from the contemporary studio crafts, with *In Parenthesis* by the poet and artist David Jones (1895–1974). Jones, whose work is characterised by a Blake-like combination of text and image, begins *In Parenthesis* with an acknowledgement to the printer. From this intersection between art and craft Reid can clear a large, airy space for himself and his reader.

Traversing this area at an easy walking pace, more graceful than Leach but with some similar sleight of hand, he suddenly turns the nettle into a flower:

> the fondness of the Crafts Council for spoof jugs and unwearable jewellery is, to say the least, paradoxical. Misleadingly it is work of the latter kind that tends to be brought forward as evidence when the alleged duality of 'function'and 'non-function' is discussed within the context of today's crafts. I should like to consider the problem differently, offering a conception of function that would accommodate even the most Dadaistic and intentionally rebarbative whim of the avant-garde craftworker's mind. For it seems to me that whenever taste or moral bias plays a part in the choice of one pot, or rug … above another, then as consumers we are acknowledging the metaphysical quality of the piece as part of its function. It acquires a symbolic value that may be entirely private to us, but that is nonetheless an important factor in our relationship to it and, through it, to the world. (n.p.)

Reid selected objects from both sides of the line that seemed, then, to divide the studio crafts so absolutely from the traditional: a pot by Ewen Henderson, a length of Indian silk, a jar from Kenya. In its breadth his approach was prescient. It is hard to remember now why function seemed such an intractable issue. The answer may appear in part when we come to consider the writing of history in relation to the studio crafts. For the moment, however, let us stay in the heady 1980s.

If the examples of writing that I have offered so far as admirable have been, on the whole, moderate in tone, that is not because I dislike polemic. If a subject is important it will arouse passionate debate and the

debate will in turn make the subject more important by attracting attention. A good row does wonders for raising interest, and to be 'good' a row
must have something to be said on both sides and a proper issue in the
middle. This was the case with the furore surrounding the avant-garde craft
work of the 1980s, the 'spoof jugs and unwearable jewellery' that made
Reid's hackles rise and which became the eponymous 'new ceramics' and
'new jewellery' of Peter Dormer's books. They also provoked some of the
late Peter Fuller's most fruitfully furious outbursts.

Fuller, an art critic of the far left who took up so many extreme
positions that he eventually went through the full 180 degrees and found
himself on the right, carried the battle deep into the enemy camp.
Reviewing, in 1983, a Crafts Council jewellery exhibition in the Council's
own magazine, he wrote:

> The discredited ethic of a collapsed Late Modernist Fine Art tradition is
> now being transplanted into each of the several crafts .... Predictably this
> tragic vandalism is backed with public money .... (What else would one
> expect from a Government that gave us Cruise, Cable Television, and a
> run-down of arts and crafts education)? Nonetheless the 'discourse' which
> surrounds this destruction ... apes left-wing 'revolutionary' theory ....
>
> But just look at this new jewellery. It lacks intricacy, workmanship,
> sense of beauty or mystery, celebration of nature or affirmation of tradi-
> tion. It is neither pretty, attractive, precious nor ornamental .... Indeed, it
> is not really jewellery at all .... I hope we never see the like of ... The
> Jewellery Project again. (reprinted in *Images of God*, p. 269)

This is pure Fuller, lambasting everyone – the right, the left, and
modern art – making a direct appeal to a highly romantic sense of tradition before ending like a public-school headmaster. Yet each of these
apparently wild hammer-blows hits a nail on the head. Fuller acknowledges the connection between Modernism in fine art and studio craft, he
sees the new jewellery as political and radical. This was exactly how it saw
itself, albeit from the opposite end of the telescope.

Peter Dormer, no stranger to the knockabout school of criticism
himself, was able, in *The New Jewellery*, to turn this kind of criticism to his
advantage in calm, almost statesmanlike tones.

> The frequent play that [Otto] Kunzli makes with geometric shapes, with
> the block, cube and stick, has outraged jewelers and critics alike. They

have responded by thinking that such activity is tomfoolery ... in any case, they ask, who would wear this work? Who indeed? The first point is that cube-and-block jewelry is not seriously intended as commercial ornament but as a reflection on jewelry and the limited conventions within which it works. Kunzli makes us reflect on the narrowness, at any given point in history, of what society finds acceptable in dress. And the interest is not simply in reminding us that the conventions exist, but in highlighting the fact that they are arbitrary – that what is permissible changes. (p. 146)

The outrage is, as Dormer makes clear, part of the point. This work is meant to challenge and question, it is work at the edge of pre-existing definitions, it ought to attract hostile criticism.

Its supporters saw the new crafts as an avant-garde and provocation therefore as one of its distinguishing features. In the exchanges between Reid, Fuller, Dormer and others through the 1980s the debate spread from individual reviews through catalogue essays and longer articles into books. These, often glammed up to look 'designer-ish' for the 'designer' decade, took the studio crafts and some of their ideas, via coffee tables, back into magazine and newspaper articles addressing general audiences. Compared with the attention paid to fine art it was still not much, but the mid-1980s marked a high point in post-war interest in the crafts.

Ten years later the balance has shifted. Popular interest and, it might appear, Crafts Council patronage, have moved towards the more decorative, workshop-based crafts, towards makers who see themselves more as small businesses than artists. Perhaps the focus has changed only because the craft scene itself has been transformed. The avant-garde has passed, as it was bound to, and its place has been taken, at the more analytical end of writing about craft, by an interest in history.

Rather like Molière's *bourgeois gentilhomme* suddenly realising that he had been speaking prose all his life, the crafts, or at least those who wrote about them, began to notice that they had a past. Certain continuities emerged. Critics began to take account, for example, of the fact that 'non-functional' ceramics, whether Egyptian grave goods or Victorian fairings, had been around for some time. Suddenly all the intractable questions about teapots seemed to matter less. The new jewellery's reaction against precious materials had, perhaps, some precedent in the

199

nineteenth century when experimental designers' use of enamel, glass and sea shells seemed as radical as perspex.

Consider the difference between Edward Lucie-Smith and John Houston at the beginning of the 1980s and Alan Powers in the mid-1990s.

Lucie-Smith's *The Story of Craft* (Oxford, 1981) was conceived by Phaidon as a companion volume to the immensely popular *Story of Art* (Oxford, 1950) by Sir Ernst Gombrich. Lucie-Smith is one of the few critics taken equally seriously for his writing on art as on craft. He is perceptive and well informed. The curious failure of the last chapter of *The Story of Craft* is therefore illustrative of a more general problem of craft writing at the time. Lucie-Smith has terrible trouble trying to squeeze his narrative into the Gombrich model, to which it does not belong. He commits the solecism, unforgivable in a book with the subtitle *The craftsman's role in society*, of captioning David Drew 'traditional basket-making' and putting him next to a picture of a smock and a toothless French lacemaker in a straw hat.

On the penultimate page Lucie-Smith finds himself defeated by the effort to incorporate contemporary studio craft into his account and leans on John Houston for a moment to catch his breath. Houston is quoted to this effect:

> Our modern reactions to the words craftsman and artist are the result of innumerable struggles about status and expression, marketing and sensibility. In the last six hundred years their meanings have been bombarded by the words around them, a swarming cluster of meaning perpetually in motion .... The continuing arts–crafts debate is largely about historical categories and definitions, but these precedents are usually and confusingly expressed as opinions because the historical process which formed them has been discounted or forgotten. (p. 280)

This now seems a considerable overstatement, but that was how it felt – immensely complicated, baffling, uncharted. Perhaps the self-absorption was another concomitant of the avant-garde, certainly it had advantages in generating debate.

By 1985 Christopher Reid, in *Craft Matters*, distancing himself from the 'new' crafts, was hinting at a longer view. In 1988 *Craft History*, a short-lived but important quarterly magazine, took the bold step of assuming a continuity between the Arts and Crafts movement and the contemporary scene, including essays whose scope embraced Wally Keeler's teapots and Philip Webb's 1886 house, Willinghurst.

Since then the quantity of historical writing on the crafts has increased, not least because the activities of the 1980s are now themselves history. Books like Dan Klein's *Glass: A Contemporary Art* (London, Collins, 1989) and, to a greater extent, Oliver Watson's catalogue *British Studio Pottery* (Oxford, Phaidon, 1990) were made possible by the catalogue essays and magazine articles which populate the footnotes.

The quality of historical writing has also risen. Witness Alan Powers in *Crafts* (March/April 1996) on English block-printing as a test case for Modernism, both as an aesthetic and as a historicist philosophy:

> Block printing is neither within nor outside the story of modern architecture. Joseph Hoffmann designed textiles for the Wiener Werkstatte but, it would be argued by many critics, that was the point at which Hoffman's architecture began a slide into neo-classicism and the Werkstatte enterprise as a whole to lose its place in the progressive narrative. The Viennese architect Josef Frank designed some interesting if not canonic flat roof houses before emigrating to Sweden where he designed rich, almost rococo floral textiles for Svensk Ten, many of which are still in production. He understood that the otherness [of textiles] extended not only to the textile medium but to its content. Classic English block printing, combining austere and decorative qualities even in the same piece, defies their use as polar opposites of good and bad. Block printing is a serious part of the culture of its time, particularly so in England where it was so strong and architecture, on a scale of international comparison relatively weak. (p. 34)

Houston's cloud of historical unknowing has dissolved to reveal a wide, clear view. While some may regret the relative decline of critical writing based closely on contemporary work, an essay like Powers's in fact elevates the status of its subject by demonstrating what Leach (for all his philosophical allusions) did little more than assert, namely that craft is a fit subject for philosophical argument – that it has, like all important art and science, something to tell us about the human condition.

13 ✧ *Writing about objects we don't understand*

JONATHAN MEULI

The public that visits art galleries in Europe and America has two stubborn ideas in its collective head: the genius of the artist and the importance of originality. We (representing that public) have had a tendency to feel both that originality is in some way objectively real and demonstrable, and that the quality of originality is in itself something to strive for. 'Our' artists, the artists working in this tradition, may not always be admired for their artworks (which, in the case of minimalist, conceptual, performance and body arts, for instance, are often derided), but they are given credit for the supposed intellectual and spiritual pursuit of originality itself. This chapter discusses the nature of the pursuit of originality by artists and the way in which some works tend to be perceived both by artists and by the art-viewing public as 'original', whereas others (apparently created in a very similar way) tend to be viewed as 'traditional'.

The idea of individual genius and of the originality of the products of that genius are intimately connected. (In fact it is hard to think of a 'traditional' or 'conservative' artist who has a reputation within the Western canon as an artist of genius.) It is inevitable that when the idea of the individual artist of genius began to be critically examined, the associated idea of originality would also have to be reassessed. As it is feminist art history which has figured most strongly in demythologising the artist as individual of genius, it is not surprising that some of the most interesting recent criticism of the idea of originality has also come from feminist theory. For example, the model suggested by Griselda Pollock in her writing about the avant-garde in Paris in the late nineteenth century is a particularly interesting one. Instead of basing her analysis on 'conventional histories of modern art, which tell its story through heroic individuals, each inventing his (usually) novel style as an expression of individual genius',[1] the author proposes three terms: *reference*, *deference*, and *difference*.

> To make your way in the avant-garde community, you had to relate your work to what was going on: *reference*. Then you had to defer to the existing leader, to the work or project which represented the latest move, the last word, or what was considered the definitive statement of shared concerns: *deference*. Finally, your own move involved establishing a *difference* which had to be both legible in terms of current aesthetics and criticism, and also a definitive advance on that current position.[2]

The advantage of Pollock's model for understanding the pursuit of originality by the post-Impressionists (in this particular case she is discussing Gauguin) is that it contextualises and makes relative the idea of originality, and this makes it easier to study. The old idea of the artist's genius and originality as in some way absolute or transcendent characteristics made them difficult to discuss in any meaningful way. It seems to be no accident that Pollock chooses the adjective 'novel' in the passage quoted above, rather than 'original'; novelty, in having less high-flown connotations, is a more appropriate term for these meditations than the value-rich 'originality'.[3]

It is not only the artists of the Parisian avant-garde whose originality has been reinterpreted. There has been a propensity in the art history of the last ten or twenty years to begin to prefer models of artistic development which stress sociological contextualisation of the labour of individual artists rather than their separateness and the irreproducibility of their talents. For several hundred years, one of the most famous models of artistic originality has been Leonardo da Vinci's *Last Supper* in the refectory of Santa Maria delle Grazie in Milan. In the second edition of his *Lives*, published in 1568, Vasari wrote of Leonardo as 'an artist of outstanding physical beauty who displayed infinite grace in everything he did and who cultivated his genius so brilliantly that all problems he studied he solved with ease'.[4] Of the *Last Supper* in particular, he wrote that Leonardo

> brilliantly succeeded in envisaging and reproducing the tormented anxiety of the apostles to know who had betrayed their master; so in their faces one can read the emotions of love, dismay, and anger, or rather

sorrow, at their failure to grasp the meaning of Christ. And this excites no less admiration than the contrasted spectacle of the obstinacy, hatred, and treachery in the face of Judas or, indeed, than the incredible diligence with which the work was executed. The texture of the very cloth on the table is counterfeited so cunningly that the linen itself could not look more realistic.[5]

The characteristics of realism and the depiction of emotion have been regarded ever since as saliently characterising both the *Last Supper* and the novelty of Leonardo's contribution to the progressive movement of art history, to the extent that the painting became almost an icon of secular 'originality' ('the power of creating or thinking creatively') rather than a religious meditation. The iconic nature of the *Last Supper* as a symbol of secular creativity and power is figured in Vasari's telling of an anecdote in which Leonardo finds a more sympathetic ear with Duke Ludovico Sforza than with the Prior of Santa Maria delle Grazie, and threatens to depict the Prior as Judas. The story serves to set the values of the secular world (secular politics, humanism, scientific advance, art) against those of the religious world. The important contact is between the temperamental man of genius, his powerful secular patron and the artwork.[6]

Recently, a different art-historical approach has been taken to this most famous fresco. It has been noted that the painting, while certainly possessing novel characteristics, may also be seen as part of a Florentine tradition of last-supper paintings in refectories which antedate Leonardo by 160 years, and that the painting is novel neither in its representational aspirations nor in its iconographical significance.[7] Taddeo Gaddi, in the Franciscan monastery of Santa Croce, Florence, in the 1330s, Andrea Orcagna (or someone close to him) in the refectory of Santo Spirito, *c.* 1365, and Andrea del Castagno in Sant'Apollonia, *c.* 1450 all painted *Last Supper* frescoes characterised by representational illusionism – Gaddi's figures appearing in 'real space' in front of the painted architectural decoration, and the later artists developing ever more elaborate perspectival and *trompe l'oeil* effects.[8]

The reinterpretation of Leonardo's work as part of an older tradition both stylistically and iconographically also takes note of the large size of Christ – a characteristic seen as archaic.[9] It is interesting that Vasari noted the difference between the treatment of Christ and that of the Apostles – not in point of size but in facial appearance:

Having depicted the heads of the apostles full of splendour and majesty, he deliberately left the head of Christ unfinished, convinced he would fail to give it the divine spirituality it demands ... for [the head of Christ] he was unwilling to look for any human model, nor did he dare suppose that his imagination could conceive the beauty and divine grace that properly belonged to the incarnate Deity.[10]

Thus, within the text of Vasari, we find information about the traditional nature of the work – but it forms an anecdote revealing the painter's piety, sense of decorum, or humility, and is not perceived by Vasari or many of his subsequent commentators as revealing Leonardo's debt to the 'old manner'.

It is interesting to speculate on why art historians in a number of fields, from Renaissance to *fin-de-siècle* Paris, have begun to dismantle the myth of artistic originality. Much is due to Marxist and feminist analysis. The endeavour has been given added urgency, also, by the growth in studies of the cultures of the colonised,[11] and by the manifest imbalances which these studies have only begun to reveal in the structures created in the aesthetic meeting of the colonising and the colonised. The process of what has been called 'provincialising "Europe"'[12] (i.e. trying to describe Europe as peripheral rather than central) has enabled us to begin to construct more accurate models of the real nature of artistic novelty.[13]

As in the West we have arguably overestimated the reality and the significance of artistic 'originality', so we have consistently undervalued it in other cultures. Even among those Westerners who claim both a knowledge of and a liking for the arts of other cultures, the propensity to view their artistic productions as possessing qualities *other* than our own is very strong. Thus, for instance, while individuality and originality are accepted unquestioningly as characteristic of the best Western art, anonymity and adherence to tradition are still predicated for the non-Western. The interesting thing is that a lot of non-Western art is not anonymous:

no work of art is anonymous; an artist (or artists) is always identifiable. If African sculptures are anonymous, this is the result of white collectors having taken no interest at all in the artist's identity.[14]

Taken out of context, this remark might seem merely petulant and a little exaggerated. In fact, it reflects a sad truth about priorities in collecting non-Western art. There has been a similar approach in many parts of the

205

world. According to one author who knows the field well, there is, for example, much more information about individual artists from Suriname than might be expected, for those who are patient enough to dig it out.[15] Historic art from the northwest coast of America (British Columbia and southeast Alaska) is almost always exhibited as the anonymous production of a tribal people, but in fact there is a great deal, both published and in the archives, about individual artists.[16] Even where archival information is not available, close examination of style, and matching of information about date and provenance, can build a picture of individual and workshop characteristics.[17]

Simply inveighing against racist prejudices or colonialist attitudes will probably not change the practices of the art world, however. A connoisseurship for non-Western art analogous to that of Western art is not likely to become established unless the market creates it. After all, if Berenson and his contemporaries had not been competitively interested in buying and selling early Italian primitives, the world's great art galleries would probably still be mixing up Duccio with Cimabue. The problem that affects historic non-Western art is that so *much* of it is owned by museums (almost all of it in the case of Native American art, for example) that a really active market is unlikely to develop in the foreseeable future. In the case of Native American art, a very few experts, mostly in museums, know enough to be able to recognise individual artists' work; but this in-depth knowledge is not viewed as a prerequisite for scholars studying the field.

However, even if we have to wait for the vagaries of the free market to create enough funding for specialist connoisseurships to develop, there is scope, meanwhile, for analysing Western responses to non-Western art generically, to see whether our assumptions about it stand up to scrutiny. Take, for example, the apparently harmless and value-free judgement of 'African' music as preoccupied with rhythm. The implicit counterpoint to this is 'where Western music is preoccupied with melody'. Implicit values are associated with rhythm (primitive, erotic, earthy, Black) and melody (ethereal, soulful and spiritful, uplifting, White). That there may be differences in the musical expressions of different groups of people at different times is obvious, but the danger of such commonplaces is that their continued reiteration provides an anecdotal basis for a biologically and racially deterministic view of culture for which there is no empirical evidence whatever. Thus 'African' as a generalisation becomes 'African' as a category, and this in turn quickly becomes 'Black' as a category. Characteristics of 'African music' are extended to 'African culture' as a whole, and an aesthetic arises founded only on platitudes and misconceptions about 'race' and 'ethnicity'.

In an article entitled 'Repetition as a Figure of Black Culture',[18] James Snead gives an interesting account of how repetition may be a cross-culturally desirable component of aesthetic enjoyment.[19] However, his analysis, as indicated by its title, concentrates almost entirely on 'Black Culture'. It does not consider 'Black Culture' in a *political* sense and so begs the question of exactly what 'Black Culture' is supposed to be. The implication is that repetition is characteristic (presumably) of 'Black' people. How 'Black' you have to be, to be especially interested in repetition, is not made evident. His further discussion of how repetition and rhythm may reflect 'ritual and annual cycles' and of how '"happiness" accrues through a perpetual repetition or apparent consensus and convention that provide a sense of security, identification and "rightness"',[20] casts in an incongruously bucolic light the work of contemporary rap artists who also contribute to 'Black' culture without being overly concerned with when to bring in the harvest.

I have mentioned Snead's analysis because it is cited by Susan Vogel in *Africa Explores*, a publication by the Center for African Art in New York, which is one of the few published works to illustrate and discuss contemporary African art.[21] Vogel views African visual art, also, as a rhythmical repetition of themes. The art historian Joseph Cornet is also cited:

> above all linked to the deep psychology .... There exists ... a sort of cultural parallel to the desire for security, a real satisfaction in repetition, which is so different from modern Western art's spirit of adventure. This refuge in repetition can be seen even in the most recent Zaïrian arts.[22]

Vogel's own commentary reads:

> One of the insights gained from an overview of African arts is that the idea of the artwork as a reprise of familiar themes lies deep in the African conception of creativity. Where originality, the ability to create something never before known, remains a fundamental concept, however strongly contested, in the Western idea of the artist, the African artist is more likely to be seen as a continuum or continuity of artists drawing on preexisting

forms. (Since all artists re-use existing forms, this distinction between the Western and the African artist may be more a matter of emphasis than a real difference.) ... [but] Where repetition in European art is often directed toward perfecting the model, the African reprise is an end in itself, designed not to develop or improve on the basic theme but to embody it in a given instance or to play off it.[23]

Vogel cites, as examples, the Zaïrian artist Cheri Samba's paintings from various dates on the theme of Mami Wata and Papi Wata, and the Kenyan potter Magdalene Odundo's 'sensuous pots [which] return again and again to the millennial African round-bottomed, swell-bodied form without ever exhausting it or repeating it'.[24] Quite what 'millennial' means in this context, and why it is seen as something particularly African, is not easy to explain; still less the other characteristics. Vogel points out that artists often repeat earlier successful designs at the request of patrons, and goes on: 'A certain kind of repetition, such as that seen in Kane Kwei's coffins, is thus the sign not of a failure of imagination but of success.'[25] Kane Kwei makes coffins in the form *inter alia* of onions, limousines, aircraft and cocoa pods. It is hard to see, within the genre of coffin-making, how it would be possible to be more original.

> In addition to reprise of earlier forms, rhythmic repetition of forms within the same work is a minor aesthetic trait of African art. Photographers all over Africa enjoy multiple printings of the same negative for aesthetic effect ... [artists repeat various motifs, maskers wear similar masks,] [and] visitors to Africa are always amazed to see groups or families dressed alike for special occasions, a popular expression for the same taste for rhythmic repetition.[26]

It is evident that much of the above is transnationally characteristic of art. Naturally, artists repeat successful motifs: Ivon Hitchens and Ben Nicholson spring to mind. Were Lucy Rie's or Hans Coper's pots really so different in their use of repetition and originality from Magdalene Odundo's? In which case are they, too, millennial and round-bottomed? What about Perugino's many *Crucifixions* and Raphael's innumerable *Madonnas* repeated at the request of patrons? Contemporary installation artists exhibited by the Saatchi and Tate galleries repeat similar conceptual themes with only the subtlest of variations. Businessmen in the City of London are known to dress alike for special occasions without thereby displaying their deep-seated need for the consolations of repetition.[27]

The examples that I have given may seem particularly crude, and perhaps too soft a target for this criticism. There are, however, three things to point out about Vogel's publication, which has become the subject of fairly routine criticism by academics on these and other grounds. The first is that it does us great service by publishing widely the work of a number of African artists whose work is too little known: there are remarkably few works available on contemporary African art of any sort. The second is that it is particularly influential, precisely because so alone in the field, and is read by many lay readers whose knowledge of non-Western or Western art history is not so good as to make them aware of the somewhat doubtful premises of its arguments. The third is that the assumptions it makes about the racial character of certain art forms are far from atypical: they are the norm rather than the exception – errors that we *all* fall into, almost subconsciously – and do not reflect badly on Vogel, who is in fact a friend and supporter of African art, so much as on the false understanding that we *all* share about ethnicity.

Vogel's essay happens to display a relatively large number of assumptions about the racial character of art within a small space. Other academics whose subject is not ethnicity *per se* let slip their guard without realising it. Helen Codere, for example, an excellent historian of Kwakwaka'wakw ('Kwakiutl')[28] culture, describes an episode involving the confiscation by the Canadian authorities of a large collection of masks and ceremonial art objects that were being used in an illicit Native feast or 'potlatch' in 1921 in the following terms:

> [A] dramatic series of events [which] involved the Royal Canadian Mounted Police, native informers jealous of the potlatch-giver and pressures brought to bear on the [Indian] agency by a highly missionized half-Kwakiutl.[29]

The phrase 'a highly missionized half-Kwakiutl' is interesting for the assumption that it inadvertently reveals. Missionisation may indeed be relevant to the individual's dislike of the continued potlatching, in that the missionaries were ideologically opposed to what they saw as a pagan practice. However, the description of that individual as 'half-Kwakiutl' is gratuitous, given that some of the most significant Kwakwaka'wakw ('Kwakiutl') artists and supporters of 'traditional' culture were also 'half-

Kwakiutl' or, in some cases, not 'Kwakiutl' at all. The greatest authority on all aspects of Kwakwaka'wakw culture, himself a Kwakwaka'wakw chief, was half-Scottish and half-Tlingit (another Native American group). There were numerous other intermarriages between ethnic groups among all representatives of 'traditional' Kwakwaka'wakw culture. However, Codere reinforces the academics' idea that 'real' Indians are *only* those that accept without reservation their 'traditional' culture (always provided that the tradition conforms to that defined by the anthropologist).

The first danger that this example (an assumption accidentally revealed) and the essay by Vogel (an explicit argument) highlight so clearly is that of racial or ethnic essentialism in the descriptions of what is 'typical' about an art form. The second is that where this essentialism forms part of our preconceptions about *non-Western* art forms, it tends to lead us to stress their 'repetitiveness' and 'traditionalism' as opposed to our own (supposed) freshness and originality. This is no new phenomenon either. A recent essay shows how dealers marketed a Native American basket-maker (Louisa Keyser) as 'quintessentially' Washoe, although Keyser's designs were in fact entirely original and non-traditional.[30]

That originality might be viewed as an essential attribute of artworks in some non-Western art traditions is little known. A Native American reminiscence from the northwest coast recalls the rivalry between the great chiefs Tsibasa and Legaix: 'Also in the winter ceremonials, each would always try to outdo the other in having the best powers and the most modern and theatrical devices.'[31] Tsibasa goes on to amaze and confound his rival by installing a set of revolving steps ('one of my most difficult and secret powers') in the ceremonial entrance to his great house. The rivalry between the chiefs was predicated upon the ability of artists to produce 'original' work of all sorts, and northwest-coast society cannot be well understood without that knowledge, and yet most of us tend to think of Native American cultures as 'essentially' traditional. There is a sense in which Pollock's model of *reference, deference* and *difference* applies as closely to nineteenth-century northwest-coast art production as it does to nineteenth-century French.

The view of Euro-American culture about what is rightly and typically non-Western presents serious problems for contemporary artists from outside the Euro-American tradition. In North America, for example,

We must also re-consider a recent development which legitimizes as 'Art' only certain types of native art, namely that which refers to, or operates within the 'avant-garde' or conceptual western art tradition. In a curious form of discrimination, artists of native ancestry who continue to work exclusively within their own cultural traditions are often condemned for being conservative, catering to the white art market, and ignoring the pressing social and cultural issues of modern society.[32]

We have this trouble with subject matter. We're either not supposed to refer to our own people and our own situation at all, or we're supposed to exclusively refer to that .... One of my real goals is to broaden the tradition.[33]

There is obviously some relationship between ethnicity and artistic production, even if it is not as clear-cut as we would like to think. The 'avant-garde' of nineteenth-century Paris may have been no more and no less 'avant-garde' or 'traditional' than a contemporary workshop in central Africa or North America, but the products of the three groups of artists are recognisably different from each other. If it is misleading to state that there is anything 'essentially' 'Black' about African art, or 'essentially' 'Italian' about the art of Florence in the fifteenth century, we are still left to wonder why it is that certain products (styles, types of artefact, means of expression) are created and, more significantly, continue to be made in certain places.

At least one model now being considered amongst economists would seem to offer possible explanations. W. Brian Arthur, Professor of Population Studies and Economics at Stanford University, and a number of other economists (Paul Romer at Berkeley, Paul Krugman of MIT, Kenneth Arrow of Stanford) 'have begun to question – even to reverse – some of the basic assumptions underlying their field'.[34] One example of an assumption both challenged and subsequently better explained is that of economic activity being subject to diminishing returns.

This notion, which dates back to the English economist David Ricardo in the 1820s, asserts that any expanding economic activity eventually experiences a negative feedback. For example, easy-to-reach coal can be mined cheaply, but expansion into more difficult veins becomes expensive. This in turn dissuades people from expanding further, and they may look for an alternative to mining coal. The same goes for oil. So the economy strikes a natural balance between usage of coal and oil. This equilibrium outcome ... is attractively predictable and stable .... It depends only on consumers' wants, available technology and raw materials – not on the whims or accidents of history. But .... Many parts of the economy – the high-technology sector, for example – do not experience diminishing returns. To produce a new ... drug, computer ... program, or passenger jet, perhaps hundreds of millions of pounds must be spent on research and development. Once in production, however, incremental copies are comparatively cheap. The average cost of producing high technology items falls off as more of them are made. There is a positive, not negative feedback: once a product gets ahead of its rivals, it gains further cost advantages, and can get even further ahead. High technology is subject to increasing returns.[35]

During the 1980s, Arthur and others at Stanford and MIT began to develop theories of economies of increasing returns.

The idea was that countries or regions that get an early start or adopt clever strategies to establish a lead in a high-tech industry forge ahead. So whole industries may end up concentrated heavily in a single country, as with pharmaceuticals in Switzerland, consumer electronics in Japan, or computer software in the US. There is nothing magic about Switzerland, Japan or the US; which country will be linked with which industry cannot be predicted theoretically .... Increasing returns have interesting implications for the characteristics of economies. There are many possible patterns of world production and consumption, so it is not possible to predict which one will occur. The particular pattern that falls into place builds up organically – that is, new firms and industries grow on what is already there. This is partly the result of historical accidents such as who set up what firm, where, and when. Once in place, such concentrations become hard to dislodge; they are 'locked in'. The resulting pattern probably does not coincide with the best allocation of resources. Even if all countries start with equal concentrations of each industry, the slightest tremble in the market place tilts the outcome into an asymmetric one. So with positive feedback, in the form of increasing returns, the economy acquires very different properties.[36]

Is it possible that the production of certain types of art in certain cultures (fresco painting in Italy, landscape gardens in England, theatrical masks in British Columbia, pottery in southwestern US pueblos) could be explained in this way without resorting to racially essentialist theories? There is an obvious sense in which art is 'high-technology' as soon as it moves beyond the absolutely utilitarian (which is very soon indeed). The way in which Arthur explains the movement of markets in high-tech industries may be applicable to many of the characteristics of art markets.

It remains to be seen whether we are able or willing to shake off the comfortable assumptions about ethnicity that we all grow up with. The problem in so far as it concerns art is that being 'racially essentialist' is – or has been historically – a part of what constitutes the symbolic capital of art – in other words it has formed an important part of the way in which we assess (and rank) artworks (national schools, regional schools, 'African' art, are valued in large part *because of* their nationalism, region-alism, Africanism, etc.). It not only becomes self-repeating ('locked in') in *production* in the way that Arthur describes for innovative industrial products, but also, unlike those industrial products, in *consumption*. The Italians are loved by the English for their 'Italianness', which exists (partly because of historical accident) but becomes artificially reproduced indef-initely because we (English) continue to want to consume 'Italianness'.[37] We have come to love the 'traditional' virtues of Native American cultures (their supposed ecological ideals, for example), and those cultures are finding it extremely difficult to shake off that image; they are continuing to produce it because (and in some cases only because) we are continuing to consume it.

International Euro-American high culture reproduces in many forms through the agency of many media the view that much of the world's history is soured and defaced by 'ethnic' conflicts. Many of us (all of us?), as representatives of Euro-American high culture, lament this, and support political activity to try to resolve such conflicts. At the same time (still helplessly (?) representatives of Euro-American culture), we also reproduce again and again the view that the spiritually uplifting qualities of art are a form of universal solace or redemption, without recognising that many of those qualities in which we find solace are precisely those irrational appreciations of ethnicity that, through their more violent expression in the form of ethnic warfare, have given rise to our need for solace in the first place. There is a poignant irony here, and sadly, we need to come to terms with it.

Notes

1 Pollock, 1992, p. 14.

2 *Ibid.*

3 *The Concise Oxford Dictionary* (8th edn, 1990) defines the words as follows: 'Novelty; newness, new character – originality – a new or unusual thing or occurrence – a small toy or decoration *etc.* of novel design – having novelty; Originality; the power of creating or thinking creatively – newness or freshness – an original act, thing, trait, *etc.*' The dictionary's correlation of power/originality/creativity is an interesting one in the context of this debate.

4 Vasari, 1965 [1568], p. 255.

5 *Ibid.*, p. 262.

6 Vasari also emphasises the novelty of the Leonardo, as so often in the *Lives*, by making implicit comparison between the new work and another older and more traditional one, in this case a 'painting of the Passion done in the old manner, on the end wall' [by Montorfano], seen by Leonardo 'while he was working on the Last Supper, in the same refectory'. Vasari, 1965 [1568], p. 263.

7 'Although Leonardo's treatment is very different from that of any earlier depiction of the scene … neither the choice of subject nor the illusionism of its representation is a novelty. On the contrary, the tradition of decorating monastic refectories with a large-scale, realistic semblance of Christ and the disciples partaking of bread and wine evolved in Florence in the course of the fourteenth century, when the great urban monastic complexes were built. (There is an earlier example which may be archetypal, in the fresco of the Last Supper in the refectory of San Paolo fuori le Mura in Rome, 1073–85, but as only a few fragments survive it is difficult to judge the degree of illusionism attempted.)' Langmuir, 1986, p. 61.

8 *Ibid.*, pp. 64–5.

9 'You might not expect such an archaic, symbolic, anti-realistic formula to figure in this late work. Yet, if you compare the seated figure of Christ with the standing disciples on the left and right of the table, you will realise that, subtly but unmistakeably, Leonardo has painted Christ on a larger scale than the other figures. This, if nothing else, should alert the viewer to Leonardo's debt to his predecessors.' *Ibid.*, pp. 63–4.

10 Vasari, 1965 [1568], pp. 262–3.

11 Said, 1978; Bernal, 1987– ; Bhabha, 1987, 1990; Mitter, 1992 [1977], 1994.

12 Chakrabarty, 1992, p. 19.

13 The connection between feminist scholarship and the study of relationships between colonist and colonised is a close one. Price, cited below as an authority on Surinam art, points out some of the connections between the

views that Euro-American culture has historically taken of the cultural achievements of women and those that it has taken of the cultural achievements of the non-Western societies it has colonised. So too do Duncan, 1993 [1973, 1982] and Torgovnick, 1990.

14 Martin, 1989, cited in Deliss, 1990, p. 12.

15 Price, 1989, pp. 104–5.

16 Marius Barbeau, for example, collected and published information about scores of individual artists and their work (Barbeau, 1929, 1950). His notebooks and manuscripts, kept in archives at the Museum of Civilization in Hull (Quebec), contain still more. There is a great deal wrong with Barbeau's theoretical approach to his material (see Duff, 1964), but the value of his primary data is not diminished by that.

17 Vansina, 1984.

18 Snead, 1990.

19 'We may either deny or own to the repetitions of material existence – or ... own that repetition has occurred, but that given a "quality of difference" compared to what has gone before, it has become not a "repetition" but rather a "progression", if positive, or a "regression", if negative ... even if not in intentional emulation of natural or material cyclicality, repetition would need to manifest itself. Culture as a reservoir of inexhaustible novelty is unthinkable.' Snead, 1990, p. 213.

20 Snead, 1990, p. 214.

21 Vogel, 1991.

22 Cornet, 1989, pp. 55–6, cited in Vogel, 1991, p. 19.

23 Vogel, 1991, p. 19.

24 *Ibid.*

25 *Ibid.*, p. 20.

26 *Ibid.*

27 Or perhaps they *are*, in fact: the point is that we don't think or say that they are.

28 Kwakiutl and Kwakwaka'wakw are approximately synonymous; however, the term Kwakiutl is an academics' term which is inaccurate and disliked by many of the people who have had to bear it. Kwakwaka'wakw is an alternative suggested by Native groups themselves.

29 Codere, 1961.

30 Cohodas, 1992.

31 Watt, 1992.

32 Danzker, 1991, p. 91.

33 Jimmie Durham, Native American artist, born in 1940 in Arkansas. He studied at the Ecole des Beaux Arts in Geneva and since the mid-1980s has exhibited internationally – at Documenta 9, Kassel (1992); the Whitney Biennial, New York (1993); a solo exhibition at the Palais des Beaux Arts, Brussels; and one at the ICA in London: 'Original Re-runs', 17 December 1993 – 20 February 1994. This information and the artist's comment quoted above are taken from the exhibition handout from the ICA exhibition.

34 Arthur, 1993.

35 *Ibid.*

36 *Ibid.*

37 On the whole, high-tech industries are more ruthlessly managed than art markets. However, even here consumption plays a part in *locking in* an idea of ethnicity: we 'buy British', or 'buy American' or may decide that we like or dislike French or Japanese cars *generically*. However, the connection with ethnicity is not so deep-rooted as to override commercial viability – whereas it evidently is in the case of art. We, as consumers, do not 'allow' Native Americans to produce art that is relevant to anything apart from their ethnicity, whereas we don't blink at consuming their products if they happen to be computers, cars or skyscrapers; and yes, Native Americans do produce computers, cars and skyscrapers.

References

Arthur, W. Brian, '"Pandora's Marketplace" in "Complexity"', *New Scientist* supplement, 6/13 February 1993, pp. 6–8.

Barbeau, Marius, 'Totem Poles of the Gitksan, Upper Skeena River, British Columbia', National Museum of Canada *Bulletin*, 61, Anthropological Series, no. 12, 1929, Ottawa.

— *Totem Poles*, 2 vols, National Museum of Canada *Bulletin*, 119: 1, 2, Anthropological Series, no. 30, 1950, Ottawa.

Bernal, Martin, *Black Athena: The Afroasiatic Roots of Classical Civilization*, Vol. 1 (1987): *The Fabrication of Ancient Greece 1785–1985*. Vol. 2 (1991): *The Archaeological and Documentary Evidence* (London, Free Association Books, 1987).

Bhabha, Homi, 'Of Mimicry and Man: The Ambivalence of Colonial Discourse', in Annette Michelson *et al.* (eds.), *October: The First Decade, 1976–1986* (Cambridge, MA, MIT Press, 1987), pp. 317–26.

Bhabha, Homi (ed.), *Nation and Narration* (London, Routledge, 1990).

Chakrabarty, Dipesh, 'Postcoloniality and the Artifice of History: Who Speaks for "Indian" Pasts?', *Representations*, 37, winter 1992, pp. 1–26.

Codere, Helen, 'Kwakiutl', in Edward H. Sapir (ed.), *Perspectives in American Indian Culture Change* (Chicago, Chicago University Press, 1961), pp. 431–516.

Cohodas, Marvin, 'Louisa Keyser and the Cohns. Mythmaking and Basketmaking in the American West', in Janet C. Berlo (ed.), *The Early Years of Native American Art History* (Seattle, London and Vancouver, University of Washington Press/UBC Press, 1992), pp. 88–133.

Cornet, Joseph-Aurélien, *et al.*, *60 ans de peinture au Zaire* (Brussels, 1989).

Danzker, Jo-Anne Birnie, 'Organizational Apartheid', *Third Text*, 13, winter 1991, pp. 85–95.

Deliss, Clementine, 'Lotte or the Transformation of the Object', in Clementine Deliss *et al.*, *Durch, 8/9: 'Lotte or the Transformation of the Object'*, essays associated with an exhibition at the Grazer Kunstverein (Graz, Grazer Kunstverein/Akademische Druck- u. Verlaganstalt, 1990), pp. 2–28.

Duff, Wilson, 'Contributions of Marius Barbeau to West Coast Ethnology', *Anthropologica*, new series, 6:1, 1994, pp. 63–96.

Duncan, Carol, 'Virility and Domination in Early Twentieth Century Vanguard Painting', in *The Aesthetics of Power: Essays in Critical Art History* (Cambridge, Cambridge University Press, 1993). [First published in *Artforum*, December 1973, pp. 30–9, revised and reprinted in Norma Broude and Mary D. Garrard (eds.), *Feminism and Art History: Questioning the Litany*, Cambridge, Cambridge University Press, 1982, pp. 292–313.]

Langmuir, Erika, 'Case Study of Leonardo's *Last Supper*', in *The Open University Arts: A Third Level Course; Art in Fifteenth Century Italy, Block I, Introduction* (Milton Keynes, Open University Press, 1986), pp. 58–77.

Martin, Jean Hubert, *Magiciens de la Terre*, catalogue of exhibition (1989) at the Musée National d'Art Moderne, Centre Georges Pompidou and La Villette, Paris.

Mitter, Partha, *Much Maligned Monsters: History of European Reaction to Indian Art* (Oxford, Clarendon, 1992 [1977]).

— *Art and Nationalism in Colonial India: Occidental Orientations* (Cambridge, Cambridge University Press, 1994).

Pollock, Griselda, *Avant-Garde Gambits 1888/1893: Gender and the Colour of Art* (London, Thames & Hudson, 1992).

Price, Sally, *Primitive Art in Civilized Places* (Chicago and London, University of Chicago Press, 1989).

Said, Edward, *Orientalism* (London and Henley, Routledge & Kegan Paul, 1978).

Snead, James, 'Repetition as a Figure of Black Culture', in Russell Ferguson *et al.*, *Out There: Marginalization and Contemporary Cultures* (Cambridge, MA and London, MIT Press, 1990), pp. 213–30.

Torgovnick, Marianna, *Gone Primitive: Savage Intellects, Modern Lives* (Chicago and London, University of Chicago Press, 1990).

Vansina, Jan, *Art History in Africa* (Harlow, Longman, 1984).

Vasari, Giorgio, *Lives of the Artists*, trans. George Bull (Harmondsworth, Penguin, 1965 [1568]).

Vogel, Susan, *Africa Explores: 20th Century African Art*, with contributions by Walter E. A. van Beek *et al.* (New York and Munich, The Center for African Art and Prestel Verlag, 1991).

Watt, Henry, 'A Challenge Feast of Tsibasa', told by Henry Watt (Nisnawhl) to William Beynon, *c.* 1948, in George F. MacDonald and John J. Cove (eds.), *Tsimshian Narratives*, Vol. 2, *Trade and Warfare*, collected by Marius Barbeau and William Beynon (Canadian Museum of Civilization, Mercury Series, Directorate Paper No. 3, 1987, Ottawa), pp. 112–15.

14 ⬧ The language and practical philosophy of craft

PETER DORMER

There are two arguments in this short chapter. The first is that when craft is practised as a disciplined piece of knowledge, it is inevitably an activity of self-exploration in the sense that one learns about oneself through searching for excellence in work. It has been said of Aristotle that he conceived of moral philosophy 'as an exercise in self-clarification on the part of individuals who seek to live excellently' (see Allan Janik, *Tacit Knowledge, Rule Following and Learning* (Berlin, Springer-Verlag, 1989)). There is a sense, which I will argue for, that the craftsperson's determination to work excellently is an exercise in self-clarification and, in Aristotle's meaning, moral.

However, the second argument is that there can be no general theory covering the craft disciplines, and that consequently whatever clarification of motives and values the craftsperson achieves can be inferred from the work and what he or she does but cannot, with any depth, be put into words.

The reason for calling craft a practical philosophy is that almost nothing that is important about a craft can be put into words and propositions. Craft and theory are oil and water. Because of this some people might question whether craft should be called a philosophy at all. But a disciplined craft is a body of knowledge with a complex variety of values, and this knowledge is expanded and its values demonstrated and tested, not through language but through practice. It makes craft difficult to write or even talk about with clarity and coherence.

219

Following the rule book

For the past thirty years some crafts have been redefined in their content, aspirations and in how they are taught by theories of education that emphasise the importance of learning through finding out things for oneself. There are some crafts, however, such as classical dance, surgery or flying an aircraft, where such theories have never made inroads into practice because they are simply inappropriate.

A medical school that allowed its students to discover for themselves, by trial and error and without the benefit of existing hard-won knowledge, the disciplines of even minor surgery would soon come to be criticised by the public. Also, except for one or two latent sadists, the majority of the students would probably recoil with horror. A flying school based on the principles of flight through self-discovery is equally inconceivable. In the other example, classical dance, students could in principle be left to work it out on their own, but in practice they would find it quite hopeless. The choreography of classical dance is a language and there is no way of learning it to the right levels of excellence through books; dancers have to be taught and have to mimic their tutors and mimic them for hours on end. Each of these crafts and many more like them are rightly called disciplines, and each, in its own terms, can be creative.

In fact all crafts, be they pottery or painting, lettering or sculpture, were once regarded as disciplines in the sense that there was a body of knowledge to be learned and the standards of excellence that one tried to attain were set by other people – professional practitioners both dead and alive – as well as by oneself.

Of course, rigid instruction does not always encourage creativity. For one thing, instruction, as distinct from teaching, is non-negotiable (no matters of opinion are debated between a flying instructor and a trainee pilot, for example). Instruction is based on the principle that there is a right and a wrong way of doing things.

Teaching is arguably a broader activity than instruction because teaching is less determined by specific vocations. A recognition of the difference between instruction and teaching came into its own after the Second World War, when a general liberalisation of education encouraged children and students to ask questions about what they were learning rather than receive information passively. And, bearing in mind that the plastic arts (other than design and architecture) are not like surgery or learning to fly in their responsibilities to health and safety, it was clear that no harm and probably some good could be achieved by shaking these activities free from the assumptions of instruction and the framework of rules and formulas.

To damn the theory and practice of education that is based on individualism and learning through self-discovery would be foolish. Given appropriate frameworks, where a teacher has established matters in such a way that each student does not become lost in confusion, then the setting of problems or projects for individual exploration can be immensely fruitful.

But it is arguable that in the enthusiasm for questioning rules and throwing away formulas an assumption was made that has never been justified empirically, even though it is widely held ideologically – the assumption being that rules, formulas and instruction are necessarily restrictive upon creativity. Yet in reality the use of rules and formulas is pragmatic: they are an efficient means of helping novices become experts. The knowledge required to be expert in the discipline of almost any craft is usually complex, and the transfer of knowledge from one person to another is often done through demonstration and structured teaching using formulas which are conceptually clear and simple.

The formulas vary from discipline to discipline. In drawing they include a mass of different ways of breaking down the anatomical structure of a human being or beast. In modelled clay portraiture there are schematic approaches for constructing the basic volumes of the head and neck, the eyes, nose and mouth; these schemata enable the struggling student to make sense of what are otherwise extremely confusing objects. The value of formulas in art is discussed at length and with great insight by Sir Ernst Gombrich in *Art and Illusion* (London, Phaidon, 1960).

Honest work

Growing alongside the interest in self-discovery through art or education there has been a strengthening of interest in the general issue of personal identity. Intellectuals have rediscovered the subject since its last high point of topicality in the 1950s, when Existentialism was the rage.

However, discursive philosophies such as Existentialism are not the only or even the main areas in which people seek clarification of who they are and what they stand for. People most often find coherence and clarification of their values through what they actually *do*. Thus in the craft disciplines, one finds practitioners with a profound understanding of what they are and what they stand for. This understanding is, in part, the result of the search for excellence in their work. Indeed, craftspeople quite often use the phrase 'honest work' when they want to praise one of their peers for the quality of what they have produced.

For someone who has never made anything, the full weight of what it means to make something 'honestly' may never be understood. Yet a good many art students and professional artists know about honesty in work because they cheat. The temptation to cheat in making comes in two broad forms – (a) continuously changing one's mind during the course of making an object and (b) hiding one's ignorance from oneself. For instance, suppose one sets oneself a goal such as making a figure in clay with the theme 'man and cat' but it ends up as a woman in a long overcoat *sans* animal of any description. How might this have happened? Well, conceivably (and I know this from personal experience because I am the one who cheated on this particular occasion), because at every challenge – getting a figure to stand on two legs, making a cat look like a cat – one gave up and found some simpler form instead. (Making a woman in a long overcoat means you can use the overcoat as the structural support for the figure: the engineering is much easier than trying to create a figure on two legs.) It is frequently easier to change the subject than to solve the challenges to one's knowledge that are raised by the original theme.

Yet craftspeople committed to practising their craft honestly as a discipline work strenuously to clarify their goals and seek out rules, not only of making, but also of procedure, that will keep them to the sticking-point. The difference between rules of making and rules of procedure is that the rules of making are 'how to' rules which, once assimilated by a craftsperson, can be forgotten or even broken. Rules of procedure are those rules that a craftsperson uses to keep him- or herself on track for the intended goal.

To make this distinction clear and to show how rules of procedure are tied to the concept of 'honest work' consider the following example. Professor Neal French, author of one of the chapters in this book, has described to me the work and instruction of his teacher at the Royal College of Art in the early 1950s, T. Huxley Jones. Huxley Jones was a prominent sculptor and portraitist who worked in clay. Once he had achieved the basic three-dimensional form of the head Huxley Jones built his portraits using small flattened pellets of clay. He was adamant that once you placed a pellet on the head then that was it: his rule was – you do not move that pellet.

What Huxley Jones says in his book, *Modelled Portrait Heads* (London, Tiranti, 1968), is:

> I would suggest that at first, until experience is gained and a personal technique evolved, the head should be built up by adding pellets of clay with the thumb. Obviously much bigger pieces can be used when starting than in later stages. At all stages it is important to make the clay 'work', that is the pieces are not just put on arbitrarily: they must mean something in relation to the form they are intended to express. (p. 15)

The last stage of Huxley Jones's work was to make the pellets disappear by merging them into one surface with the use of wooden modelling tools. In so doing he sometimes managed to create an effective sensation of human flesh – as though, having ensured he had the underlying structure, first of the bones, then the muscles, he was able in his final act to create the skin. He created a surface that was alive.

Huxley Jones's method is not the only way of proceeding; as we now say in our condescending way, 'the rule worked for him, we must discover our own rules'. Perhaps. But before doing so we need to understand what 'working for him' means and why he recommended his rule to his students.

First, by not moving the clay around the modeller was not 'deadening' the surface by 'tiring' the material. Both those words 'deadening' and 'tiring' have meaning for someone working clay. The sort of surface that practitioners dread is that which is akin to a cheap plastic bucket: unresponsive to light and shade, no material depth, and, as it happens, no plasticity.

Second, if the modeller knows he is going to place small pieces of clay in position and never move them again then it makes him think hard before committing himself. His questions are: why am I adding this piece of clay here? Is it because it contributes to this part of the form? Or is it because I am trying to disguise inadequacies in my construction? Do I really understand what I am doing?

At first the rule of not moving the clay pellet once you have placed it is impossible for a non-expert to follow, but its existence acts as a standard for the student to reach. When one can genuinely place something exactly then this is the proof to oneself that one knows what one is doing. It is the standard implied by the rule which is important – knowing how to measure a head, knowing the proportions, knowing the structures of bone and muscle. Eventually there is no reason why the accomplished student should follow Huxley's particular rule, only that he follows some rule to *maintain* the standard he now demands of himself.

Huxley Jones's rule was his means of helping himself towards finding and then maintaining the truth of what he was doing, and it was a means of helping students do the same for themselves. He wanted each piece of work to be 'honest'. This meant that to the best of his ability he tried to ensure that from the basic structure to the finished surface he had constructed a representation which he could justify empirically.

There is an element of profundity here. For an activity such as portraiture does allow the maker a degree of cheating that other people may never recognise. For unless the audience for the portrait knows the sitter very well, there is no sure way that it will know whether or not Huxley Jones took a few short cuts or gave up on the difficult bits. But Huxley Jones himself would have known. *His* rule is an affirmation of his self-respect. It helped him maintain his integrity; it was a part of the process of self-clarification through striving to produce excellent work.

On wanting to be right

Some craftspeople believe they are involved in an activity in which they think they can get something right, and this means more than that they simply think they are doing something that is right for themselves: they think they are doing something that is right *in itself*.

There are various different senses of rightness that a craftsperson might be interested in. The simplest category concerns fitness for function in which a specific category of tool has to perform a specific range of functions. This following example was coined by Tom Stoppard in his play *The Real Thing* and is paraphrased here. Consider the difference between a cricket bat and any piece of wood shaped to look like a cricket bat. Made up of several pieces of wood the real cricket bat is carefully put together to be supple and springy like a dance floor. In the right hands this bat can be used to knock a cricket ball and send it flying several hundred feet. The piece of wood that is merely shaped like a bat will not only not knock the ball very far but will send such a jarring sensation up your wrists and forearms that you'll be left dancing up and down with your hands in your armpits. And as Stoppard's play emphasises, the cricket bat is not better than the lump of wood because there is a conspiracy among certain elitists against using humble lumps of wood as bats; it is better simply because it is better for its purpose.

Much more elusive categories, which combine aesthetics and function, can be found in the design and making of alphabets, tableware, furniture or anything in which there is a claim that both looking right and performing right are inseparable. Here there are bound to be many more arguments than there are in the case of cricket bats versus lumps of wood. For in the case of the cricket bat its superiority is easily experienced by almost anyone big enough to hold the bat. However, in cases where an aesthetic rightness is being claimed most people will assume that what is under discussion is a matter of taste and not a matter of fact.

And yet in some craft disciplines those who practise them will insist that there is a right and wrong design. This is particularly the case in the design of alphabets or typefaces, where the aesthetics of the design of the letters and how they are spaced will contribute to legibility, readability and, perhaps, the more elusive expressiveness of the text for which the lettering/type is used. But one of the practical difficulties arising from this is that whilst craftspeople and connoisseurs may recognise and appreciate the refinement of design present in the understanding of craft nuances, a lot of other people will not. They will not care about craft connoisseurship because they simply cannot see it, they do not experience it.

Each craft involves connoisseurship, and connoisseurship is a part of tacit knowledge – that is, it is learned through experience. Thus the wood specialist will come to value nuances in surface finishes that are unnoticed by the non-specialist. Some woodworkers prefer to scrape the surface of timber rather than use sandpaper, which gives a 'mushy' surface. The crafts are full of these nuances.

The word 'connoisseurship' makes some people uncomfortable; it has gained connotations of mystery and elitism. The mystery aspect associated with connoisseurship is usually overdone. It is often relatively easy for a connoisseur to demonstrate the knowledge by producing different samples for the novice or student to compare and test. Connoisseurship is knowledge that is hard to describe, but the connoisseur who wants to pass on her or his knowledge can do so by pointing out differences in examples and providing a variety of samples.

The charge of elitism that connoisseurship receives occurs when a craftsperson or a connoisseur claims the right, by virtue of his or her experience, to be trusted to pronounce on matters that other people say are a matter of taste or opinion. In public life this can lead to clashes and incomprehension.

I have watched a small group of knowledgeable men and women, members of a civic society, trying to educate local politicians and traders in a small, historic town in the north of England to take more care of the town's buildings. In particular the civic society wants shopkeepers to understand and respect the original proportions of the town's eighteenth- and nineteenth-century shop-fronts. The aim of this education is to prevent the use of inappropriate windows, fascias, lettering and signage and encourage the use of appropriate materials in refurbishment and repair.

A handful of councillors and shopkeepers have begun to grasp the civic society's message, but a few, with considerable belligerence, see all attempts at asserting 'right' and 'wrong' approaches to the design of their shops as an attack on their liberty.

The civic society members are laying claim to an objective body of knowledge. In this instance they want the knowledge applied for the good of the town's aesthetic well-being. The nature of their claim, like the claims of many craftspeople, is interesting. They are not making a claim about taste; they are making a claim about knowledge. They are not saying 'this should be done like this' because they like it better, but because they claim to know it is objectively better – just like a cricketer faced with the choice between the bat and the lump of wood knows that the bat is better.

Accordingly, to explain the objectivity of their knowledge, the civic society members have begun producing booklets with drawings to explain what they mean by appropriate lettering, letter proportions, spacing and so forth. They know they cannot easily explain their connoisseurship; but they think they may be able to demonstrate it.

Yet in craft, as in many practical activities, there may be more than one right way of doing a particular thing, there may several right ways (and there might be several wrong ways). Craftspeople overstep the mark when they claim not that their approach is right and objectively good in its content, design and process but when they claim that it is the *only* way.

For example, when Bernard Leach wrote *A Potter's Book* (London, Faber & Faber, 1940) he helped the status of studio ceramics by giving it a practical philosophy. Leach was determined to raise understanding and appreciation of studio ceramics by revealing the criteria governing good and bad work in the craft. We know from Leach's first paragraph what kind of book we are about to read:

> Very few people in this country think of the making of pottery as an art, and amongst those few the great majority have no criterion of aesthetic values which would enable them to distinguish between the genuinely good and the meretricious. Even more unfortunate is the position of the average potter, who without some standard of fitness and beauty derived from tradition cannot be expected to produce, not necessarily master-pieces, but even intrinsically sound work. (p. 1)

Leach felt confident he could tell a good pot from a bad pot and that people would accept that he had a right as a connoisseur to pronounce on this. He saw the task of writing about pottery as a means of improving its status by improving its practice. *A Potter's Book* is a prescriptive book offering a variety of rules. Here, for example, is Leach writing about the making of handles:

> The butt end ought to be attached to the pot much as a branch of a tree grows from the trunk, and an oval section for the handle is more graceful, comfortable and strong than a round one. The loop should project only far enough to allow room for the fingers, and with few exceptions, the handle should bridge that part of the pot which is concave (e.g. the neck of a jug), thus avoiding unnecessary projection. (p. 89)

Thus we learn Leach's criteria for good handles.

The point is that all that Leach says is right and should be taken note of – it is the knowledge of a man who has studied and clarified the facts of his subject – but it is not the only way of being right. Other, equally disciplined connoisseurs may offer alternative approaches.

Yet this does not mean that the different approaches are justifiable only on the basis of taste. For whilst it is the case that connoisseurs may have their own preferences, this does not mean that they are thereby saying that the approaches they do not prefer are wrong. This obvious point is important and it gets overlooked. The knowledgeable practitioner, expert or connoisseur is interested in the quality, integrity and rightness of a craft approach. But he or she does not have to *like* all of the approaches, only acknowledge their quality (or lack of it).

Equally, ideas, objects and craft disciplines exist in relation to other ideas, objects and craft disciplines, and in talking about the facts and the integrity of the facts of a craft there is no need to assert that they are absolute and hold for all time and for all places. The facts discussed here are relative to the task in hand. So, for example, some of the facts about lettering and shop-front proportions that are applicable to a debate about the function and aesthetics of a small historic northern town may not be applicable in the context of a new shopping mall. Similarly, Leach's strictures on handles may not be applicable, because of production requirements, in the context of a pottery manufacturer. A part of the search for the integrity of a practice is clarifying the nature of the context.

A non-theoretical activity

I do not know how many practitioners who call themselves craftspeople would regard their craft as a discipline. It is my impression that for many practitioners, especially younger ones, the practice of a craft has a more casual connection with the craft's tradition. Craft seems to have become a loose kind of art, and art itself is far less dependent upon craft disciplines. How many people, for example, now learn to paint in any structured way?

Moreover, there are many people producing 'craft' who do not place the emphasis upon making. Their emphasis is upon ideas that have an existence that, they say, is separate from and not dependent upon making. Where this is the case then there can be theory. For if the ideas are separable from the object then they must exist in some form, and presumably that form is language. Conceptual crafts exist primarily in words, with the objects acting as symbols or pegs. The goals of such practitioners can be fought out in discussion and in philosophical debate.

But the kind of craft and connoisseurship that I have been defining is placed differently to conceptual craft. In non-conceptual craft the thinking is in the making, the connoisseurship in making can only be demonstrated, words – even Leach's – are inadequate. Moreover, the precious rules and the formulas of craft that make up non-conceptual craft are vulnerable to theorists and their scepticism. Hardly a rule or a formula can be defended by a craftsperson's own verbal argument once the theorist's scepticism has been turned on full heat. Why this rule and not another? How can you justify that this approach is intrinsically better than that? Every blessed thing the connoisseur or craftsperson says can be destroyed philosophically.

The problem has already been touched upon. The craftsperson cannot very easily explain the rightness of what she or he has achieved; other people have to recognise it. They have to see it. And because craftspeople cannot explain the reasons behind their work they are in an unhappy position in our society. Unless a person can explain the principles of his or her activity – unless there is a theory about it – then he or she may be credited with having skill but not understanding. This makes it easy for theorists to view the craftsperson as naive. And then, because we have made our minds up that craftspeople do not understand the real meaning of what they are doing, we look elsewhere for explanations and in so doing miss the integrity of a whole other world of knowledge – that of the craftsperson.

Ironically, it is one of this century's leading theorists and philosophers who comes to the rescue of the 'traditional' craftsperson. Craft, as I have defined it, with making as its central activity, is all bound in with tacit knowledge and connoisseurship – knowledge that cannot be described very easily but which can often be demonstrated. Because it cannot be described in a language it will not easily be theorised and it is very hard to draw down into general principles. But the facts of the knowledge can be demonstrated through example and comparison. And it is here that the most fashionable Western philosopher of the twentieth century, Ludwig Wittgenstein, comes to the rescue because he recognised the fundamental distinction between knowledge that can be described in words and knowledge which can only be shown. On 19 August 1919 Wittgenstein wrote to Bertrand Russell that the cardinal problem in philosophy was the difference between what can be expressed theoretically in propositions – language – and what cannot be expressed theoretically but only shown

(Ray Monk, *Ludwig Wittgenstein*, London, Jonathan Cape, 1990, p. 64). What can only be shown cannot be written about, and to those who think there can be a theory and a critical language of craft that is a warning worth heeding. If they do not then they will distort the integrity of the very subject they profess to respect.

INDEX

237